Alistair MacLean's War

Alistair MacLean's War

How the Royal Navy
Shaped his Bestsellers

Mark Simmons

Pen & Sword
MARITIME

First published in Great Britain in 2022 by
Pen & Sword Maritime
An imprint of
Pen & Sword Books Ltd
Yorkshire – Philadelphia

ISBN 978 1 39901 938 5

Typeset by Mac Style
Printed and bound in the UK by CPI Group (UK) Ltd,
Croydon, CR0 4YY.

Pen & Sword Books Limited incorporates the imprints of Atlas,
Archaeology, Aviation, Discovery, Family History, Fiction, History,
Maritime, Military, Military Classics, Politics, Select, Transport,
True Crime, Air World, Frontline Publishing, Leo Cooper, Remember
When, Seaforth Publishing, The Praetorian Press, Wharncliffe
Local History, Wharncliffe Transport, Wharncliffe True Crime
and White Owl.

For a complete list of Pen & Sword titles please contact

PEN & SWORD BOOKS LIMITED
47 Church Street, Barnsley, South Yorkshire, S70 2AS, England
E-mail: enquiries@pen-and-sword.co.uk
Website: www.pen-and-sword.co.uk

Or

PEN AND SWORD BOOKS
1950 Lawrence Rd, Havertown, PA 19083, USA
E-mail: Uspen-and-sword@casematepublishers.com
Website: www.penandswordbooks.com

Grateful acknowledgment is made to HarperCollins Publishers Ltd for permission to quote from the published works of Alistair MacLean. All rights reserved.

Broadsword Calling Danny Boy.
Broadsword Calling Danny Boy.

Where Eagles Dare

The singer, musician and composer James Moyer Franks used the call-sign as the title of his 2006 pop song produced by Tomcraft and Geoff Dyer used it as the title of his 2018 book about the film *Where Eagles Dare*.

Contents

Foreword
by Lee Child

I was delighted when Mark Simmons asked me to write the foreword for this book – mostly because the request implied the book had actually been written and was ready to go. It's a subject I have long wanted to see covered, and finally it has been. Excellent!

Alistair MacLean was a giant figure when I was growing up. I started reading him when I was nine or ten. My dad had a couple of titles in paperback, and I got the rest from the library, in editions with treated board covers, always slightly greasy, with thin musty pages all printed with dense grey type. I loved the patient way MacLean set up a story and sucked me in, slowly, with great self confidence. Often the first many pages covered actions only seconds long. Ahead lay the promise of reveals and reversals and triumph in the end. Bliss!

Soon I had read enough to make sense of what MacLean was doing. His first three novels were *HMS Ulysses*, *The Guns of Navarone*, and *South by Java Head*, all set during the Second World War. His next three were *The Last Frontier*, *Night Without End*, and *Fear is the Key*, all set post-war, but crucially with plot and character backstories firmly rooted in the recent conflict. It was clear that wartime experience served as a permanent and automatic calibration for everything, in terms of peril, tension, stakes, worth, and duty.

As it did in real life. I was conscious that my parents – and all my friends' parents – had been radically changed by their experiences between 1939 and 1945. I assumed that the same must have been true of MacLean himself. So much so that some years ago, when I was asked to write a foreword for a reissue edition of *Fear is the Key*, I started with the following two paragraphs.

The Second World War changed everything, including how authors become authors. Case in point: a boy was born in Scotland, in 1922, and raised in Daviot, which was a tiny village southeast of Inverness, near the remote northern tip of the British mainland, closer to Oslo in Norway than London in England. In the 1920s and 30s such settlements almost certainly had no electricity or running water. They were not reached by the infant BBC's wireless service. The boy had three brothers, but otherwise saw no one except a handful of neighbours. Adding to his isolation, his father was a minister in the Church of Scotland, and the family spoke only Gaelic at home, until the boy was six, when he started to learn English as a second language. Historical precedent suggested such a boy would go on to live his whole life within a ten-mile radius, perhaps as a land agent or country solicitor. Eventually the BBC's long-wave Home Service would have become scratchily audible, and ghostly black and white television would have arrived decades later, when the boy was already middle aged. Such would have been his life.

But Hitler invaded Poland in 1939, and the isolated boy turned 18 in 1940, and joined the Royal Navy in 1941. Immediately he was plunged into the company of random strangers from all over the British Isles and the world, all locked cheek-by-jowl together in a desperate rough-and-tumble for survival and victory. He saw deadly danger in the North Atlantic and on Arctic convoys, and in the Mediterranean and in the Far East, where ultimately his combat role was pre-empted by the atom bombs and the Japanese surrender, no doubt to his great relief, but where he saw horrors of a different kind, ferrying home the sick and skeletal survivors of Japanese prison camps. Like millions of others, the boy came out of the five-year crucible a 24-year-old man, his horizons radically expanded, his experiences increased many thousandfold, and like many of the demobilized, his nature perturbed by an inchoate restlessness, and his future dependent on a vague, unmasked question; well, now what?

Those paragraphs were informed by the little I knew, and filled out by imagination and speculation. Now, at last, Mark Simmons has brought us real facts and rigorous analysis, for which I'm grateful, even at the risk of having my earlier foreword rendered moot and inaccurate. How authors become authors interests me, and I can't wait to read on and get closer to the truth.

Lee Child
Colorado
2021

Introduction

Few first novels have had the impact of Alistair MacLean's *HMS Ulysses* published by Collins in 1955. The book remarkably sold a quarter of a million copies in hardback in the first six months, a record at the time. It was after winning first prize, £100 in the *Glasgow Herald* short story competition, that MacLean came to the attention of Ian Chapman who worked for the publishers Collins in the Glasgow office. It was Ian's wife Marjory, who had been reduced to tears by *The Dileas*, Alistair MacLean's short story that first drew her husband's attention to the author.

After some gentle persuasion and the offer of an advance of £1,000 Ian Chapman, who would become a lifelong friend to Alistair, managed to convince the reluctant author to write a novel.

It was hardly surprising that MacLean turned to his wartime experiences in the Royal Navy to tell the story of *HMS Ulysses,* based loosely on his own time on the cruiser HMS *Royalist* and drawing heavily on the stories of many of the infamous Arctic Convoys to Russia. He would go on to draw on his store of wartime experience with the next two books. *The Guns of Navarone* and *South by Java Head* following in the wake of *Royalist* as she moved from Arctic waters to the Mediterranean and then the Far East and the war against Japan. Arguably these were his best books.

Yet his editor at Collins, Milton Waldman, advised that he scrap *South by Java Head* and move away from World War Two stories. William Collins, the chairman, came to the rescue by selling the film rights to Danny Angel and backed the story of the fall of Singapore. Waldman would seem to have misjudged the market at the time. War stories were very popular and sold in their millions in austerity Britain of the 1950s and 1960s, rationing did not end until 1954, coupled to that was the painful retreat from Empire and the Suez fiasco of 1956. Readers wanted to look back to 'Britain's finest hour'. Indeed, *HMS Ulysses* published in 1955 had followed in the wake of Nicholas Montserrat's *The Cruel Sea* and Herman Wouk's *The Caine Mutiny* both published in 1951 and both made into films. One of my all-time favourites from the era was Christopher Landon's *Ice Cold in Alex,* also made into a memorable film.

The Guns of Navarone was published in 1957 and based loosely on the Dodecanese campaign of 1943 sometimes known as 'Churchill's Folly', although the island of Navarone is a fictional invention by MacLean he later wrote that there was *'no such island as Navarone, but there were one or two islands remarkably like it...'*

South by Java Head followed in 1958 and it is these three novels we will concentrate on, for this is not a biography of Alistair MacLean, rather a study of where his remarkable success started and where it came from. In 1959 in his next book *The Last Frontier* he turned away from the Second World War, although even then the roots of the book were firmly embedded in the conflict. The setting in this case was the Cold War and it proved to be another excellent thriller.

Yours truly first came across Alistair MacLean when I saw the 1961 Carl Foreman film of *The Guns of Navarone* with its star-studded cast. Yet remarkably for the time it was the author's name that got top billing emblazoned across the screen even before the title. Even today *Navarone* and *Where Eagles Dare* remain regulars on TV and remain firm favourites with the viewing public. The effect was to get me reading Alistair's books. I like to think his spare style also influenced my own novels.

Ian Rankin said of *Where Eagles Dare* that it was *'Probably the first grown-up book I read. I'd have been about 11 and it may have belonged to my dad. It's real boys' own stuff and none the worse for that. I stumbled across a copy in a second hand bookshop a couple of years back. So got the chance to re-read it. Great Stuff.'*

We will also look at his later Second World War books including *Where Eagles Dare* (1967), and *Force 10 from Navarone* (1968) and his unpublished story *Tobruk* (1960?). In *Force 10 from Navarone,* unusually for MacLean, he brings back the characters of Captain Keith Mallory the mountaineer, Corporal Dusty Miller the explosives expert, and Andrea the Greek resistance fighter, from the first Navarone book. In *Partisans* (1982) he would use some of the unused plot lines from *Force 10* with both books set in Yugoslavia and finally two excellent books returned to the Second World War toward the end of his life, as if it was his swan-song. With *San Andreas* (1984) he was back to the war at sea and Arctic waters, in *The Lonely Sea* (1985) we find a collection of short stories and short pieces of non-fiction, many from the war at sea.

Glossary and Acronyms

AB	Able Seaman Royal Navy
Abwehr	German Military intelligence service, meaning 'defence' in German
AIO	Action Information Office on board ship
AVH	The State Protection Authority Hungarian Secret Police
Buzz	Royal Navy slang for rumour or gossip
Charlie	Royal Navy slang for German Focke-Wulf Condor 200 reconnaissance aircraft
DEMs	Defensively equipped merchant ships
Dockyardie	Royal Navy slang for Dockyard Worker
DNI	Director Naval Intelligence
E-boat	Allies designation for German Motor Torpedo Boat (German S-boat)
EAM-ELAS	Greek Communist Partisans
Gestapo	*Geheime Staatspolizei*, German secret state police
GRU	Soviet military intelligence
HO	Hostilities Only Rating Royal Navy
IGY	International Geophysical Year Station
KGB	Soviet Intelligence Service
Leading Hand or Killick	Royal Navy rank equivalent to Corporal Army/RAF
LRDG	Long Range Desert Group
LTO	Leading Torpedo Operator
Manse	A house provided for a minister in Scottish Presbyterian Church
MI5	Military Intelligence Section 5, British Counter Intelligence service
MI6	Military Intelligence Section 6 British espionage service, often known as SIS
MGB	Motor Gun Boat Royal Navy

Mod	Gaelic Festival of song, arts and culture
MTB	Motor Torpedo Boat Royal Navy
OSS	Office of Strategic Services, replaced by CIA, USA
PO & CPO	Petty Officer, Chief Petty Officer Royal Navy equivalent to Sergeant/Colour Sergeant Army
Pompey	Royal Navy slang for Portsmouth
R-boats	Small German Minesweepers
RAMC	Royal Army Medical Corps
Run-a-shore	Royal Navy Slang for night-out
SAS	Special Air Service
SBS	Special Boat Service
Scuttlebutt	US Navy/ Royal Navy slang for rumour or gossip
SD	*Sicherheitsdienst*, secret service branch of the SS
SIS	Secret Intelligence Service, British, also known as MI6
SOE	Special Operations Executive, British Section D of SIS
SS	*Schutzstaffel*, or 'protection squad', the original title for Hitler's bodyguard
Two-badger	Eight years unblemished service Royal Navy as evidenced by two good conduct badges strips worn on left uniform sleeve
Uckers	Royal Navy slang for the game of Ludo
Waffen-SS	Military arm of the SS
X-Craft	Midget Submarine, British

Chapter One

Life before the Navy

April 1922 saw Joseph Stalin at Lenin's suggestion take up the minor post of Communist Party General Secretary, while the troubled land of Ireland was on the verge of civil war, warned Michael Collins. This was the world Alistair Stuart MacLean arrived in on the 21st of the month.

His family had a sea-going tradition, yet it was a vocation his father Alexander, who was known as Alistair, did not take to. He took a Bachelor of Divinity degree at Glasgow University completing it in 1909. His first ministry was in the parish of Tarbert, a small fishing town on the western shore of the entrance to Loch Fyne. He preached in Gaelic to his congregation and soon gained a reputation as a fine speaker. By 1913 he had moved on to the much bigger Glasgow parish of Shettleston. It was there he met Mary Lamont who was a renowned singer and had won a gold medal that year at the Mod, a Gaelic Festival of song, arts and culture. The couple were married in Glasgow at St. Columba Church in November 1916. Shortly after, the Reverend MacLean set off for the Western Front as a chaplain to the Black Watch.

At home Mary gave birth to the first of their boys, Lachlan. Alistair Senior returned in 1918 and soon their second son Ian was born. The young Alistair came along a few weeks before the family moved to Daviot in the Highlands in complete contrast to the city of Glasgow. In effect the Reverend MacLean was going to take over his late uncle Alexander Stuart's parish, who had unexpectedly died. The congregation knew him well for he had preached there for his uncle while on leave. His doctor even advised him to make the move as he had been gassed on the Western Front and the fresh air of the Highlands was much better for him than the polluted streets of Glasgow.

The MacLean family proved to be a welcome addition to the parish of Daviot and Dunlichity, Mary's singing voice immediately invigorated the services, and their boys would increase the school roll by ten per cent.

The parish near the northern end of Loch Ness was an idyllic setting for the young Alistair growing up with a keen imagination. Inverness and the Moray Firth with the lure of the sea were not far away and the area was resplendent with Scottish history. The field of Culloden was close by and the legends of Bonnie Prince Charlie, and Mary Queen of Scots who had passed through Inverness, and St. Columba, who had sailed into the region bringing Christianity to the wild Picts.

There is a reserved understated quality in Alistair's writing about his childhood. There are gripes about having to drive *grouse across the bleak wind-swept Grampian moors for the benefit of short-sighted American Millionaires'* and of the churches that were equally bleak on the inside as the moors outside; of the intense cold of his attic bedroom that exposing any bare part of the body from the protection of the blankets risked a *'condition only one degree removed from frostbite'.* Yet there are many happy reflections, *'sleeping under the stars on... new-mown hay'.* Of being in his father's study along with *'half the men of the Parish'* to listen to the Scotland – England international soccer match, from Hampden Park on his father's radio, the only one in the area.[1]

The Reverend MacLean was of a short stocky stature, who wore shoes with thicker soles and large hats to try and match his wife's height. He had an easy-going nature, and time for everyone. Active in local affairs, he served on the council and had a wide range of friends and acquaintances from all classes.

The fourth MacLean boy, Gilleasbuig (who later would become known as Gillespie) was born in 1926 and the next year Alistair junior set off on the road of education at Daviot Public School. Unlike the English Public Schools the Scottish establishments were truly for all. Miss Joan Mackintosh was the headmistress of the two-roomed two-teacher school and was also the organist at Daviot Church. With these limitations the emphasis was strictly on the three Rs – reading, writing and arithmetic. Miss Barbara Mackintosh was the second teacher and related to Joan. She was the first to teach young Alistair and recalled the first day at school for the new pupil. He came to school in a *'MacLean tartan kilt'* and he *'was so like his father'.* She found him *'a quiet little boy who gave no trouble at all'.*[2]

It was there he met Tom Fraser who would become his life-long friend. The son of a railway surface man who had died aged 32, his mother had to bring up four children alone. There was no such thing as social standing in such a small community especially among children, their bonds of friendship were formed on fruit scrumping raids, they would often give imaginary sermons from Alistair's father's pulpit with much waving of arms and dramatic gestures.

In the spring and summer the MacLean boys, to save on shoes, went barefoot to school, which might appear penny-pinching considering their father's income was £700 a year when the average labourer at the time was paid a pound a week. The family employed Janet MacNeill as housekeeper; she had been with the Reverend since his first days at Shettleston. The Reverend MacLean's Uncle Stewart had employed more servants and a gardener and generated income from land – the 'glebe' – that went with the manse. Given the austerity of the times the Reverend of Daviot was known as a generous man. Tinkers and tramps were often picked up on the road as he did his rounds in his red Clyno car, in its day the biggest manufacturer of vehicles after Austin and Morris. He sometimes brought them home to be fed and they always left with some money in their pocket, much to the vexation of Mary and the equally stern Janet who was very much part of the family.

A few bird-line miles north of Daviot two hills squat on the edge of the Moray Firth, the north and south Sutors. Between them flows the sea to form a large sheltered natural harbour. Like a big lake that can hold many ships, anchored in safe, deep waters of the Cromarty Firth, the tiny town of Invergordon lies on the eastern shore. In September 1931 about 1,000 people lived in the town and some 12,000 sailors of the Royal Navy lived on ships at anchor nearby. The sailors of the lower deck had little to do but brood over the pay-cuts, particularly at that time.

In 1929 the economic foundations of post-war Britain began to unravel. That year the world boom collapsed, triggered by the New York stock market great crash. A Labour Government was elected in May committed to ending unemployment and increasing public spending; as the world went into crisis the new administration raised unemployment benefit. The result, sterling came under pressure and the new Government needed to borrow to protect the pound yet foreign bankers wanted the budget deficit eliminated. Spending would have to be reduced by £120 million, half the budget for the year. A report recommended an increase in taxation to raise £24 million and a drastic reduction in unemployment pay. Government employees also faced pay cuts of 10–20 per cent. This included the armed forces, that a report pointed out rather harshly: '*No officers or men serving His Majesty has any legal claim to a particular rate of pay.*'[3]

The King worried about revolution and there were riots outside parliament. Labour tried to avoid the cuts, but eventually they had little choice and taxes were raised even more than expected. Unemployment benefit was cut by 10 per cent, and state salaries by the 10–20 per cent recommended.

Navy pay proved more complicated, men being paid on the 1919 scales were placed on the lower 1925 rate. The result was that some men lost 25 per cent of their pay, officers about 11 per cent, while the Army and Air Force were down 10 per cent. Young married ratings were particularly hard hit. Even worse to foster resentment, the lower deck got the buzz of what was happening before the official announcement, which fostered the feeling it was all underhand. The Atlantic Fleet, anchored at Invergordon, got the official notification on 12 September 1931. There were soon ominous signs of unrest. In an attempt to head things off three days later the fleet was ordered to sea but the crews of four battleships refused to raise steam. The news stunned the world. The pound went into free fall losing a quarter of its value in a few days. The Government was forced to abandon the Gold Standard, and realigned navy pay-cuts to the same rate as the other services.

On board the cruiser HMS *Dorsetshire* Able Seaman 'Ginger' Le Breton recorded on the morning of the mutiny '*we all decided not to turn to*'. After breakfast on deck they cheered other ships that had gone on 'strike'. The captain of HMS *Dorsetshire* Arthur John Power, extremely popular with the crew, eventually managed to persuade his men to return to duty. Ginger found it a '*remarkably moving moment*' as the men came to attention and followed their captain, 'a *moment that I will remember forever.*'[4]

In the fleet seven captains were relieved of their commands. Captain Power was the only ship's captain from the mutiny to obtain further promotion. In a long career he would become Admiral of the Fleet Sir Arthur John Power. Of the admirals only one commanded again while 124 mutineers were drafted ashore, many of whom were discharged from the service, while the ships, to try and avoid further trouble, were dispersed to their home ports.

The young Alistair MacLean, aged nine at the time would have been well aware of the mutiny. He was on the cusp of following his older brothers to school at the Inverness Royal Academy. Inverness was only a few miles away but travel was difficult so the boys took up residence at a boarding house supervised by the Academy; this worked well with the even tempered Lachlan but not with the more rebellious Ian. He hated Hedgefield and stubbornly refused to attend. The Reverend MacLean solved the problem along with another minister Hector Cameron at Moy, not far from Daviot, who also had several children attending the Academy, by organising a bus. This also allowed young Alistair to attend the Academy while still living at home.

No doubt the Invergordon Mutiny lodged in Alistair's subconscious mind. Was this the inspiration for the opening pages of his first novel *HMS Ulysses* in which the opening scene had Vice-Admiral Vincent Starr, the Assistant Director of Naval Operations, talking to the senior officers of the *Ulysses* assembled in Rear Admiral Tyndall's day cabin? He has had to fly hurriedly from London, interrupting his busy schedule at the bequest of the First Sea Lord to investigate what had taken place aboard the ship. The men had gone on strike on the return from operations against Lofoten Island off the coast of Norway close to Narvik. Starr does not understand why '*Commissioned officers in His Majesty's Navy, including a flag officer, sympathise with – if not actually condone a lower deck mutiny*.' He questions why the *Ulysses*' own Marines were not used to restore order, instead of asking another ship for assistance?

Tyndall comes to the defence of Captain Dick Vallery and tells Starr it was on his orders. '*Turn our own Marines against men they've served with for two and a half years? Out of the question! There's no matelot-bootneck antipathy on this ship, Admiral Starr*.'

Starr is rather taken aback and returns to the report and the boarding party of Marines from the *Cumberland* and the fight that takes place when they attempt to arrest the ringleaders resulting in '*2 dead, 6 seriously injured, 35–40 minor casualties*'. He likens it to a battle.[5]

In general the Marines at Invergordon were not used for the same reason MacLean had used in his novel. Other than brief confrontations on HMS *York* and HMS *Norfolk*, on other ships some Marines joined what they considered a 'strike'.[6] Andrew Browne Cunningham, a later Admiral of the Fleet, felt: '*A mutiny it certainly was. It had no other name*.'

Although he did concede the action was directed against the Government and not against the officers.[7]

Are there echoes of the popular Captain Power of HMS *Dorsetshire* in the fictional saint-like Captain Vallery of the *Ulysses*, both of whom would reach flag rank? Vallery is promoted in action, but only after Tyndall had died of frostbite and shock. A signal arrives from the Admiralty that is read over the ship's loudspeaker system: '*Their Lordships expressly command best wishes Rear-Admiral, repeat Rear-Admiral Vallery. D.N.O, London.*' Vallery felt it '*Dead men's shoes*' and considers saying so but in the end said nothing on that point for it had cheered the crew.[8]

As Britain lurched from one crisis to another in the 'Great Depression' and unemployment reached 3.5 million, for the MacLeans it was as if they were far removed from the effects in their Highland home. In his study the Reverend MacLean was able to lose himself in his books; few things gave him as much pleasure. He had written his own book published in 1928, the *High Country*, a collection of essays upon the theme of the role of Christianity in life. *The Living Church* magazine reviewed the book, finding that it '*tingles with wholesome Scottish simplicity*' even though its references to Scottish literature were rather obscure.[9] He also reviewed books himself for the *Glasgow Herald* under the pseudonym 'Bookworm'. After the rigours of a large Glasgow parish and the horrors of the Great War, he was now happy with his ministry and his family. He probably had no inkling his third boy would become a bestselling author.

Ian felt his brother Alistair was not that bright, '*just a dour wee customer who was quietly introspective*' and his reading did not extend much beyond '*the Wizard or the Hotspur just like any other Highland boy.*'[10]

Dr Donald John Macdonald, the headmaster of the Royal Academy in Inverness remembered his famous pupil. He even taught Alistair English and in later life read his books, but at the time he had no idea he might be special: '*One of the lessons you learn in a lifetime of teaching is to keep an open mind about young people.*'

In 1934 the Reverend MacLean celebrated his twenty-five years of ministry. The church at Daviot was full; he paid tribute to his uncle and the congregation that had asked him to take over the parish of his youth; it had been like coming home. He added that he was happy and fortunate in his '*beloved wife*' and his four boys and to have a friend like Janet MacNeill. Most expected the forty-nine year old popular minister would have many more years before him. However it was not to be: two years later he died of a cerebral haemorrhage.

For Mary MacLean and her sons they had not only lost a beloved husband and father but their home as well. Now she had to provide a home for her and the boys. Gillespie was 10, Alistair 14, while Lachlan was 19 and had started studying medicine at Glasgow University. Mary was no doubt relieved in one sense that Ian had already gone to sea having joined the British India Navigation Company as a cadet.

Glasgow had been the home of Mary's youth and with Lachlan attending the university it was the obvious choice for her and the boys to return there, albeit coupled with a complete change in her financial position, her income consisting of a not too generous Church of Scotland pension.

Alistair was 15 when the family moved back to the city of his birth yet he would never forget the Highlands for he had '*only to smell a primrose and I am back again on the banks of the River Nairn in Inverness-shire*'. Although he had no love of Glasgow he had '*one burning ambition and that was to take advantage of the first opportunity to leave it…*'[11]

The MacLeans' new Glasgow home was a tenement flat on Carrington Street. Mary had to let two rooms to students to supplement her pension. Alistair had gained a bursary to Hillhead High School which he did not like as it was run more like an English Public School, while Gillespie went to Woodside Secondary.

For some time Lachlan had not enjoyed the best of health and had had an operation at Inverness Infirmary. Shortly after the family return to Glasgow he was rushed to hospital and another operation revealed stomach cancer. He died just short of his twenty-first birthday. It was as well Mary MacLean was strong-willed, already having lost her husband, her eldest son, and her home within two years. Janet had stayed a while, but had to find a living herself so even she had to move on, although she was not far away in service and was still a frequent visitor.

For Alistair the loss of Lachlan was a sorrow he never got over. He had been someone he looked up to who had protected him against Ian's bullying. Two of the Cameron boys, the sons of the Reverend Hector Cameron from the Daviot days, by then studying in Glasgow, often dropped in at Carrington Street. The talk usually got around to football with Alistair which helped bring him out of his shell and all became supporters of Glasgow Rangers. Archie Lamont, Mary's brother and the boy's uncle, stayed with them for a period and could be relied upon to get match tickets.

The sea seemed to offer Alistair a means of escape. Letters from Ian talked of distant exciting places and kindled in him a wish to set sail. Instead Adolf Hitler interrupted; he would go to sea – but in the Royal Navy.

Chapter Two

Joining Up

Only a few weeks after his nineteenth birthday Alistair MacLean left his native Scotland for the first time in the spring of 1941 – his destination HMS *Victory* in Portsmouth. Nelson's old Flagship, launched in 1765 had been 40-years-old at Trafalgar, and was under restoration at the base which had been turned into a training establishment for new ratings arriving every week to be housed in the Victorian barrack blocks.

In the summer of 1939 Alistair had left Hillhead High, his school in Glasgow, gaining his Higher Leaving Certificate with good marks; and was listed as coming third in English, quite a remarkable result as he later wrote: '*I had to go to school to learn English and was forbidden to speak it at home until the age of fifteen.*'[1] His headmaster was disappointed he did not return for the sixth-year studies, however Alistair needed to help support his widowed mother and younger brother Gillespie. Thus he took up the position of clerk in the offices of F.C. Strick. Frank Clarke Strick, a London shipbroker, had founded the London and Paris steamship company in 1887. The Strick Company Glasgow office was opened in 1920.

Alistair's ambition at the time was to follow his older brother Ian's lead and go to sea, although he had seen little of Ian who had been home only three times in five years since joining the Merchant Navy. He did return to Glasgow early in the war to sit his Second Mates examination after which he returned to sea aboard the ill-fated SS *Domala*, a passenger liner of 8,000 tons launched in 1921 and built for the India route. She was bombed by the Luftwaffe in the English Channel on 2 March 1940; badly damaged and on fire, the ship was beached off the Isle of Wight to save her. Around 100 people died in the attack but Ian was lucky and survived. Salvaged and renamed *Empire Attendant* she was sunk by *U-582* in 1942, in the submarine's log she was entered as the *Domala*.

When Alistair set off south for Portsmouth in 1941 he may not have felt so confident in leaving Scotland at that time although no doubt this was coupled with an element of excitement. Much later he wrote about leaving Scotland in general that the *'most striking feature about Scotland is not Scotland itself but the vast droves of its loyal citizens who regularly depart from their enchanted homeland with a fixed and avowed determination never to return to it again.'*[2]

Many young men, who would be considered boys today, in the Second World War volunteered to join the Royal Navy by choice, in many cases to avoid conscription into the Army. The National Service Armed Forces Act at the time required all able men between the ages of 18 and 41 liable for conscription to register. By the end of 1939 1.5 million men had been conscripted to join the armed forces. Of these, 1.1 million went to the army, the rest being split between the Navy and Air Force. By volunteering you were far more likely to get your choice.

Like Alistair and others the Cornish poet Charles Causley became a HO, 'hostilities only rating' and volunteered for the navy after watching his father, a veteran soldier of the Great War who had served on the Western Front, an invalid because of that war, die in 1924 all too young from its effects. Thus Charles *'didn't fancy the army'*; he also had a long train journey from Launceston in Cornwall, in his case to HMS *Royal Arthur* at Skegness in Lincolnshire for his rating training.[3] Many years later Alistair MacLean would buy Jamaica Inn high up on Bodmin Moor not far from the market town of Launceston.

The Senior Service was the most prestigious of Britain's armed forces and of the world in 1939. The lure of the Navy's aura of history and duty was attractive to many. In the early months of the war, like the other services, the navy had plenty of volunteers. From a force of less than 200,000 regulars and reservists before the war it would grow to over 900,000 by 1945. There would be over half a million 'Hostilities Only' ratings by the war's end. A further 70,000 served in the Royal Marines, while the Women's Royal Navy Service ballooned from 6,000 in 1940 to 75,000 by 1944. Well might a Government report in 1941 highlight that men were attracted by the *'personal prestige'* which being part of the senior service imbued on the individual.[4]

Like Alistair, Stuart Pent another Scot left from Glasgow Central Station for London. He found the train was full of soldiers and airmen and he got little sleep. On arrival in London, he had to change stations from Euston to Waterloo, for which he took a cab, where he caught the Portsmouth train. He spent nine weeks training as a seaman at HMS *Collingwood,* before he was found to be colour blind and was transferred to engineering and became a stoker with three more weeks training at the main barracks at HMS *Victory.*[5] Here Alistair embarked on his basic training on 3 June 1941 and was issued his kit and given his service number JX282131, a number drummed into every recruit and learnt parrot-fashion and something never forgotten. Stan Bowman found the drill tough at HMS *Victory* barracks drill ground in September 1940 and recorded in his diary after one period that *'14 collapse on the parade ground out of 30.'*[6]

Alistair's specialist training in the torpedo branch took place at HMS *Vernon.* Generally a six week course, it had been located at Gunwharf Portsmouth but enemy bombing of the harbour area forced its dispersal to various sites around the country. *Vernon R* was established at Roedean School for girls, Brighton in May 1941. The course included electrical theory and work with depth charges, mines and torpedoes. At the time, like Alistair, many men *'were fresh out of basic training and were still wet behind the ears, while seasoned hands found Roedean a big change'.* The navy still used hammocks at the time, both at sea and in many cases ashore, slung in large communal spaces, each man carried his own hammock from ship to ship as a part of his personal kit. In the naval ratings' handbook there are four pages devoted to care of the hammock and an elaborate illustration for slinging a hammock. At Roedean: *'Instruction was given Monday to Friday and Saturday mornings, involving marching six or seven hundred men into the workshops in and around Brighton twice a day for instruction and back. Some as far away as the Dreadnought Garage site in Hove.'*[7]

Roedean, being close to the beach, was under the constant threat of attack and regular defence exercises were held. Other sites around the town were targeted by enemy aircraft. In October 1942 two Me 109s strafed the St. Dunstan's building, one rating was killed and another wounded.

In one of his last novels *San Andreas* (1984) MacLean mentions Roedean through his character Bosun Archie McKinnon who, after the wounding of the captain and the death of senior officers, takes command of the ship. The *San Andreas* was a British Merchant Navy Hospital Ship on her way back from Murmansk in Russia. He unmasks a spy-saboteur whose cover is blown, as an RN LTO (Leading Torpedo Operator), because his pay-book states he qualified at Portsmouth. Confronting Simons, the spy, he tells him.

> '*I was a Torpedo Gunner's Mate in the Navy. No L.T.Os qualified in Portsmouth in early nineteen forty-three, or indeed for some considerable time before and after that. They qualified at Roedean College near Brighton....*' which was a girl's college before the war. '*You're a fraud and a spy, Simons.*'[8]

There must have been an element of excitement when Alistair, carrying his kitbag, walked up the gangplank of his first ship HMS *Bourne,* a requisitioned paddle steamer on Thursday 19 March 1942. He would have been all too familiar with this type of vessel that plied the Clyde and the salt water lochs of the Western Isles. Indeed the *Bournemouth Queen* had been built on the banks of the Clyde in 1908 and was considerably modified for naval service. Alistair would have noted on the foredeck her 12-pounder gun of First World War vintage and aft where the saloon had once been had been cut away to accommodate mine-sweeping gear; this would be his action-station as a torpedo rating. She was then based on the Tyne and Forth as an anti-aircraft vessel, although she would also have been able to deal with mines. In Alistair's book *The Lonely Sea,* a collection of short stories, there is a tribute story to minesweeping in *They Sweep the Seas,* which has a trawler off the West Coast of Scotland fulfilling that role, commanded by two veterans of the First World War. '*The Lieutenant (RNR) wore three rows of ribbon*'; he had seen action in the Dardanelles '*and walked with a pronounced limp – a memento of Zeebrugge.*' No doubt he was referring here to the April 1918 raid on Zeebrugge. The skipper was even older and he '*had swept mines*' in the earlier conflict. Could these have been a profile of the type of men who might have commanded HMS *Bourne?*[9]

The east coast from the Tyne to Harwich was known as 'E-boat Alley' in 1941. There was a shortage of MGBs (Motor Gunboats), and MTBs (Motor Torpedo Boats) and Corvettes to combat the fast German boats and air attack at the time, so all sorts of craft were pressed into service. Not that the *Bourne* would have been capable of taking on an E-boat. Her role was in the rivers and estuaries as there was still a threat of invasion at the time, as well as sailing as part of the escort with the coastal convoys.

Eric James Craske was a naval gunner who served on DEMs for most of the war (Defensively Equipped Merchant Ships). In 1940 he joined the SS *Birker Force*, '*1,100 tons of coal-dust-caked collier*' forming up with a convoy on the Tyne. They were bound for Beckton gas works in London. Off the Humber they sailed past the results of the work of the '*Luftwaffe, E-boats, U-boats, mines, masts sticking up out of the water, marked by a mass of wreck buoys.*'

Near Yarmouth, German aircraft attacked the convoy; they '*came out of the sun. The armed trawler escort let fly with her 12-pounder, everybody firing every which way.*' He did four trips on the *Birker Force* '*up and down the Tyne, and you know you can actually get to like a little coal carrier, if you love ships*'. The only trouble he found was that in bad weather she '*rolled something awful*'.[10]

By the time HMS *Bourne* arrived on the Clyde the most important ship in Alistair MacLean's life had been laid down and building for over a year. HMS *Royalist*, pennant number 89, was a modified *Dido*-class light cruiser ordered from Scotts of Greenock which had been laid down on 21 May 1940.

Alistair said goodbye to HMS *Bourne* in February 1943; later in the war she became an accommodation ship at Fort William. Refitted after the war, the *Bournemouth Queen* did another ten years plying the south coast before going to the breaker's yard in 1957.

Then Alistair spent four months at HMS *Roedean* in Brighton before moving back to Scotland and HMS *Spartiate* in June 1943 for two months, a shore establishment based on the St. Enoch hotel forming the grand Victorian frontage of St. Enoch railway station, which the navy had taken over to move personnel away from the dockyards that lined the Clyde that were a prime target for enemy aircraft. The shore establishment is mentioned in the novel HMS *Ulysses*, when assistant cook McQuater, trapped in the Y-turret magazine, speaks with Captain Vallery as a fire is raging above and he switches on the sprinklers to flood the magazine. Vallery asks him over the intercom if there is any message he might like to send: '*Me? Ach, there's naething Ah'd like….Well, maybe a transfer to the Spartiate, but Ah'm thinking maybe it's a wee bit over late for that.*'[11]

The Clyde River Patrol was also run from the hotel, its main task to keep open the narrow dredged channel that led west to the Firth of Clyde. Any ship that got damaged in the channel would be like a cork in a bottle and could be disastrous. The main danger was mines, and watching posts were strung along the banks of the channel manned by the Home Guard or Naval ratings in transit like Alistair. Fourteen launches manned by volunteers from the Northern Yacht Club under the command of the RNVR also patrolled the channel, any mines found were dealt with by minesweepers.

Room 504 in the hotel housed a small office of Naval Intelligence run by Lieutenant Commander Edward Seagar who had a direct line to the Admiralty and he ran a string of agents in Glasgow. Through them he came across intelligence that the Philips Radio factory in Eindhoven was providing most of the radios in German tanks. This led to the RAF raiding the site and wiping out radio production.[12]

Chapter Three

HMS *Royalist*

After the anti-aircraft cruiser HMS *Royalist* was launched at the end of May 1942 the young Alistair MacLean joined the ship in August 1943. Scott's yard at Greenock had been building ships since 1711 and would build 114 for the Royal Navy. Around the dockside and on the ship would have been a hive of activity, the ship's company key personnel would have started to arrive a few at a time, so as not to get in the way of the dockyard workers affectionately known as 'dockyardies'. As the commissioning day approached more would arrive from all over the country, and the officers would be briefed by the commanding officer. That officer was Captain Markham Henry Evelegh who was 45 in 1942, and had been appointed to command HMS *Royalist* at the end of June 1941. He had joined the navy at the start of the First World War and remained in the navy afterwards.[1]

Next would come contractors' trials after which HMS *Royalist* would be commissioned into the fleet. Midshipman John Roberts described the process that took place aboard the destroyer HMS *Serapis*:

The ship's company arrived in the morning and in the afternoon we took in all our stores. It was a busy day, the workmen still trying to finish jobs, and we trying to sort ourselves out. Dust and smoke from recent welding while everywhere the smell of new paint mixed with that of the first meals being cooked in the galleys.[2]

However, HMS *Royalist* as ships go did not have an easy birth, as she was a modified version of the *Dido* class light cruisers designed as AA ships in the fleet role. Displacing about 7,000 tons fully loaded, some ten ships were ordered from 1936–1938 while in 1939 five of the modified ships were ordered. HMS *Royalist* would be further redesigned to act as an escort carrier squadron flagship immediately on completion.[3]

The general modifications of what became known as the *Bellona* class of five ships arose because of shortages and, to improve stability, the third super emplaced 5.25in turret 'Q' was omitted and in its place, a smaller multiple anti-aircraft mounting was built. This saved weight and space, permitting the bridge superstructure to be moved forward and the two funnels to be straightened, making a clearly different silhouette compared to the earlier *Dido* ships.

Inside the rear hardback cover of the Collins 1st Edition of *HMS Ulysses* is an excellent line drawing of the cruiser. Very similar to the *Royalist*, it shows the Admiral's quarters No.19 and the For'ard pom-pom No.6 that replaced the Q turret, behind which is the Fighter Direction Room No.8 also a modification. This is also explained in the text that '*Ulysses*' was one of a kind, a '*modification of the famous Dido type, a forerunner of the Black Prince class.*'[4]

In fact both HMS *Royalist* and HMS *Black Prince* were part of what became known as the *Bellona* class. Yet it was only HMS *Royalist* that was further modified inside where two compartments were changed and fitted out as communications rooms for carrier operations. One of these was for the Action Information Office (AIO), an early operation room for plotting and display of tactical positions, a feature of most modern warships to this day. This was to help with the ship's role in operations against the German capital ships *Tirpitz* and *Scharnhorst*. However, it increased the size of the crew by over 100 and affected the sleeping arrangements on board making them cramped and uncomfortable.[5]

In *HMS Ulysses* it is one of the reasons the crew are tired, as it is the only ship able to fulfil the role of carrier command and air operations.[6] The ship returning from one operation has to immediately re-store and be ready to set out on an Arctic convoy, which sparks the mutiny.

In September 1943 HMS *Royalist* was on acceptance trials, however the result was more delay for '*defects and installation problems*'.[7] Repairs and alterations continued into October and would not be completed until January 1944. Through this extended period the crew would have been, in the majority of cases, surplus to requirements.

Courses and training would have been high on the list 'to keep the men busy'. Alistair's advancement from ordinary seaman to able seaman was '*governed by the time served in the lower rate and is subject to the man being qualified and recommended*'. Educationally all that was required was

'*A simple test in arithmetic and dictation…,*' as the naval ratings handbook tells us.[8] Leave was another way to use the time and was good for morale, but was always subject to conditions: '*Leave with full pay and allowances is granted in accordance with the regulations whenever possible, but always subject to the exigencies of the service generally, to the safety and efficiency of the ship in particular, and to the local circumstances which may prevail.*'[9]

On leave Alistair returned to visit his school in Inverness. He must have been on leave or liberty when he saw a huge fight on '*Princess Street, Edinburgh, between our own forces and the American Navy*' and by our own forces he literally meant Scots because he found that '*none of the casualties to whom I spoke later had an English, Irish or Welsh accent.*'[10]

By February 1944 HMS *Royalist* had started run-up trials in the Clyde area and then finally in March she joined the Home Fleet at Scapa Flow. Her first sortie would be against the mighty German battleship *Tirpitz*, sister ship to the *Bismarck*. Immensely powerful ships weighing over 50,000 tons fully loaded, they had double bottoms and twenty-two water tight compartments and armour belts 8.7–12.6 inches thick. With their wide beams they were extremely stable. Alistair wrote of the *Bismarck* that this '*provided a magnificently stable firing platform for her eight 15-inch and twelve 6-inch guns – and the German gunnery, far superior to ours…….*' and they were fast with a top speed of 30 knots (35 mph). *Tirpitz* was laid down in 1936, launched in 1939 and entered service in February 1941.[11]

Two years before in January 1942 under direct orders from Hitler the new battleship *Tirpitz* was moved to Norway. The Fuhrer's 'intuition' was that the Allies might invade Norway. He declared that: '*Every ship which is not stationed in Norway is in the wrong place.*'[12] The Germans managed to get *Tirpitz* to Trondheim undetected by using the Kiel Canal, yet the movement of such a large ship could not be hidden for long. The loss of her whereabouts by the British prompted Admiral Sir John Tovey, commander of the Home Fleet, to cover the northern passages into the Atlantic and postpone the sailing of the next Russian convoy PQ9. It took air reconnaissance a week to find her. The battleship was anchored under camouflage nets in Aasfiord 15 miles from Trondheim.

For many months *Tirpitz* and other German surface ships would influence British convoy operations to Russia and in the North Atlantic, albeit for most of the time these ships did very little anchored in Norwegian Fjords. Soon *Tirpitz* was joined by the pocket battleship *Admiral Scheer* and the heavy cruiser *Prinz Eugen*. Although the submarine *Trident* torpedoed the cruiser, badly damaged, she limped back to Germany.

The presence of German heavy units in Norway and in particular *Tirpitz* cast a long shadow over the deployment of the Royal Navy's capital ships. Churchill did not like the use of these ships in this manner or the First Sea Lord, Sir Dudley Pound's insistence that at least three of Britain's most modern battleships of the *King George V* class remain in home waters.[13]

In February the German battle cruiser *Scharnhorst* joined *Tirpitz,* a potential confrontation with these ships of the Kriegsmarine obsessed senior Royal Navy officers, who were willing to use the Russian convoys as bait. *The Times* in an editorial went as far as to comment that Admiral Tovey '*would probably much prefer to find them at sea than to know that they continued to lurk in a lair so conveniently placed. If the Russian convoys prove a magnet to draw them to sea he will know how to deal with them.*'[14]

Captain Vallery in *HMS Ulysses* over the loudspeaker system 'clears lower deck' and speaks to the crew shortly after they set off, he does not '*minimise the dangers*'. He says they face four problems '*abnormal weather conditions*'; second there would be no time to pick up survivors; third there were '*possibly three–U-boat packs*' waiting for them, and '*finally, we have reason to believe that Tirpitz is preparing to move out.*'[15]

In March *Tirpitz* had put to sea in an attempt to intercept the British convoys PQ.12 outbound and QP.8, the homeward convoy, both were large of sixteen and fifteen merchant ships respectively. A long range Focke-Wulf Condor reported the outbound convoy on 5 March and on that information *Tirpitz* put to sea with three destroyers. The Condors are known as '*Charlie*' in *HMS Ulysses* when they find FR.77, three arrive at the same time which meant trouble. By this time all four escort carriers, the main reason *HMS Ulysses* has been deployed with the convoy, have been lost.[16]

On the evening of 6 March the submarine *Seawolf* patrolling off Trondheim reports a heavy ship having sailed. The Home Fleet puts to sea with two *King George V* class battleships, the battle cruiser HMS *Renown* and the aircraft carrier HMS *Victorious* and attendant destroyers. However, the weather is bad, preventing the launching of search aircraft.

The next day the two convoys passed each other 200 miles south-west of Bear Island; at that time all elements were within 90 miles of each other. *Tirpitz* had just missed them passing within a few miles of both convoys. The German destroyers were detached to sweep to the north and one of them sank a Russian merchant ship which had dropped astern of the homeward convoy. These ships soon had to abandon their search to refuel. *Tirpitz* with much bigger fuel tanks and range continued to search alone but by then the gap between the two convoys had widened. Tovey and the German commander Vice-Admiral Otto Ciliax continued to play blind man's bluff. With better weather, aircraft from HMS *Victorious* did locate *Tirpitz* heading for home and a torpedo bomber attack was launched on 9 March. The Albacore's attack failed to hit the battleship while two aircraft were lost. That evening, *Tirpitz* anchored off Narvik and the next day the Home Fleet reached Scapa Flow.

Lack of fuel would severely curtail the use of German heavy ships. It was not until PQ.17 sailed in June that *Tirpitz* was ready for action along with the heavy cruiser *Admiral Hipper* and six destroyers which sortied from Trondheim. A second group of the slower pocket battleships *Lutzow*, *Admiral Scheer* and six destroyers would operate from Narvik, although soon after sailing *Lutzow* ran aground and had to return to port. The convoy had a covering escort of the battleships HMS *Duke of York* and the USS *Washington* with the carrier HMS *Victorious*.

Intelligence reports passed on to the Admiralty by the naval attaché in Stockholm, Captain Henry Denham, were enough to convince them to disperse the convoy with disastrous results. Admiral Pound made that decision on 4 July on a report of inactivity and was trying to anticipate moves rather than waiting. The actual sailing was reported the next day:

Telegram (C) Most immediate Arctic Convoy:
1. *At 14.30 Sunday 5 July naval forces unspecified then at Rolfso sailed to attack convoy.*
2. German air force was given orders to cease attacks on British warships at 16.00 Sunday 5th. (In case by mistake they attacked their own ships.) *After this attacks only to be made on convoy and aircraft carrier. 1258/6 July.*

Yet the next day Denham reported that: *Telegram (E) Immediate Arctic Convoy:*

German naval forces have been ordered to abandon operation to attack
convoy by 22.00 on 5 July........1714/7 July.[17]

The question is why did Pound wish to avoid a confrontation with German surface ships when Tovey's strategy had been to bring on a fight? Pound was responsible for all fronts and at the time the Royal Navy was stretched very thin in the Mediterranean, the huge effort of Operation *Pedestal* convoy was being made to keep Malta in the war. The Battle of the Atlantic was at its height and the US Navy was hard pushed in the Pacific, although had sent some ships to the Home Fleet to help support the Russian convoys. As Donald McLachlan indicates in his book on Naval Intelligence:

If Hitler and Raeder were afraid of losing big ships because they had so
few, so then were Churchill and Pound. They were not in the mood for a
death or glory battle against the mighty Tirpitz *and her squadron. But,*
on the Royal Navy's aggressive record to date, the German Naval Staff
could not count on that; indeed, they seem to have assumed the opposite.[18]

The result was twenty-three ships with valuable cargoes sunk by U-boats and aircraft. At the time Dudley Pound was ill and how much this affected his judgment is hard to say, but the obstinacy he displayed in not reversing the order is hard to explain otherwise. A few months later he suffered a stroke, a brain tumour was discovered and he died on Trafalgar Day, 21 October 1943.

'*Do another PQ.17?*' says Commander Turner in *HMS Ulysses* observing: '*The Royal Navy could never stand it….*'[19] Unusual for a novel there is an extensive footnote covering the bottom of two pages about the ill-fated PQ.17. In that note MacLean is clear he does not '*presume to assign blame.*
Curiously enough the only definite conclusion is that no blame can be attached to
the actual commander of the squadron, Admiral Hamilton. He had no part in the
decision to withdraw.' (MacLean refers to Rear Admiral L.H.K. Hamilton commander of the 1st Cruiser squadron, the convoy's close cover.)[20]

After PQ.17 *Tirpitz* went into an extended period of refit at Trondheim which was not completed until December 1942. *Scharnhorst* arrived in Norway in March 1943. As part of their sea trials the two ships attacked Spitzbergen which then housed a British weather station and refuelling facility. *Tirpitz* fired her 15-inch main armament in anger for the first and last time.

The British were determined to neutralise the ship and after several ineffective bombing raids, X-Craft (midget submarines) were used to lay mines under the *Tirpitz*. The X-Craft were the most potent and effective of all midget submarines used during the war. The craft used against *Tirpitz* were 50ft long, weighed 27 tons, carried a charge of 4,480lbs and had a crew of four. They were towed by a conventional submarine and then released once close to the target. In September 1943 three out of ten of the tiny vessels breached the defences surrounding the battleship and two laid mines. The explosion resulted in extensive damage to the hull. Fear of returning the battleship to Germany for repairs meant they were carried out by the repair ship *Neumark*, a remarkable achievement albeit they were not completed until April 1944.

Rear Admiral Claud Barry summed up in his dispatch about Operation Source the X-Craft attack on *Tirpitz*:

In the full knowledge of the hazards that they were to encounter, these gallant crews penetrated into a heavily defended fleet anchorage. There, with cool courage and determination, and in spite of all the modern devices the ingenuity devised for their detection and destruction, they pressed home their attack to the full... It is clear that courage and enterprise of the very highest order was shown by these gallant gentlemen, whose daring attack will surely go down in history as one of the most courageous acts of all time.[21]

Alone the battle cruiser *Scharnhorst* attempted to intercept convoy JW 55B at the end of 1943. On this occasion the convoy was ordered to reverse course, while a trap was hatched by British cruisers covered by the battleship HMS *Duke of York*, with the advantage of radar controlled guns. *Scharnhorst* floundered about in bad weather until she was surprised by the cruiser HMS *Belfast*, in a running fight the battle cruiser managed to damage HMS *Norfolk* which had joined the fight. With the odds mounting against him, Admiral Erich Bey, the German commander tried to run back to port, however, they sailed south into the path of HMS *Duke of York*. The first salvo from the battleship scored a direct hit on *Scharnhorst* and with cruisers on one side and HMS *Duke of York* on the other there was no escape. Destroyers finished her off with torpedoes. *Scharnhorst* capsized and sank at 19:45 on 26 December; only 36 of her crew of near 2,000 were picked up.

Chapter Four

March–May 1944, Northern Waters

On 30 March 1944 HMS *Royalist* set sail from Scapa Flow at 1715, flying the flag of Rear Admiral Arthur William La Touche Bisset. He commanded Force 8, with four escort carriers and the fleet carrier HMS *Furious*, their target the German battleship *Tirpitz* that lay at anchor in Alten Fjord Norway within the Arctic Circle. Bisset was a highly experienced commander of naval air operations having commanded the fleet carriers HMS *Formidable* and HMS *Illustrious* in the Mediterranean. A small rotund cheerful looking man, he could have been the model for MacLean's ill-fated Admiral Tyndall in *HMS Ulysses*, who is a west country man known affectionately as '*Farmer Giles*' with '*ruddy features, usually so cheerful and crinkling....*'[1]

The Admiralty had alerted C-in-C Home Fleet in January: '*In view of the great importance of putting* Tirpitz *out of action, it is requested that you will plan to attack* Tirpitz *in Altenfjord with naval aircraft during the period 7–16 March.*'[2] The operation was code-named 'Thrustful' but later changed to 'Tungsten'. The dates of the operation were postponed to the end of March, beginning of April as a radar update on the carrier HMS *Victorious* overran. Some 42 Fairey Barracuda Fleet Air Arm dive bombers, carrying either 500lb or one 1,600 lb bombs would make the attack from the fleet carriers and would be escorted by 88 fighters flying from the escort carriers.

HMS *Victorious* had sailed at noon with a powerful Home Fleet escort including two battleships under the C-in-C Admiral Sir Bruce Fraser. To cover the later sailing of Force 8 a fake radio net was set up to confuse the enemy operating for five days with transmissions from the shore establishments Hatston air station, Loch Erriboll and Scapa Flow, and ships not involved in the operation, including the battleship HMS *Rodney* and the depot ship HMS *Tyne*.

Zero hour was 3 April at 0415 and Lieutenant Richard Walker was on the destroyer HMS *Wakeful,* part of the escort force. He watched the aircraft take off in two waves three-quarters of an hour apart: *'It was a beautiful clear morning with a light breeze and a calm sea. We could see the snow on the Norwegian Mountains about sixty miles off to the south.'*[3]

Four aircraft were lost during the attack but *Tirpitz* had been hit fourteen times. The ship's heavy armour prevented serious damage against relatively light bombs, yet a further three months of repairs would be required.

Both HMS *Victorious* and HMS *Furious* moved closer to the shore to recover aircraft which was completed by 0758. Vice-Admiral Sir Henry Moore who had planned the operation signalled the Admiralty: *'Tungsten completed Admiral Von Tirpitz hit by at least one 1,600lb bomb and many other bombs 3 Barracudas one fighter lost. Fighter pilot safe.'* He considered renewing the attack the next day, but the *'fatigue of air crews'* and the favourable reports of damage already inflicted, plus a deterioration in the weather convinced him the fleet should return to Scapa Flow. Meanwhile the fleet also covered the passing of convoy JW 58 to Murmansk.[4]

The convoy had departed Liverpool on 27 March with forty-eight merchant ships and was the biggest convoy ever to sail on the north Russia run, and much was done in a hurry to give it better protection. Unusually it was to have two escort carriers to accompany it, HMS *Biter* and HMS *Tracker*. However the former was not ready in time so HMS *Activity* was hurriedly despatched from Greenwich to Scapa Flow on 24 March. She had not been 'arcticised' with steam heating at gun mountings, flying stations, and catapult mechanisms and she only had three Swordfish and seven Wildcats on board. HMS *Tracker's* air crews were rusty as there had been no time for either carrier to work up. Two days later, off Iceland, HMS *Starling*, a *Black Swan* class sloop and one of the most successful anti-submarine ships in the Royal Navy, sank *U-961*. By now the convoy was supported by the Second Escort Group from the Atlantic. North-west of Norway three more U-boats were sunk, two by aircraft from the carrier HMS *Tracker*. Apart from one merchantman forced to return all JW 58's forty-eight ships reached Kola Inlet on 5 April.[5]

The Arctic convoys took a million tons of supplies to the Soviet Union, including 5,000 tanks and 7,000 aircraft. The Royal Navy lost eighteen warships and 1,994 men in the years 1941–1945, while 98 merchant ships were lost with 829 men. The Kriegsmarine lost one battleship, three destroyers, and 32 submarines and the Luftwaffe numerous aircraft. As Glyn Prysor observed in his book *Citizen Sailors*, '*Judged simply by relative casualty rates, this was the most dangerous convoy route, but the human cost went further. Physical and psychological trauma continued to take their toll long afterwards.*'[6] Yet it was not until 2012 that a campaign medal, the Arctic Star, was awarded retrospectively after much lobbying, for service in the Arctic Convoys and was awarded for service north of the Arctic Circle.

In Jack Webster's excellent biography of Alistair MacLean he writes that: '*MacLean's ship took part in only two full runs to the outskirts of Murmansk, it was heavily-engaged in bombing German oil installations on the Norwegian coast.*'[7] A confusing statement, as movements for HMS *Royalist* in the Admiralty Diary do not support this in that the ship was only involved with one convoy JW 58 and then only as distant cover as part of Operation Tungsten.[8] Webster may have been influenced by Tom Brown, a Glaswegian and ship mate of Alistair's, although he never knew the future author at the time which is not all that surprising in a crew of over 600. Brown spent his war on HMS *Royalist* and told Webster that they '*ran through these hell-trips to Murmansk with nothing worse than a hole in the funnel.*'[9]

However, HMS *Royalist* did take part in strikes against shipping and installations on the Norwegian coast in Operations Hoops and Potluck. For Hoops they left Scapa Flow on Sunday 7 May. HMS *Royalist* was flag ship and in the force were three escort carriers, the cruiser HMS *Jamaica* and six destroyers. The next day at 0700 strikes were launched against a German north bound convoy of five merchant ships with ten escorts close to Kristiansand. One merchant ship was damaged while two Wildcats of the strike force were shot down. On return to the carriers the force was jumped by Me 109s and Fw 190s which were driven off by Hellcats. A strike was launched against oil tanks at Khjen and the force shot down two float planes. After the strike force was recovered the ships withdrew, returning to Scapa Flow on 9 May.[10]

Three days later HMS *Royalist* sailed again on Operation Potluck, this was to create a diversion for Operation Brawn, another attack on *Tirpitz*. With HMS *Royalist* were the escort carriers HMS *Emperor* and HMS *Striker*, the cruiser HMS *Sheffield* and six destroyers. Arriving off the south central Norwegian coast two days later they began to be shadowed by German aircraft which meant they had fulfilled part of their mission. That afternoon they were attacked by a group of Me 110s. Gunfire from HMS *Royalist*'s high angle 5.25 inch guns, firing 'proximity shells' that detonated close to the target rather than on contact, was particularly effective and forced them away, chased off by Sea Hurricanes from HMS *Striker*. Closing the coast, a strike was launched against the fish oil factory at Fosnavag and two armed coasters found close inshore. A Focke-Wulf 200 Condor started shadowing the force but was chased off by Wildcats and was last seen disappearing into cloud with a port engine smoking.

MacLean had a grudging respect for the giant German reconnaissance aircraft, nicknamed 'Charlie' and would later write *'the most effective air weapon the Germans had was the essentially non-combative Focke-Wulf Condor 200'*. With its remarkable flying range as far as the Arctic Convoys were concerned, it could cover all the northern seas high up into the Arctic Circle and even the dreaded Denmark Strait, between Iceland and Greenland. It was through that strait that the Russian-bound convoys from Canada and the United States passed. To see a Condor could mean disaster.[11]

Bad weather curtailed any further operations and the force withdrew arriving back at Scapa Flow 0600 Tuesday 16 May. As for Operation Brawn, designed to be a repeat of Tungsten, weather conditions over Tirpitz were bad with low cloud and the strike force from HMS *Victorious* had to abandon the mission and return to the carrier.[12]

In the novel *HMS Ulysses* MacLean uses his own experiences of life onboard HMS *Royalist* but also weaves in well documented events of other ships and men to create his fictional Arctic Convoy FR77. First the men of *HMS Ulysses* are confronted by the weather as the mercury in the barometer keeps falling, the waves get higher, the troughs deeper. The experienced sailors know what's coming, Carrington, who had spent years in the West Indies and been through several hurricanes, *'Admits he's seen a barometer lower but never so low with the pressure still falling so fast'*.[13]

The description of weather conditions are among some of MacLean's best writing: *'It was a dull glaring purple, neither increasing nor fading, faintly luminous and vaguely menacing in its uniformity and permanence.'* And as the storm struck, *'serried waves of greenish-grey'* and there was *'500 feet between crest and crest'*.[14]

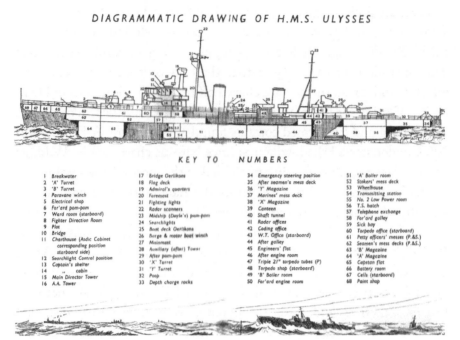

DIAGRAMMATIC DRAWING OF H.M.S. ULYSSES

KEY TO NUMBERS

1 Breakwater	17 Bridge Oerlikons	34 Emergency steering position	51 'A' Boiler room
2 'A' Turret	18 Flag deck	35 After seamen's mess deck	52 Stokers' mess deck
3 'B' Turret	19 Admiral's quarters	36 'Y' Magazine	53 Wheelhouse
4 Paravane winch	20 Foremast	37 Marines' mess deck	54 Transmitting station
5 Electrical shop	21 Fighting lights	38 'X' Magazine	55 No. 2 Low Power room
6 For'ard pom-pom	22 Radar scanners	39 Canteen	56 T.S. hatch
7 Ward room (starboard)	23 Midship (Dayle's) pom-pom	40 Shaft tunnel	57 Telephone exchange
8 Fighter Direction Room	24 Searchlights	41 Radar offices	58 For'ard galley
9 Plot	25 Boat deck Oerlikons	42 Coding office	59 Sick bay
10 Bridge	26 Burge & motor boat winch	43 W.T. Office (starboard)	60 Torpedo office (starboard)
11 Charthouse (Asdic Cabinet corresponding position starboard side)	27 Mainmast	44 After galley	61 Petty officers' messes (P.&S.)
	28 Auxiliary (after) Tower	45 Engineers' flat	62 Seamen's mess decks (P.&S.)
12 Searchlight Control position	29 After pom-pom	46 After engine room	63 'B' Magazine
13 Captain's shelter	30 'X' Turret	47 Triple 21" torpedo tubes (P)	64 'A' Magazine
14 „ cabin	31 'Y' Turret	48 Torpedo shop (starboard)	65 Capstan flat
15 Main Director Tower	32 Poop	49 'B' Boiler room	66 Battery room
16 A.A. Tower	33 Depth charge racks	50 For'ard engine room	67 Cells (starboard)
			68 Paint shop

Diagram of HMS *Ulysses* as it appears in the end pages of the first edition of the book. (*Courtesy of HarperCollins*)

Frank Pearce sailed on the cruiser HMS *Trinidad* on convoy PQ 13 right into an Arctic gale. The waves as '*high as sixty feet*' crashing into the ship yet while deep in the trough the quiet was eerie. Then the climb began, the ship vibrating to another '*foam lashed crest*' where they were struck by the '*unbridled force of the tempest…*'[15]

Then there was the intense cold that numbed the bones of drained men already tired from lack of sleep. Ordinary Seaman Dick Wilder served on the destroyer HMS *Impulsive* and his ship joined PQ 18 in September 1942. Even submarines were deployed along the Norwegian coast to attack any German surface units that might be tempted to come out. Some sixty-five warships were there to support the thirty-two merchant ships, probably a reaction to the disastrous PQ 17. Wilder remembered being at defence stations for the entire passage '*four hours on four off*' and that '*lack of sleep was probably the hardest thing to bear along with the cold*'. He '*wore three jerseys, long johns, no 3 trousers, and my overalls, topped with a duffle coat, Cossack hat, scarf and gloves*'. Yet he still felt cold.[16]

Ice was another problem; it could add hundreds of tons to the weight of a ship, even change the centre of gravity, more a problem for the destroyers and even worse for the top heavy carriers. Their flight decks became sheets of ice for the crew to try and clear, in such conditions with hand tools and steam hoses it was extremely hazardous, in bad weather impossible.

With PQ 18, for only the second time in the war an escort carrier HMS *Avenger* was part of the convoy. MacLean in *HMS Ulysses* has four accompany FR 77 but they do not last long. The novel is split into seven days starting on Sunday afternoon. On Tuesday morning the first of the carriers *Invader*, hits a rogue drifting mine; badly holed she is sent back to base with two escorts. That afternoon with the storm gathering fury *Defender's* flight deck is torn open and she is sent back to Scapa Flow, along with the old destroyer *Portpatrick*, one of the lend-lease former US Navy First World War destroyers, as her bow plates had started leaking. That night *Wrestler's* steering gear is damaged so she too has to be sent back. Finally at 0702 on the Wednesday, the storm having abated, *Blue Ranger* the last carrier is torpedoed by a U-boat, on fire burning within minutes she is gone. Admiral Tyndall immediately contacts the Admiralty asking for another carrier or permission to return to base. The reply soon comes back which he shares with Vallery and Brooks in the captain's cabin.

'*D.N.O to Admiral commanding 14 A.C.S, Tirpitz reported preparing to move out impossible detach Fleet Carrier, FR 77 vital: proceed Murmansk all speed, good luck: Star.*'[17]

It is effectively a death sentence, over the next three days FR 77 has to battle submarines, air attack and even surface ships, but not the *Tirpitz*. The ship that had dominated British North Atlantic strategy for two years, her sister ship had destroyed HMS *Hood* the most loved ship in the Royal Navy, sent to the bottom within minutes with only three survivors from her crew of 1,418.

The cruiser HMS *Royalist* had been modified to act as a Carrier Flagship with aircraft direction facilities and advanced radar. So MacLean was clearly drawing on this for the role of *Ulysses* in the novel, although the ship does not fulfil her premier role.

Below decks there was little comfort for the men. Everything was damp and cold and they slept where they could, still fully clothed. Anywhere they could find a space near the galley was popular as it generated some

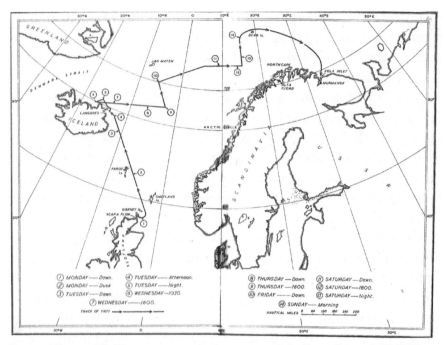

Route of Convoy FR 77 as appears in the front pages of the first edition of *HMS Ulysses*. (*Courtesy HarperCollins*)

heat, yet their rest was always tinged with apprehension of being trapped below in a sinking ship. Everything was covered in condensation, an ideal breeding ground for TB, the fear of Commander Brooks.[18] In his prologue to his novel *San Andreas*, MacLean writes about the poor living conditions aboard Merchant Navy ships prior to the Second World War and how the death rate for seamen was 47 per cent higher than the national average, mostly the result of '*tuberculosis, cerebral haemorrhage and gastric or duodenal ulcers*'.[19]

Captain Vallery is suffering from pulmonary tuberculosis. He tries to keep it to himself but the ship's doctor, the Irish Surgeon-Commander Brooks, known as 'Socrates', has suspected it for some time as the disease was all too common on the lower deck. It is not until the Monday afternoon that Vallery allows Brooks to examine him. Afterwards the Junior Medical Officer Lieutenant Johnny Nicholls, related what Brooks said to him to some other officers in the wardroom that he cannot take much more or he will die.[20]

Some of the more notable scenes in *HMS Ulysses* were based on real events, like the men trapped in the lower power room on Saturday evening, while it is filling up with oil from a fractured fuel tank. They are in danger of drowning in oil, however Petersen, with superhuman strength, manages to rescue the last three who were clinging exhausted to the ladder.[21]

Royal Marine bandsman George Lloyd faced the real experience on the cruiser HMS *Trinidad*; he worked in the transmitting station, a compartment near the bottom of the ship alongside the oil fuel tanks. At 0630 on 29 March 1942 the cruiser was engaging some German destroyers. The ship was hit on the port side by one of its own torpedoes. The explosion ruptured one of the oil fuel tanks and oil started pouring through the hatch into the TS compartment which was the only way in or out. The senior rating there, Warrant Officer Gould, ordered them to shut the hatch. Lloyd recorded; *'Everyone seemed to be completely paralysed with fear glued to his position. Just like so many hypnotised rabbits, standing waiting to be drowned.'*

One man went to the ladder and tried to climb it but the force of the oil knocked him off. Lloyd went to help him; *'Suddenly I became really angry.'* He pushed the other man from behind, both men covered in oil. Together they managed to get up the ladder. Lloyd reflected that he had

> *no memory of what happened after this until I crawled out of the hatch two decks up. They later found that another sailor had tried to get out after me, but the hatch had come down and broken his back. So I was the last person to get out of the TS. All the rest were drowned in that cold black oil.'*

It was a picture that haunted him for the rest of his life, *'those silent men standing motionless, the tiny emergency light bulb giving its dim light, the cold black oil engulfing their bodies'.*[22] Bandsman George Lloyd, also a composer, had written the ship's official march, which was performed at the Royal Albert Hall during the Last Night of the Proms in 2013 in the presence of the last surviving crewmen from HMS *Trinidad*.

The likely explanation as to why one of HMS *Trinidad's* own torpedoes hit the ship was a frozen gyro. This would have drastically reduced the speed of the torpedo from the 46 knots, over 50mph, to a crawl. The ship was zigzagging at the time which put her in the path of the torpedo. However, one of the ship's officers had another explanation; he had seen the torpedo leave HMS *Trinidad* heading toward the enemy destroyer when a salvo from the cruiser's 6-inch guns fell short into the path of the torpedo, throwing it off course. It hit the Royal Marines mess deck on the port side, rupturing the oil fuel tank and flooding the forward boiler room, killing several men instantly. Two decks below in the TS room, opening the hatch to try and find out what was happening let oil and water pour into the compartment.[23]

HMS *Trinidad* limped into Murmansk where temporary repairs were made. In May she headed for home escorted by four destroyers at reduced speed. However, a day out she was attacked by a swarm of Ju 88 bombers, damaged again and on fire with another sixty-three men lost. It was decided to sink her and the destroyer HMS *Matchless* torpedoed the cruiser and she sank in the Arctic Ocean, in much the same area the fictional *HMS Ulysses* is sunk.

The Arctic Convoys continued almost to the end of the war, even as the Red Army was advancing into Germany. In February 1945 JW 64 was under frequent air attack from the start. As they approached the Russian shore Lieutenant Peter Cockrell on board HMS *Campania,* an escort carrier, wrote in his diary: *'Russian destroyer Churchill (ex USA) came out to meet us and was torpedoed with very heavy loss of life outside Kola Inlet.'*[24]

In *HMS Ulysses* we are told the ship is due to head for the Mediterranean for its next assignment after she returns from FR 77.[25] This was where *Royalist* and MacLean would go next, after first a visit by the King to the ship at Scapa Flow in May and a cruise into the Arctic Circle during the D-Day Landings to try and draw off U-boats that may have been tempted to enter the channel to attack the invasion shipping. After this the cruiser went to a shipyard on the Tyne for a short refit. Before setting off south Captain Markham, who had been Mentioned in Dispatches for his service on Operation Tungsten, was relieved of command on 28 June by Captain John Graham Hewitt DSO, 42-years-old in 1944. The new captain was an experienced Mediterranean sailor and had won his DSO commanding the sloop HMS *Auckland* during the 1940 Norway Campaign. His ship, damaged by a German bomb, still managed to evacuate troops from Andalsnes and Namsos. In the Mediterranean while escorting a convoy HMS *Auckland* was attacked by Axis aircraft and sunk off Tobruk in 1941. He then went on to command the light cruiser HMS *Dauntless* serving with the Eastern Fleet before joining HMS *Royalist.*[26]

Chapter Five

July–September 1944, Western Mediterranean

H MS *Royalist* had docked in Newcastle at the end of June 1944. On 12 July she sailed in convoy for the Mediterranean. By then she had been designated as the flagship for the British carrier group TG881 for the Allied landings in the South of France. Her first port of call was Naples, by then a city under Allied occupation.

Norman Lewis serving in the Field Security Police was one of the first to enter the city in October 1943 and found it *'smells of charred wood, with ruins everywhere, sometimes completely blocking the streets, bomb craters and abandoned trams. The main problem is water. Two tremendous air-raids on August 4 and September 6 smashed up all the services….'* The retreating Germans had also blown up anything that might have been of use to the city or the Allies.[1]

By the time Alistair arrived Lewis was observing the overcrowding of the city. *'In the Vicaria district up to three people occupy every two square meters in a basso.'* Even the prostitutes' rooms were not exempt *'there will be tenants in the room – such as bedridden old people lying in wall bunks'* during the nubile proceedings but they *'turn their faces to the wall. All things in Naples are arranged with as much civility as possible.'*[2]

The story 'Rendezvous' appeared in Alistair's collection of short stories *The Lonely Sea* (1985). It concerns the MGB (Motor Gun Boat) F 149 operating largely within the triangle Malta, Sicily, Naples. The skipper, Lieutenant McIndoe, is detailed by Admiral Starr to operate along the Italian coast landing and picking up agents, spies, and saboteurs, under the command of Major Ravallo, an American of Italian descent. This Admiral Starr doesn't seem to be the same character that we came across in *HMS Ulysses*: he is described as weighing *'Two hundred and fifty pounds'* and has a *'red face, white hair, and bushy eyebrows.'*[3] It is a story of betrayal and double dealing, resolved years later.

These clandestine operations did take place, John Steinbeck, the celebrated American author, spent months in the area as a war correspondent often going on patrol and operations with what he called *'The Plywood Navy'*, made up of American torpedo boats and British MTBs. On one such operation they dropped five commandos, *'the great swashbucklers'*, on an island near Naples where the Germans were holding an Italian admiral the Allies were keen to rescue. Steinbeck was not overly impressed by their appearance.

They were small-tired-looking men who might have been waiters or porters at a railway station. Their backs were slightly bent and their knees knobbly and they walked with a shuffling gait. Their huge shoes, with thick rubber soles, looked far too big for them. They were dressed in faded shorts and open shirts, and their arms were an old-fashioned revolver and a long, wicked knife for each.[4]

Yet they achieve all they have to as the MTB waits in moonlight for an hour for the return of the rubber boat which carries back the admiral and his woman, they even make another trip for her luggage. They have also disposed of the seven German guards and the one they were not told about.

HMS *Royalist* sailed for Malta at the end of July where the assault carrier force for Operation Dragoon, the invasion of the South of France, was being assembled. Task Group 881 was to be commanded by Rear Admiral La Touche Bisset who had used the cruiser as his flagship in actions against the *Tirpitz*. However, he was taken ill and command fell to Rear Admiral Thomas Troubridge, a versatile officer. Prior to this he had commanded the battleship HMS *Nelson* and the fleet carrier HMS *Indomitable*. He also commanded Operation Brassard, the capture of Elba, from 17–19 June.

Task Group 881 consisted of five escort carriers, the anti-aircraft cruiser HMS *Delhi*, HMS *Royalist*, the flagship housing the fighter direction operations unit, five British destroyers and the Greek destroyer *Navarinon* – one wonders if this name may have influenced Alistair for the title of his later book. TG882, the other carrier group, consisted of two USN escort carriers and two RN carriers, two British cruisers and six American destroyers. Their main role was to gain air superiority over the invasion beaches and support the ground forces.

Operation Dragoon had a stormy birth and came close to permanently damaging relations between Britain and America. Winston Churchill saw it as a dangerous move for Europe merely to satisfy Joseph Stalin, the leader of Soviet Russia. In August 1943 Churchill and the US President Franklin Delano Roosevelt met at the Quebec Conference to assess the strategic situation and Italy and France were top of the agenda. Churchill strongly favoured Operation Overlord, the cross-Channel invasion of France. As for Italy he later wrote he wanted to

'drive Italy out of the war' and *'second we should seize Sardinia and Corsica and then press against the Germans in the north of the peninsula to stop them joining the fight against Overlord'. There was also Anvil, a projected landing in Southern France in the neighbourhood of Toulon and Marseilles and an advance up the Rhone Valley. This was to lead to much controversy later on.*[5]

Churchill was in favour of Operation Overlord being delayed so the Allies could capture the Dodecanese, push on in Italy and bring Turkey into the war. This was the line he took at the Cairo Conference with Roosevelt from 22–26 November 1943, by which time the war had become bogged down in Italy. Churchill and his generals wanted another amphibious landing in Italy, whereas Anvil was seen as a distraction. General Maitland Wilson, the Allied Supreme Commander in the Mediterranean, wanted to launch a seaborne landing at the head of the Adriatic followed by an advance eastward to Zagreb and then into Austria and the Danube.

In MacLean's *Force 10 from Navarone* (1968) the operation planned by Commander Jensen RN, Chief of Allied Intelligence, Mediterranean, who first crops up in *The Guns of Navarone*, is an attempt to keep German divisions tied down in Yugoslavia and away from Italy, as he informs Captain Keith Mallory, who has come direct from Navarone to Termoli on the Italian Adriatic coast at his bequest, along with Corporal Miller and Andrea Stavros, the latter having been dragged away from his wedding nuptials at Mandrakos with the none-too-pleased Maria. All the airfields *'between here and Bari are jammed with dummy bombers and gliders'*. Near Foggia is a huge military camp with just two hundred men, while the harbours of Bari and Taranto are full of landing craft all made of plywood, and convoys of trucks and tanks move about the area. He asks Mallory if he was in the German High Command what would his conclusion be? Mallory says he would think it meant an invasion. *'But I wouldn't be sure.'* Jenson informs him the Germans are worried and they have sent two divisions from Italy to Yugoslavia to combat the threat, and it will be Mallory's job to keep them there.[6]

By the time the Allied leaders moved from Cairo to meet with Stalin in Tehran, Churchill was already uneasy as Roosevelt had seemed distant. Although it was publicised as a meeting of 'The Big Three' the British were largely cold-shouldered. Roosevelt even stayed at the Soviet Legation. The Americans were impressed by the sacrifice of the Soviet people who were desperate for a second front to take the pressure off the Red Army. They had already suffered more casualties than Britain and the United States combined would suffer for the entire war. Stalin felt only a direct attack on France would significantly draw down large numbers of German troops. He did not want the Allies interfering in the Balkans or Eastern Europe as he considered this his sphere. It was music to Stalin's ears as General Alan Brooke recalled at the conference when he approved Roosevelt's plan to transfer six divisions from Italy to invade Southern France. *'I am certain he did not approve such operations for their strategic value, but because they fitted in with his future political plans.'*[7]

The naive American thinking aided Stalin and his plans for hegemony over Eastern Europe. Depriving Overlord and the Italian front of these troops, Roosevelt even promised Stalin they would not interfere in the Balkans either. This drain on troops even went as far as to affect operations in Burma. It set Churchill against the Allied supreme commander General Dwight Eisenhower. For over a month the British PM opposed the plan even threatening to resign which might have brought down the government. Operation Dragoon was such a draw on manpower and resources that it could not be launched at the same time as Operation Overlord, and even then Eisenhower vacillated over launching it, leaving it so late that the Germans were already retreating from France. The Allies would never break out of Italy leaving Stalin to control Eastern Europe. Later Eisenhower was graceful enough to admit the Americans had been wrong.

The initial Dragoon landings went well; the Operation's name had been changed from Anvil on 1 August. HMS *Royalist* was in the thick of it as the flagship of Admiral Troubridge who commanded all the escort carriers split into two groups. The US Eighth Fleet of some 880 ships was responsible for putting the assault forces ashore on the beaches of the Riviera and was commanded by USN Vice-Admiral H. Kent Hewitt. It was the largest amphibious operation ever conducted in the Mediterranean. The assault commenced at dawn on 15 August, two days before Allied troops had entered Florence, but by then their offensive strength was exhausted. While 150,000 Allied troops were landing only 350 miles to the north-west eventually over half a million would be committed to Dragoon.

The fleet was exposed to attack by the Luftwaffe throughout the first day and into the night; most effective were the Donier 217 bombers equipped with glider bombs which Alistair had seen in action describing them as '*highly effective…and the bombs once released, were virtually impossible to shoot down…*'[8] They accounted for several landing craft being damaged and the destroyer USS *Le Long*.

Churchill had got there just before the landings were about to begin, and met with Marshal Tito and the soldier adventurer, Alistair's namesake, Fitzroy MacLean, who was the Prime Minister's representative in Yugoslavia. They would meet again after the war. Tito had been waiting for Churchill's arrival for a week and had been discussing affairs and strategy with General Maitland Wilson during that time. When Churchill arrived Fitzroy MacLean felt the Prime Minister was diplomatic, '*….with a touch generally light and friendly…He was generous in his praise of Tito's elderships and in his recognition of the Partisans' contribution to the Allied cause; generous too, in his estimate of the help they would need to achieve the liberation of their country and to rebuild it once the war was over.*'[9]

Later in the visit they lost the Prime Minister only to hear he had gone for a swim in the Bay of Naples. Fitzroy had to go and find him in an MTB. At the time the invasion fleet was moving toward the South of France. Naturally the commander of the MTB did not want to get entangled with the mass of shipping:

It was then that we noticed something unusual was happening. As we watched, one of the troopships slightly slackened her speed as if to avoid something. Simultaneously there was a burst of excited cheering from the troops on deck, and a small bright blue object shot across her bows. On inspecting this through a pair of glasses, I recognised it was the Admiral's barge and there, standing by the coxswain, wearing a boiler suit and a broad-band Panama hat, smoking a cigar and giving the V-sign was the object of my search.[10]

At 0800 on D-Day, Churchill boarded the destroyer HMS *Kimberley* to accompany the invasion fleet; there is still a feeling of rancour as he wrote to his wife Clementine:

One of my reasons for making such a public visit was to associate myself with this well-conducted but irrelevant and unrelated operation. Here we saw long rows of boats filled with American troops steaming continuously to the Bay of St Tropez. As far as I could see or hear, not a shot was being fired either at the approaching flotillas or on the beaches. The battleships had now stopped firing, as there seemed to be nobody there.[11]

By the time Churchill got there much of the firing had stopped. The carriers and the longer range bombers of the Air Forces flew 4,200 sorties against targets along the coast that day, while Hewitt's battleships, cruisers and destroyers pounded the area and at 0755 rocket ships added 30,000 rockets to the bombardment of the German positions. The initial landings and airborne assault resulted in very light casualties, some 200 killed and 385 wounded. In September the Allied advance slowed to a virtual crawl due to lack of supplies, however Operation Dragoon was seen as a success having liberated the South of France and opened up important ports in that area.

The carrier aircraft directed from the fighter control room on board HMS *Royalist* were the first aircraft to patrol over the invasion beaches and to spot the fall of shot of the bombarding ships. Most aircraft were Seafires (modified Spitfires) which Admiral Troubridge called the *'aristocrats of the sky'*, although he admitted the American Grumman Wildcats were more robust in carrier operations being designed for that purpose and less prone to landing and take-off accidents. His five carriers flew 170 sorties on D-Day. At night the carriers withdrew south out of the assault area returning at dawn to resume the air patrols. The carriers in rotation went back to the naval base of Magdalena, Sardinia; HMS *Royalist* spent 48 hours at the base during this period. Once the Nineteenth Tactical Air Force had begun operating from air fields ashore, they took over responsibility for defence of the beaches. On 27 August

Troubridge's ships were released and sailed for Alexandria. During the period in support of the Dragoon landings forty-three aircraft were lost, many of which ditched in the sea.[12]

Before following HMS *Royalist* into the Aegean we will look at the Adriatic area, Italy and what was once Yugoslavia. There is no evidence that the cruiser went into these waters however Alistair set two of his wartime books there and was always keen to base his stories in places he knew well. In 1967 with producer and film director Geoffrey Reeve, who would direct three films based on MacLean stories, he went to Yugoslavia to research the background of *Force 10 from Navarone*. He returned in 1978 to look into setting the *Partisans* (1982) there, based on a story he had heard on an earlier visit during the filming of *Force 10*. It concerned a female double agent who had operated from Mostar. Later Alistair would live in the Villa Sandia near Dubrovnik, he was 57 then and spent eight months of the year there virtually until the end of his life. He rented part of the villa, a ground floor apartment, from Avdo Cimic who lived there with his wife Inge and daughter Sandra. It was an idyllic setting with views across the Adriatic Sea which Alistair found an ideal place to write. In time Avdo would become his right-hand-man.

The small Italian coastal town of Termoli, a fishing port 120 miles north of Bari would become the base from which his characters in both books set off for their adventures in Yugoslavia. In the *Partisans* the town in winter was '*grey, bleak, bare grimy and seemingly uninhabited except for a few half-hearted blacked-out premises which were presumably cafes and taverns*'.[13] In *Force 10* when Mallory and his comrades arrive in the town they drive through the war torn streets. They meet Commander Jensen in a '*modest palace*' of '*columns*' and '*veined marble…*'[14] Later on three Royal Marine Commandos join Mallory's team; first impressions were that they had the '*look of tough and hard-bitten competence.*'[15]

No doubt Alistair had researched Termoli's war-time past and discovered that it had been taken by the Allies on the night of 2/3 October 1943, in Operation Devon by the 2nd Special Service Brigade, made up of No 3 Commando (Army), 40 Commando (Royal Marines) and elements of the Special Raiding Squadron. The force landed behind enemy lines about a mile west of the town and soon secured Termoli, capturing the German commander in his pyjamas. By daylight German paratroopers and infantry counter-attacked in strength, later supported by tanks, but the Commandos hung on and were reinforced by elements of the 78th Division, heavy fighting continuing until 6 October. In his history of 40 Commando Major J. C. Beadle called the Termoli landing 'a classic Commando operation' and went on to write:

> The Royal Navy having accomplished a long sea trip undetected by the enemy, landed the men at precisely the right time and place. There is no doubt that the complete surprise obtained contributed largely to the early successes. The overall achievement was considerable, although the cost in Brigade casualties, 45 all ranks killed and missing and 85 all ranks wounded, was high.
>
> In the operation spanning five days they overcame all attempts by a force vastly superior in numbers and armament to dislodge them and in so doing won a valuable harbour, caused the enemy to withdraw from the natural line of the Bifurno and denied them the use of the important littoral road from Naples, therefore forcing them to retreat further northwards.[16]

This puts the time-frame for *Force 10* clearly at the end of 1943, whereas in *Partisans* the town is still under Axis control with Italian MTBs operating from the port. Placing the book in 1942, the Yugoslav-born Peter Petersen seems to be in the pay of the Nazis and, trying to obtain information on the pro-German forces, he and his motley team are landed at Ploce on the Dalmatian coast. The skipper of the MTB Lieutenant Giancarlo Tremino, 'Call me Carlo', tells Peter that he has made the run 'many times and haven't been sunk yet'.[17] We will return to both these books in a later chapter.

Chapter Six

Churchill's Folly

Before following HMS *Royalist* into the Aegean, it is well to look at events there a year before, for they would have a profound effect on Alistair resulting in his most successful book *The Guns of Navarone* (1957). The opening narration to the 1961 film of the book by James Robertson Justice, who plays Captain James Jensen RN, a Naval Intelligence officer, tells us that:

> *In 1943 the Axis powers decide that a show of strength might bully neutral Turkey into joining them. Their target is a command of 2,000 British soldiers marooned on the island of Keros in the Aegean Sea. Rescue by the Royal Navy is impossible because of large radar-directed guns on the nearby island of Navarone.*

In reality Winston Churchill was equally guilty of trying to bully Turkey into the war on the Allied side. From December 1942 the British Ambassador to Turkey, Sir Hughe Knatchbull-Hugessen and his team began putting pressure on the Turkish leaders to align with the Allied cause. The war situation was much better: '*With the Germans driven back, Libya and Cyrenaica clear, and Stalingrad relieved, the position was more favourable*', wrote the ambassador.[1] Churchill had suggested to him a meeting with the Turkish President Ismet Inonu and Prime Minister M. Numan Menemencioglu in Cyprus. However, the conference was held in Adana, the city lying 20 miles from the Mediterranean coast in south central Anatolia.

The Turkish President and Prime Minister were accompanied by the Chief of the Turkish General Staff Marshal Fevzi Çakmak, with a host of advisors. Churchill came with his generals Harold Alexander, Henry Maitland-Wilson and Alan Brooke plus several others in his entourage. The conference was held in a disused railway loop, west of Adana, in the Turkish presidential train. The purpose of the meeting was outlined as *'an exploration of the likelihood and desirability of Turkey taking an active part in the war during the year [1943]'*.[2] However, Turkey was not prepared for war, but came to an understanding that the British might count on them once *'they were adequately equipped'*. Over the next few months *'detailed conversations would take place with military leaders'* and as Sir Hughe commentated: *'We were working toward a "Zero" hour timed for the autumn.'*[3]

It was thought the meeting would have been kept secret, but the Turks soon released details of the conversations. It was also common knowledge that Churchill had received an enthusiastic welcome from the people of Adana. MI6 were well aware that Turkish ciphers might have sprung a *'leak'* and that the Turkish Foreign Ministry was in the habit of keeping other diplomatic missions *'informed of the progress of British/Turkish negotiations'*.[4]

By mid 1943 it was not only the Turkish Foreign Ministry that was leaky but the British Embassy in Ankara as well. Elyesa Bazna had become valet to Sir Hughe and promptly began photographing secret documents and selling them to the Germans. He was code-named 'Cicero' and was to become one of Germany's most successful spies. Indeed, the German Ambassador in Ankara at the time, Franz Von Papen, on seeing the first of Bazna's films felt:

> *It needed only one glance to tell me that I was looking at a photograph of a telegram from the British Foreign Office to the Ambassador in Ankara. From content and phraseology left no doubt that this was the genuine article. It consisted of a series of answers from the Foreign Secretary, Mr Eden, to questions which Sir Hughe Knatchbull-Hugessen has asked in another telegram requesting guidance on certain aspects of his country's policy, particularly in regards Turkey.*[5]

The Cicero intelligence convinced Adolf Hitler of the need to hold the Aegean, to safeguard supplies of chrome ore for armoured steel, bauxite, aluminium and copper from Greece and Turkey. Also, it was vital to keep Allied long range bombers away from the crucial Romanian oil fields. In the end Cicero was betrayed by the pretty young secretary Cornelia Kapp who worked for Ludwig Moyzisch, an SD intelligence officer, and Bazna's contact at the German Embassy. Kapp at the time was working for the OSS, the American Intelligence service. MI6, informed by the Americans at the time, did not take it seriously or react quickly enough and Bazna got away. He had been investigated and interviewed by MI6 because of suspected document leaks but was dismissed as a suspect because '*the valet was too stupid to make a good spy and did not, in any case, speak or understand English.*' Indeed the story reads like a plot from a spy story.[6]

On 9 September 1943, the day after Italy surrendered and Allied troops landed at Salerno, Churchill wrote to his Chiefs of Staff: '*This is the time to play high.*' Four days later he telegraphed General Wilson: '*The capture of Rhodes by you at this time with Italian aid would be a fine contribution to the general war.*'[7] The only trouble was the Germans beat the British to the draw – on 8 September they implemented Operation Axis to take over Italian positions in the Aegean islands when Italy surrendered. The islands of Karpathos, Siros, Andros, Tinos, Zea and Naxos were quickly occupied.

The same day, Lord George Jellicoe, the commander of the Special Boat Squadron, parachuted into Rhodes in an attempt to convince the Italian commander there, Admiral Inigo Campioni, to hold the island for the British. At first the admiral was enthusiastic, however as soon as he learned it would be several days before any substantial British forces would arrive on the island, he became jittery and his support disappeared. The next day the first skirmishes between German and Italian troops began. That night Jellicoe left, his mission a failure, an Italian armed motor boat taking him to the small island of Castellorizzo.[8] Two days later the Sturm Division took Rhodes where 40,000 Italian troops surrendered to the Germans. In spite of Rhodes now being hostile and across British lines of communication, Operation Accolade, the British occupation of the Aegean Islands, went ahead. Troops including elements of the Long Range Desert Group, the SBS and several infantry battalions which were landed in Leros, Kos, and Samos. Two Spitfire squadrons were established on Kos, but much air support had to come from Cyprus, beyond the range of single seater fighters.

On 23 September the destroyer HMS *Eclipse* intercepted a German convoy with Italian prisoners from Rhodes and sank two transports and a torpedo boat. This led to the German invasion of Kos and Leros to eliminate them as British air and naval bases. The Luftwaffe had some

400 aircraft operating from Rhodes and Crete. Air attacks took revenge on the Royal Navy, sinking the destroyers HMS *Queen,* HMS *Olga,* and HMS *Intrepid* in Portolago harbour, Leros, on 26 September. They pounded the airfield on Kos and within days it was inoperable. It would be the last hurrah of the Stuka dive bombers which feature in *The Guns of Navarone.* Mallory watches them come in to attack his team: *'Even as he spoke, the flight-commander titled his gull-winged Junkers 87 sharply over to port, half turned, fell straight out of the sky in a screaming power-dive, plummeting straight for the carob grove.'*[9]

On 1 October, the Royal Navy dispatched from Alexandria all available 'Fleet' destroyers to escort to Malta the battleships HMS *Howe* and HMS *King George V.* This left only *Hunt* class destroyers in the Aegean at a time when it was known the German invasion of Kos was imminent. Destroyers and other warships were dispatched to the Levant when they became available, while six Lightning squadrons of the US Twelfth Air Force were deployed to Gambut in Libya, to support the Royal Navy.[10]

Eisenhower was far from happy with this:

If the decision to undertake Accolade depends upon a firm commitment for the diversion from our own operations of a material portion of our air force, then Accolade will have to be postponed. We will be inferior to the enemy in ground strength throughout the winter. Our air force is the asset that we count on to permit us taking the offensive in spite of the fact. Our first purpose must remain.[11]

Churchill appealed directly to President Roosevelt the next day.

I believe it will be found the Italian and Balkan peninsula are militarily and politically united and that really it is one theatre with which we have to deal....I beg you to consider this and not let it be brushed aside and all these possibilities lost to us in the critical months that lie ahead.[12]

Yet it was all too late. Kos was invaded on 3 October and by the next day the garrison had surrendered, over 1,300 being taken prisoner and 102 Italian officers who had co-operated with the British were executed, including the CO, under Hitler's 11 September order to execute captured Italian officers.

The Italians on Kalymnos surrendered to the threat of German air attack, providing good anchorages for the German Navy in the narrow bays. The invasion of Leros was delayed when a troop convoy was surprised by the Royal Navy and a ship sank with the loss of 659 men. Also, the US Lightnings were effective straight away shooting down dozens of German aircraft, but the cost to the Royal Navy was heavy. The destroyers HMS *Panther*, HMS *Harworth*, HMS *Eclipse* and HMS *Dulverton* were sunk and the anti-aircraft cruiser *Carlisle* was badly damaged and towed to Alexandria, never to put to sea again. She became a depot ship; Alistair may well have stayed on board HMS *Carlisle* while HMS *Royalist* was under refit in Alexandria over the winter of 1944/45.

German forces continued to gather while the Royal Navy at night continued to reinforce and supply the garrison on Leros. Also on the island were about 5,500 Italian sailors who had gone over to the British, half of which made up the gun crews manning the 6-inch guns which were on almost all the mountain tops, with smaller guns defending bays and harbours. The other half was the naval base personnel who were largely unarmed. There was an Italian Army infantry battalion, almost all of which were reserves recalled to active duty or men from older draft categories.

Just when the Lightnings were having a marked effect they were recalled to the central Mediterranean. The British never recovered from the loss of these outstanding aircraft.

By 12 November when the invasion of Leros began, the Germans had complete control of the air. The fighting on the island was vicious, the Germans largely arriving by sea and air during the day and the British coming in by night to aid the garrison. British destroyers bombarded German positions on the island and MTBs conducted sweeps hoping to catch German forces at sea. MTB 315 caught two German 'R' boats, small minesweepers, trying to land troops. Lieutenant Commander C.P. Everson reported:

We found ourselves within 100 yards of a small craft very similar to our LCM, obviously full of troops as the boats were easily discernible against the searchlights. Action was immediately joined; closing the range to about 50 yards both MTBs (315, 266) opened a very heavy fire with .5 inch and 20mm guns.[13]

They even dropped depth charges in the water, the destroyer HMS *Echo* later passed through the area reporting '*hundreds of men in the water screaming for help*'.[14]

Perhaps as far as *The Guns of Navarone* is concerned, an action by a lone Italian gun on the heights of Clidi may well have influenced Alistair. Captain J.R. Olivey of the LRDG, on arriving at battery Ciano on Clidi's point 320 with reinforcements, found most of the Italian gunners had fled, abandoning the 152mm coast defence guns. Only No 2 gun remained in action manned by *Sottotenente* (Sub-Lieutenant) Ferruccio Pizzigoni of the Alpine Regiment and one other Italian Marine. Olivey went on to write a recommendation for an award to Pizzigoni:

> At the approach of enemy shipping from the North East Lt. Petsigonne (Pizzigoni) showed considerable skill having later taken over command of the Marine battery on Pt 320. His guns being responsible for sinking at least two of the enemy landing craft before they could reach the island.[15]

It is revealing to note that the guns on MacLean's fictional island of Navarone also point to the north according to the map in the front of *The Guns of Navarone*, toward Kheros sixteen miles away. There is an island called Keros in the Aegean but more of this in the next chapter.[16]

The brave Italian officer continued the defence of Leros, driving off barges attempting to land on the north coast, carrying ammunition forward under enemy machine gun fire, until his gun was destroyed by enemy mortar fire. He then took a machine gun and '*...advanced to a cave to the west. His gun was heard in action up to 14:00 hrs when his position was overrun and captured by the enemy.*' No trace of him was found; when the position was re-taken Olivey concluded he was captured; it is believed he was executed by the Germans when a prisoner. Italy in time recognised Pizzigoni's bravery by the posthumous award of the country's highest award the *Medaglia d'oro al Valor Militare* (Gold Medal for Military Valour.)[17]

Yet slowly, on the island the German paratroops and Brandenburg Regiment gained the upper hand. The latter capturing the garrison CO, Brigadier Robert Tilney, who decided on 16 November to surrender the island; throughout the operation his scattered units had been hamstrung by poor communications. The LRDG and the SBS refused to surrender and escaped from the island. About 3,200 British and 5,350 Italians were taken prisoner. Tilney did manage to save most of the Italians from the threatened massacre by the Germans that had occurred on other islands, most notably Cephalonia, portrayed vividly in Louis de Bernières' novel *Captain Corelli's Mandolin.*

Admiral Luigi Mascherpa, the Italian Commander on Leros and Admiral Campioni, commander in the Aegean, were court martialled for 'high treason' and then executed at Parma by the remnants of Mussolini's followers who proclaimed themselves the legitimate government of Italy.

Churchill had virtually written off his Leros campaign a month before. In a message to President Roosevelt, he said: '*....the fate of Leros is sealed.*' And he told General Wilson '*...to order the garrison to evacuate by night taking with them all Italian officers and as many other Italians as possible and destroying the guns and defences*'.[18]

The battle of Leros was one of the last German victories of the war, due mainly to their domination in the air causing great losses to the Allies, especially in ships. In *The Guns of Navarone* Jensen tells Mallory that '*The Navy is sick and tired of the Eastern Med.*' He blames the High Command, it was just so they '*...can play round-and-round-the-rugged-rocks and who's-the-King-of-the-castle with their opposite numbers in Berlin*'. The blame for the defeat was laid at Churchill's door rather unfairly as another 'Gallipoli' disaster.[19]

Chapter Seven

September–October 1944, The Aegean

The boot for the British was very much on the other foot when HMS *Royalist* and Admiral Troubridge's carrier strike force steamed into the Aegean compared to twelve months before. The force was made up of seven escort carriers, two light cruisers and seven destroyers.

The dramatic decline in German fortunes was due to the Red Army's rapid advance in August, crossing the frontiers of Romania and Bulgaria, these two countries, satellites of the Nazis were forced to sue for peace. This placed the German forces in Greece and the Aegean Islands out on a limb and in danger of being cut off. On 27 August Adolf Hitler ordered a withdrawal of forces to a line in the central Balkans running from Corfu through Salonika across Greece, but the Russian advance through Bulgaria was so rapid that on 5 September the Germans began to reduce their garrisons in southern Greece, Crete and the islands. Troubridge's force was part of the Allied plans to stop this. Thus began Operation Outing I from 14–20 September. The destroyers on the first night sank a convoy of four vessels between Crete and the island of Thira (Santorini). During this phase, although hampered by German minefields, they still managed to sink some sixty vessels and also bombarded shore targets and landed troops on some islands. They did find it difficult to halt the withdrawal of the garrison from Crete by air at night, until the specialist fighter direction ship HMS *Ulster Queen* arrived, able to co-ordinate night fighters operating from northern Egypt. However by this time some 12,000 German troops had been flown out.

It was during this period according to the ship's log, that HMS *Royalist* suffered her only damage from enemy action when an 88mm shell passed through the forward funnel above the '*stokers mess deck*'.[1] This occurred when operating close inshore to one of the many Aegean islands.

In Alistair's short story *McCrimmon and the Blue Moonstones* the fictional HMS *Ilara* arrives in Alexandria from the Aegean with part of her *'after-funnel missing – the souvenir of a slight estrangement which had arisen between her and the 9.5 German batteries on Milos....'*[2] Most of this story takes place in Egypt although HMS *Ilara* goes back to the fight and sinks a German transport off Crete.[3]

Cliff Smith a Naval Writer (sometimes called a scribe, working as an administrator performing all clerical duties) recalled his ship HMS *Kimberley*, the same class of destroyer as Mountbatten's HMS *Kelly* which had been lost in 1941 and the evacuation of Crete. Smith called *Kimberley 'a Med fixture known as "Cunningham's Taxi".'* Her *'beat was the Dodecanese Islands, still German occupied. Here we patrolled uneventfully, except for a bombardment of Rhodes with our 4.7 inch popguns, cut short when the somnolent Germans fired back with their 12 inch, and we left in a hurry.'*[4] Here then is plenty of evidence of large calibre coastal guns being used against shipping which clearly influenced Alistair's fertile imagination.

Troubridge's carrier force maintained the pressure until the end of October, their aircraft flying 640 sorties, at little cost. Yet despite the heavy losses in ships and transport aircraft the Germans did not give up. On 3 October Hitler ordered the complete withdrawal from Greece and nine days later they left Athens. Royal Navy minesweepers quickly began clearing mines in the Gulf of Athens and the harbour of Piraeus.

From the end of August to the end of October 1944 the Germans managed to evacuate over 37,000 troops mostly by air, from Crete and the Aegean Islands. German shipping had suffered grievous losses, with the sinking of some former Italian destroyers. German maritime power, as the official British history says, in the *'long-contested waters of the Aegean, where we had suffered grievous checks and heavy losses only a year earlier, was finally extinguished'.*[5]

In October HMS *Royalist* visited the islands of Mytilene and Chios where they were given *'a rousing welcome'.*[6] Yet on Crete, Rhodes, Leros, Kos and a number of smaller islands large garrisons of German troops remained. In mid-October troops landed on Mudros and Lemnos and encountered little resistance. However attempts to land on Milos and Piskopi further south met determined resistance, air attack, bombardment by cruisers, and even the 14-inch guns of the battleship HMS *King George V*, which was passing through the Mediterranean on her way to join the Eastern Fleet, had little effect on these garrisons, who still refused to surrender. However as they posed no threat they were allowed to '*wither on the vine*'.[7]

On 6 October Rear Admiral Troubridge was relieved by Commodore Geoffrey Nigel Oliver who had recently commanded the British assault force for the Salerno landings. The force was now designated the First Aircraft Carrier Squadron, HMS *Royalist* continuing as the flagship. They continued with clearing mines in the Aegean and with humanitarian relief, Operation Manna.

Visiting Piraeus, the port town of Athens, HMS *Royalist* and other ships were given another good reception, as were the troops of the Parachute Regiment landed from cruisers who went into Athens. They were aware that in the wake of the German retreat the void might be fought over by the old Greek Government and the Royal Family opposed by the Communist Partisans the EAM-ELAS. However Major Anthony Farrar-Hockley gives a flavour of their initial welcome by the city's population:

> *When we got into Athens, the crowds gave us a colossal reception....The Greeks were going mad and the difficulty was to contain and keep together our soldiers. There were a number of very attractive Greek girls trying to secure them for parties, which didn't help.*[8]

Soon those very same British troops were engaged in another thankless task, trying to intervene in what was fast becoming a Greek civil war. The cruisers and destroyers of Oliver's command were engaged in assisting the army moving units to hotspots along the coast. Major Bill Corby of the 5th Parachute Battalion recorded being moved to Salonika by a cruiser: '*The battalion landed in assault craft on the beaches south-east of Salonica* (Salonika). *There were explosions in the sea on the run in, possibly mines being blown up by the Navy, but there was no opposition, despite the presence of many ELAS faces in the town.*'

As a torpedo rating the removal of mines from harbours and channels was a job Alistair could well have been involved in. Major Corby continued: '*A day or two later our cruiser steamed right into the harbour close to ELAS headquarters. From the shore her six-inch guns looked very threatening.*' A few hours later he witnessed '*a considerable force of ELAS communist troops, with horse or mule-drawn transport, moving out of the town to the north singing their favourite marching songs*.[9] British forces would suffer some 2,000 casualties in the coming Greek Civil War 1944–1949, which would prove to be as devastating to the country as the German occupation.

However, by November, HMS *Royalist* was leaving all that behind her, steaming out of the Mediterranean heading for her home port of Portsmouth for specialist maintenance and for the crew, some well-earned leave.

Chapter Eight

Navarone

Aquestion often asked is where is the island of Navarone? Alistair goes a long way to answering this question, when he wrote a detailed piece for the Companion Book Club broadsheet in 1958 for their edition of *The Guns of Navarone*, covering his thoughts about the book.

I wanted to write a war story – with the accent on the story. Only a fool would pretend that there is anything noble or splendid about modern warfare but there is no denying that it provides a great abundance of material for a writer, provided no attempt is made either to glorify it or exploit its worst aspects. I think it was perfectly legitimate territory for a story-teller. Personal experience, I suppose, helped to play some part in the location of this story. I spent some wartime months in and around Greece and the Aegean islands, although at no time, I must add, did I run the risk of anything worse than a severe case of sunburn, far less find myself exposed to circumstances such as those in which the book's characters find themselves.

But I did come across and hear about, both in the Aegean and in Egypt, men to whom danger and the ever-present possibility of capture and death were the very stuff of existence, these were highly trained specialists of Earl Jellicoe's Special Boat Service and the men of the Long Range Desert Group, who had turned their attention to the Aegean islands after the fall of North Africa. Regularly these men were parachuted into enemy-held islands or came there by sea in the stormy darkness of a wind- and rain-filled night and operated, sometimes for months on end, as spies, saboteurs and liaison officers with resistance groups.

Some even had their own boats, based on German islands, and operated throughout the Aegean with conspicuous success and an almost miraculous immunity to capture and sinking.[1]

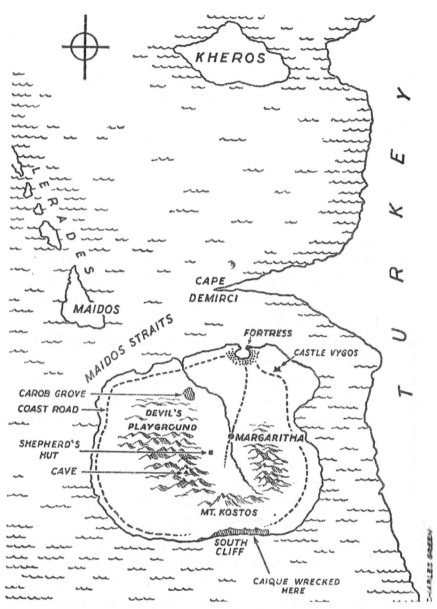

The island of Navarone as appears on page six of the first edition of *The Guns of Navarone*. (Courtesy HarperCollins)

It has been suggested that Patrick Leigh Fermor, who spent much of the war on Crete as an SOE agent serving with the resistance, might have been the model for Captain Keith Mallory. Yet the only similarity is the background with the resistance in Crete and Mallory spending eighteen months on the island in the White Mountains. More likely

MacLean's character of Mallory was influenced by George Herbert Leigh Mallory the climber and First World War soldier known as 'the human fly'. He disappeared during the 1924 expedition to conquer Everest on the northeast ridge along with his climbing partner Andrew 'Sandy' Irvine. Jensen in *The Guns of Navarone* calls Mallory '*The human fly, the climber of the unclimbable, the scaler of vertical cliffs and unscalable precipices*', because the south coast of Navarone consists of '*one vast, impossible precipice.*'[2]

MacLean continues to talk about the location:

Here obviously was excellent material for a story and it had the added advantage for the writer that it was set in an archipelago. I had the best of worlds, the land and the sea, always ready to hand. But the determining factor in the choice of location and plot was neither material nor the islands themselves; that lay in the highly complicated political situation that existed in the islands at the time, and in the nature of Navarone itself. [A factor Winston Churchill tried to take advantage of in his ill-fated Aegean campaign.]

   There is no such island as Navarone, but there were one or two islands remarkably like it, inasmuch as they were (a) German-held (b) had large guns that dominated important channels and (c) had these guns so located as to be almost immune to destruction by the enemy.[3]

In the novel the guns are described as '*a version of the 210 mm "crunch" guns....*' He could be referring here to the 21cm Morser 18, as a number of these were used by coastal artillery units. However, at 21cm [8.3-inch] they do not seem nearly heavy enough given there are only two of them to sink an 8-inch gun cruiser the *Sybaris* in five minutes.[4] In the film of the book they appear much larger, probably modelled on the 38cm [15-inch] guns that were used in the *Bismarck* class battleships and were sometimes used in the coastal gun role, and possibly the German naval 28cm [11-inch] used in various heavy ships like the *Scharnhorst*, might be a candidate. However these guns were not particularly good as coastal pieces due to their slow traverse speed and slow loading time, although they were much better under radar control, a fact of which Alistair was probably aware.[5]

   Some of the gun positions still survive on Greek islands, particularly on Crete on the Rodopou Peninsula at Cape Spatha. Most of the guns here would have been 15 cm [6-inch] similar to those used so effectively as we have seen by Lt. Pizzigoni on Leros.

Alistair continues:

Again the situation in the Dodecanese islands was dangerous and perplexing in the extreme, as it was difficult to know from one month to another whether Germans, Greeks, British or Italians were in power there – an excellent setting for a story. So I moved a Navarone-type island from the middle of the Aegean to the Dodecanese, close to the coast of Turkey, placed another island, filled with trapped and apparently doomed British soldiers, just to the north of it, and took as much advantage as I could of what I had seen, what I heard, the fictitious geographical situation I had arranged for my own benefit, and the very real political and military state of affairs that existed in the Dodecanese at that time.[6]

It is possible to roughly locate the fictional island of Navarone, for Alistair tells us it forms part of the Sporades Island Group. The map in the novel shows, four miles to the north of the island, the Turkish mainland coming to the sharp promontory of Cape Demirci, sixteen miles beyond the cape is the island of Kheros where the British soldiers are trapped. To the north-west is the Lerades group stretching away sixty miles we are told, one of which, the larger island of Maidos, is the end six miles from Navarone. It is through this strait the British ships must pass to reach Kheros but it is dominated by the guns on Navarone. The channels between the other islands are mined but the Maidos strait is too deep for mines. All these islands and the Lerades group are fictional.[7]

The Sporades and Dodecanese islands are real so we can locate the fictional group of islands on the map. In the book Mallory and his group are taken by a Sunderland Flying Boat over Cyprus to the island of '*Castelrosso*'. Kastellorizo or Castellorizo is a Greek island of the Dodecanese chain and lies a mile off the south cost of Turkey, seventy-eight miles east of Rhodes, 170 miles northwest of Cyprus.[8] From there an MTB takes them north to '*Major Rutledge's island*' through the Rhodes channel. Even given the MTB breaks down this puts them near Kos, as we are told by Major Rutledge, rather taken aback by Mallory's request for a beaten up old caique when he can get them '*a German E-boat, absolutely perfect condition…*' from Bodrum in a few hours.[9] This firmly puts them

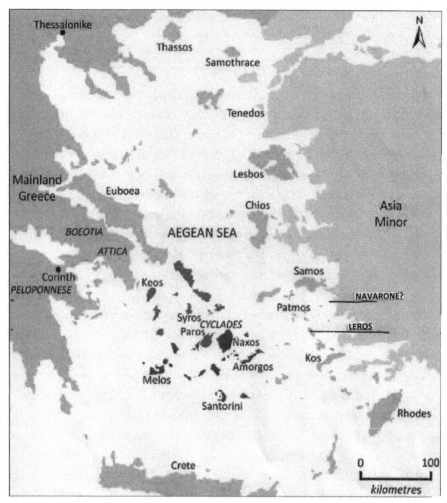

The Aegean Sea showing the likely location of the fictional island of Navarone. (*The Author*)

just north of Kos which given the time frame of the book [1943] was occupied by the Germans who had taken it in October from the British.

They head northwest from *Major Rutledge's island* in the beaten up caique with a Kelvin two-cylinder engine built on the banks of the Clyde which breaks down after a few hours. They had been making good progress '*chugging steadily north over a glassy, windless sea, …*' only a mile from the Turkish coast.[10] They were near a big island some eight miles away, probably Kalymnos, one of the most mountainous in the Dodecanese group. Intercepted by a German patrol boat, a large caique, they promptly deal with it by the bluff of being poor Greek sailors, before taking the German crew by surprise, killing them and sinking the boat. They had managed to rig some sails to get underway again and via radio they check in with Cairo, when they are told of storms in their area, the Northern Sporades, possibly force eight. They head for a small island about three miles away to take shelter and work on the engine, however, there is a German guard post on the island, but there is nowhere else close enough to shelter. Once they have moored one of the sentries comes aboard and asks him who they are and where they are going. Mallory tells him they are the '*caique Aigion*' and '*In ballast for Samos*'. He also tells him they are under orders of a German general; they have forged documents to the effect.[11]

Samos is one of the bigger islands in the Northern Sporades and this puts their caique sheltering probably northeast of Leros and therefore Navarone's location is further northeast around the tiny island of Farmakonisi or Pharmakonisi which is only 1.48 square miles. An open area of the Aegean where there is still space for a chain of islands sixty miles long running northwest away from the Turkish coast where Alistair's fictional island group fits well.

Was there a particular Greek island that was in Alistair's mind as the model for Navarone? He wrote as we have seen: '*There is no such island as Navarone, but there were one or two islands remarkably like it....*'[12]

Navarone has 400ft high cliffs on its southern coast, there are low-lying areas where carob trees grow and snow-capped mountains with a small town, Margaritha, roughly in the centre, several other villages that dot the island. The largest town is Navarone on the north coast of about 5,000 people. The town is at the base of a circular volcanic bay with a narrow entrance to the northwest.[13]

There are probably many islands that could fit the bill but three island candidates seem to stand out and have some of the features that might have influenced Alistair. Symi, part of the Dodecanese, lies thirty miles north of Rhodes, in area it is twenty-five square miles, much of the island is mountainous. The harbour town of Symi is on the north coast in a tight bay expanding into a wide bay. Nimos Island two miles north is uninhabited. It is close to the two Turkish peninsulas of Datca and Bozburun. On 12 October 1943 it was occupied by the Germans. Some scenes of the film *The Guns of Navarone* were shot on Symi.

Kalymnos, six miles north of Kos and five hours by sea from Rhodes, is much bigger at 42 square miles. Its mountains rise to a height of 2,300ft and is a popular destination for climbers, yet still having fertile valleys. It was occupied by the Italians and Germans in the Second World War and used as a base by the SBS.

Santorini (Thira) the southernmost of the Cyclades is 28 square miles. Famed for the largest volcanic eruption in recorded history about 3,600 years ago, this heralded the collapse of the Minoan civilisation on Crete 70 miles to the south and has been equated with the legend of Atlantis. Its cliffs seem a model for those on Navarone, and the horseshoe bay formed by the caldera of the volcano. During the war the island was occupied by the Italians in 1941 and in 1943 by the Germans. Even more so, in 1944 the SBS conducted a raid against the island.

By early April 1944, the Germans had set up their own coast watcher network throughout the islands of the northern Aegean. Two Kriegsmarine petty officers operated each post which was equipped with a radio transceiver under the supervision of a junior officer who was responsible for several posts. The network reported all Allied air and surface movements to the German Naval Headquarters in Salonika.

The SBS was ordered to eliminate the posts. Major Anders (Andy) Lassen VC, MC, a Dane, led the raid on Santorini. The main objectives were to destroy enemy shipping on the island, the communications and the garrison. The island had been reconnoitred by Lassen who described it as crescent-shaped *'ten miles by three sheer, sombre cliffs of black, volcanic rock'*.

The 19-strong SBS force landed on Santorini in the early hours of 23 April after sailing for three days from their Turkish base. To the Turks it was Degirmen Buku, to the British, Port Deremen, not far from Bodrum. The Turkish authorities turned a blind eye to this infringement of their neutrality. The raiders hide in a cave while their interpreter, a serving Greek officer, went to gather intelligence. They waited until dark then just before midnight they set off in two groups, one hit the wireless station which was quickly destroyed, the other the garrison's barracks. The attack on the garrison inflicted heavy casualties but two members of the SBS team were killed. The Germans took revenge on the local population executing five local men, one of which was the mayor.[14]

There is no doubt Alistair's time in the Aegean in 1944 had a profound effect on him, he liked and admired the Greeks. He found the Aegean islands to be the only ones like his beloved western isles of Scotland which had the '*quality of light, diffuse and limpid and wholly indescribable, which I have found nowhere else in the world except in the Aegean in autumn*.'[15] We will return to *The Guns of Navarone* later in the book.

Alistair did return to the Aegean for his final novel *Santorini* (1986) in which a Royal Navy electronic intelligence ship HMS *Ariadne* records two incidents in the Aegean, a strategic bomber crashing into the sea, while a large pleasure boat catches fire. The plane is carrying nuclear weapons and the survivors rescued from the boat seem to be linked somehow to the bomber coming down. The commander and crew of HMS *Ariadne* must raise the one activated bomb before it explodes triggering the volcano on Santorini to erupt and resulting in a possible worldwide nuclear winter.

Chapter Nine

Portsmouth, November 1944

When HMS *Royalist* sailed for home on 31 October 1944 the naval situation in the Mediterranean was of near total victory for the Allies. The only German naval forces left were in the north of the Adriatic, operating from northern ports Trieste, Fiume and Pula with largely light forces. U-boats had also been cleared from the sea; the last one to pass through the straits of Gibraltar was *U960* on 30 April 1944; she had been sunk nineteen days later by USN destroyers.

The escort carriers HMS *Attacker*, HMS *Hunter* and HMS *Stalker* also headed for home with *Royalist*; all were back in UK waters by 11 November. HMS *Royalist* visited her home port of Portsmouth for the first time and the crew were granted leave; some would be drafted to other ships and shore establishments while new men would join the ship.[1]

Portsmouth, affectionately known as Pompey in the Navy, had suffered grievously in the war from air raids. Between July 1940 and May 1944, the city had suffered 67 air raids, large areas had been destroyed, the Guildhall gutted, while close to a 1,000 people had been killed. After the Luftwaffe came the V1 flying bombs, the last striking on the night of 14/15 July 1944 killed sixteen people. However, most of the V1s had been falling short into open countryside or into water.[2]

Under the reign of Henry VIII the first naval dockyard had been built at Portsmouth. In the centuries that followed the shape and character of the great city has been determined as much by the geography and the recurring threat of war as by the technical and maintenance needs of the navy. The choice was largely determined by Spithead with its outlying anchorage; a deep-water channel close inshore at the approach to the harbour's narrow, readily defended entrance; and the safe, wide tidal lake inside the entrance with its obvious potential for development as a great naval base and dockyard.

In the 1930s, leaving the Dockyard main gate the streets were full of local colour which had inspired writers such as Kingsley, Marryat and

Dickens. All manner of clubs, Maltese run cafes, photographers, cinemas, bric-a-brac shops that sold Navy surplus, a godsend for those who had lost or had kit lifted. There were plenty of pubs, some showed notices 'Ladies not to stay longer than ten minutes' directed at the prostitutes also peddling their trade. There were plenty catering for the religious as well with church, chapel, synagogue and Salvation Army Hostel. There was Aggie Weston's at Castaway House providing a home from home, a bed and meals at a cheap price to members of the Fleet.[3]

However Alistair, although remaining with the ship, had headed home to Glasgow on leave. Webster states Alistair's mother '*caught sight*' of a wound in his back which he was reluctant to explain and '*The long leave, it turned out, was for the purpose of attending hospital in Glasgow.*'[4] This all seems rather strange; maybe she saw a scar, if he had had a wound that needed treatment it is far more likely this would have been done in one of the naval hospitals in Portsmouth. Also his leave would have been 'foreign service leave' and not particularly long, maybe ten or fourteen days at the most given HMS *Royalist* was only at Portsmouth for three weeks and would sail back to Alexandria early in December.[5] Indeed we are told in *HMS Ulysses* that the entire ship's company will get ten days leave in Portsmouth and then head to Alexandria for a refit. Was Alistair saying here this is what happened to HMS *Royalist*?[6]

The mysterious wound was apparently the result of a misfire on *Royalist* which hurled Alistair against a bulkhead. There is a type of misfire described in *HMS Ulysses*. In the novel pom-poms are fired against a surfaced U-boat but the muzzle covers, in the haste of the moment, had not been removed. The shells explode in the barrel, this kills four men, yet one man, Lieutenant Marshall, survives luckily being thrown clear through an open door and he smashes against the '*trunking of "B" turret....*' He does suffer broken ribs.[7]

Charlie Dunbar from Banffshire in the north-east of Scotland joined HMS *Royalist* while it was in Portsmouth. He arrived, full of apprehension as the new man on the mess deck but was in time for tea. He says Alistair was attracted by his accent and asked him where he was from. Dunbar explained he had been the projectionist for the cinema in Keith. Alistair, coming from the same area in Scotland, had introduced himself. Charlie became popular onboard as films were a favourite pastime among the crew. He kept his cinema equipment in a store under Y gun-turret near the Marines' mess deck, he brewed his own tea there, often Alistair would pop-in for a chat. The two became friends although Alistair was not a great conversationalist, but at the end of the film shows he would help Charlie put the equipment away.[8]

One of Alistair's great inspirations, Captain James Cook, who in 1755 had joined the Royal Navy as an able seaman, boarded his first ship, HMS *Eagle,* a 60-gun ship of the line lying at Portsmouth. Alistair wrote a biography of the great seaman and navigator in 1972. He recorded HMS *Eagle* was assigned to the blockade of the French coast (during the Seven Years War). Cook's first captain, wrote Alistair, '*vastly preferred the sheltered calms of Portsmouth harbour to the winter gales of the English Channel...*'[9]

Given the damage to Portsmouth resulting in fewer facilities for entertainment, and that Alistair was not the life and soul of the party on a run-ashore [naval slang for a night out], he was probably glad when HMS *Royalist* said farewell to Pompey and sailed back to the Mediterranean and the delights of Alexandria.

Chapter Ten

Alexandria, December 1944–February 1945

I t was Admiral Andrew Browne Cunningham, known affectionately as 'ABC', who selected Alexandria as his fleet base as the war clouds of what would be the Second World War were gathering, he was not unmindful that the great port had been built and named by Alexander the Great. The capital ships of the Mediterranean Fleet were moored in the ancient Western Harbour which was known from antiquity as Eunostos Haven, the Greek 'Harbour of Safe Return'. Cunningham wrote that:

> On the whole Alexandria was popular enough with officers and men. The officers had plenty of golf, tennis, and social activities, and though there was a serious shortage of recreation grounds the men found ample amusement ashore. They also had an excellent Fleet Club accommodated in the old Greek hospital and run on the lines of Claridges Club which had been such a success during the Abyssinian crisis. Here they could obtain most of the amenities they needed at very reasonable prices.[1]

'Do you know how to tell a real matelot? Sometimes I think this was the only thing I really learnt in my six years in the Navy: but it's worth knowing. You see, a real matelot uses only two swear words. And he always calls Alexandria 'Aleck.' Not Alex. Aleck, with a C and a K.'[2] So wrote Charles Causley the poet about Alexandria. HMS *Royalist* arrived in the Egyptian port in mid-December for an extended two month refit before heading east to join the war against Japan.

Ernle Bradford arrived in Alexandria aged 19 as an ordinary seaman in the Second World War and wrote:

> Alexandria to me was the city of the great Greek conqueror. It hardly existed as 19th-century French and Anglo-Egyptian collaboration. It was myth and mystery, Antony and Cleopatra, the Bull of Serapis, Pompey's Pillar, bearded anchorites, the Pharos, and a vague suggestion of infinite sexual sophistication.[3]

It would appear reading between the lines that Alistair had a fondness for 'Aleck' for here was the east so different from anything he had experienced. He had been there before but only for a day or two at a time, during the Aegean campaign, for ships to refuel and rearm, now he was there for an extended refit. He was to set one of his most amusing short stories *McCrimmon and the Blue Moonstones* in the city. It is about the attempts of Able Seaman, torpedo man, McCrimmon to get rich. We are told he is a two badger, these are good conduct badge stripes worn on the left sleeve of the uniform below the trade badge, awarded for four years good conduct or 'undetected crime', quite an achievement for McCrimmon given his penchant to be light fingered, which also tells us he must have been a regular not an HO like Alistair. He serves aboard HMS *Ilara,* we are not told what class of ship she is but likely to be a destroyer or maybe a light cruiser, she is in Aleck for repairs.

McCrimmon has come across another namesake, a dockyard worker known as dockyardies, a third or maybe fourth cousin. This McCrimmon knows a native who has '...*a fine set of semi-precious stones*' for sale at a temptingly low price. Back home they would sell for a small fortune, but the dockyardey is not due to go home for two years. However McCrimmon the torpedo man is due home soon, his cousin is a god-send, who better to trust than a kinsman, and he can sell the stones and forward his half of the proceeds. The story opens with a few words that give a flavour of MacLean's Aleck.[4]

> *The wind was blowing offshore from the native quarter, so that breathing, up-town, was only a matter of tolerable difficulty. Night, if not peace, had fallen over the city. The hour was late and all honest citizens were at home, asleep. The streets of Alexandria were thronged.*[5]

Able Seaman McCrimmon sets off to meet the '*native*' and cement the deal for the gemstones. Into the crowded streets he plunges. Yet he makes time for a game of poker in a bar, with three Armenians and a Cypriot. The opening line of Christopher Landon's great book *Ice Cold in Alex* gives us a flavour of a typical city bar, it stood '*in the lane off Mahomet Ali Square; the high stools, the marble-topped counter, the Greek behind it...*' And the noises: '*the purr of the overhead fan, a fly, buzzing drowsily, the muffled noise of the traffic seeping in through the closed door.'*[6] Landon served in the Royal Army Medical Corps in North Africa during the war.

In *The Guns of Navarone* Jensen drives Mallory into Alexandria in the big Humber staff car which clearly demonstrates Alistair's knowledge of the city for they turned right '*from the dock area, jounced their uncomfortable way over the massive cobbles of the Rue Souers, slewed round into Mohammed Ali square, passed in front of the Bourse and turned right down the Sherif Pasha.'*[7]

McCrimmon soon abandons the card game when an accusation of marked cards was broached. He walks along the Saad Zaghoul [Zaghloul], the main street, brushing off the hawkers with contempt and enters one of the clubs near Ramleh Station: '*Briskly saluting the commissionaire, whom he took for a rear-admiral...*' Inside he finds the native contact not yet there. He informs the receptionist that he will be in the restaurant, picking a table from where he can observe the cabaret. He was soon bored, especially with a couple of dancers demonstrating a waltz.[8]

Having waited an hour and consumed a few John Collins a waiter signalled him, had his contact arrived? He walks out into the vestibule, his pockets full of a '*chromium ashtray and monogrammed forks and spoons*'. No one is about, he heads for the wash room, again he drew a blank but his '*attention was drawn to a row of gleaming chromium taps*'. Somehow McCrimmon has about his person a Stilson wrench. As he is adjusting the wrench in anticipation a voice from behind says '*Meester*'.[9]

As a torpedo man Alistair would have been skilled with tools for the complexities of the weapons systems, including torpedoes, mines and depth charges. Indeed, he admitted to the film critic Barry Norman in an interview in the *Observer* to have '*...spent the war years in the navy with a spanner in my hand*'.[10]

On turning, to his relief McCrimmon was confronted by no club official but by '*a diminutive, dark-skinned individual, clad in a scarlet fez and an off-white nightgown*'. The man spoke again calling him '*Meester Creemon*'. McCrimmon felt there was no use in correcting the man. Instead he merely nodded. This was the local with the gemstones, who beckons him to follow, which McCrimmon does at a distance not wishing to appear in league with him. As they advance into the seedier part of town, he takes a good grip on the stilson wrench in his pocket, taking strength from his ancestors' deeds, who had fought on some of Scotland's most famous battlegrounds, even his father had cheered '*Glasgow Rangers to victory while imbedded in a solid phalanx of Celtic supporters*'.[11]

His guide takes him into a run-down cafe. Inside he makes out, in the smoke filled gloom, a couple of men on the floor sucking at a hookah pipe, he can perceive little else. The native introduces himself as Mohammed Ali, but given that half the male population of Aleck seemed to have the same name it does not fill McCrimmon with confidence, but he asks him to come to the point. Mohammed Ali takes from his nightgown a small bag, weighing it in his hand with a knowing look toward McCrimmon who demands sight of the stones. Would it not be harmonious, suggests Mohammed Ali, to also show the money?

There is an impasse; McCrimmon tightens his grip around the Stilsons in his pocket. Mohammed Ali starts picking his finger nails with a 9-inch long knife. McCrimmon decides against the wrench and loosens his grip, he feels magnanimous, after all '*the rude and untutored upbringing of these unfortunates entitled them to pity rather than censure.* He delves into his other pocket, the left, only to find his wallet was gone.[12]

McCrimmon explodes into a series of expletives; he curses the World and Aleck the most, for five minutes. Mohammed Ali manages to calm him down aided by copious amounts of the native brew, arrack. They agree on another meeting, this time in the better quarter at the other end of Sherif Pasha, after all look what had happened in this district. McCrimmon only leaves when the arrack no longer flows. As he tries to leave the bar a fight ensues and he crashes through the window of the bar into the arms of a passing naval shore patrol who take him back to the docks.

The shore patrols were not supplied by the Regulating Branch of the navy, the naval police. Rather they were made up of crew members of various ships. It was a duty anybody could be detailed for, usually made up of Petty Officers, Leading Hands, and Able Seamen. They were often pretty lenient, mainly ensuring the fighters calmed down and the drunks got back to their ships and onboard safely.

Charlie Dunbar recalled going on Shore Patrol with Alistair who by then was a Leading Hand. Driving the boisterous and inebriated back to the ship, one lad he recalled Alistair was frogmarching fell into the harbour and they then had to fish him out. He also took the duty seriously, checking those he had brought back did not choke on their own vomit while sleeping as it could be fatal.[13]

The next night, a Sunday, McCrimmon sets out again to conduct the deal with Mohammed Ali. In the morning he had seen his cousin and told his sorry tale. *'But there were no hard feelings amongst the McCrimmons....'* A new wallet of money would be ready for the new meeting. It was his watch that night, but he gets another sailor to take his watch for three days rum ration. Booted and spurred, setting his hat at a jaunty angle that befitted a two-badge sailor, he places the new wallet in an inner pocket this time. He climbs from his mess deck, up the rope ladder to the upper deck passage-way. Thirty minutes later he steps off the liberty-boat onto the dock and *'strode up through the native quarter, rolled his way along the vast cobbles of the Rue Soeurs, turned into Mohammed Ali square, crossed it diagonally and disappeared down the Sherif Pasha'.*[14]

At the agreed rendezvous, a restaurant, he pressed some money on *'two large Yugoslav waiters...'* in case he needed some muscle. He waited in a secluded booth, his confidence rising and heightened by the feel of the Stilsons in his pocket.[15]

Mohammed Ali arrived but he was not alone, he was accompanied by three others, all giants. McCrimmon kept his seething temper under control, calming down when he considered *'the depravity and depths of distrust of human nature...'* He greeted Mohammed Ali with a broad smile, producing his wallet of cash with a flourish, which brought a smile to the jewel seller's face, who then in turn spilled the blue moonstones from their bag onto the table.[16]

McCrimmon, who had no idea about precious stones, set about examining the eighteen as if he were an expert. He feigned disappointment with the quality of the stones. Mohammed Ali's patience began to wear thin; he stated his price at 800 piastres. But McCrimmon would not be hurried and continued to question the quality of the stones, finally opening with an offer of 500 piastres which he thought a high enough price. Mohammed Ali would not move on price. *'Both called for alcoholic sustenance; not, as the innocent might expect, from a spirit of amity but in the fervid if unchristian, hope that it might cloud the others intellect.'*[17]

Two hours later it could be said McCrimmon left the restaurant the victor with the moonstones safe in his pocket and the wallet only lighter by 500 piastres. Pleased with himself, rather foolishly he embarks on a drunken celebration of his business acumen. Finally, none too steady on his feet, he splashes out on a gharry to the dockyard gate. Climbing from his carriage he misses his footing and ends up in the gutter in a heap laughing to himself. The army guard at the No 14 gate picks him up and sends him on his way. At the quay he finds the liberty boat is long gone. Still flushed with his success he hired a local boat, a felucca, and began singing his rendering of the 'Skye Boat Song' as the two *'natives laboriously rowed out of the windless harbour'*. With the wind filling the sails he changes to 'Shenandoah' and then Rule Britannia *'as the felucca came within earshot of the Officer of the Watch of the Ilara.'* He leaps up the chain ladder having cast some *'Glasgow Corporation tramway tokens'* into the bottom of the felucca. Once onboard on the port side amidships there *'he opened the heavy steel of a small compartment and packed the bag of blue moonstones safely inside.'* He moved off *'congratulating himself at his own genius.'* He made his way toward his mess deck, climbing over the coaming of the hatchway, completely forgetting until he woke hours later in the Sick Bay that the ladder had been removed for repair.[18]

As McCrimmon lay in the Sick Bay the *Ilara* put to sea, he was beginning to recover until on the fourth day he relapsed, that seemed to be linked to the ship sinking a German transport off Crete. He asked the Sick Bay Attendant for details of the engagement and is told the transport was stopped with gunfire and sent to the bottom with a torpedo. With a voice croaking with emotion he asks if he knew which side and which torpedo tube. The answer was port and X tube. *'As the first wave of kindly oblivion swept over his shattered frame, McCrimmon momentarily and agonisingly relived those few moments folly that it was – when he had stowed the moonstones inside X torpedo tube.'*

McCrimmon does recover but is a marked man having *'destroyed the historic solidarity of the Clan McCrimmon.'* Years later members of the Clan were still looking for him.[19]

A run-ashore in Aleck was not usually the experience Alistair's McCrimmon enjoyed but could be memorable nonetheless. Here Charles Causley describes one of his:

We did the usual round of tombola in the Fleet Club, the pictures, sending home boxes of horrible-looking marshmallows, buying cameras that wouldn't photograph, pens that wouldn't write and watches that fell to pieces as soon as you wound them up...... And like all matelots, we ended up in the bar of the Blue Anchor Club, where we'd booked beds for the night, drinking John Collinses, eating peanuts and listening to an Egyptian band tearing the life out of a selection from Follow the Fleet.

As the night wore on the *'place gets noisier and noisier'*. Even when they did get to sleep they were woken by screams they thought came from the street below the window. However they eventually realise it is the *'Stoker'* in their room from another ship who had had a nightmare, dreaming someone had been trying to cut his throat. He explained he was off *'the Merman. Destroyer. Just got back from seven day's leave in Cairo. Ad a row with a gharry-driver up at Ramleh Station. Said e'd cut my throat, so I punched 'im on the gob.'* They all go back to sleep. When Causley and his ship mate Tug Wilson get up and are ready to leave, the stoker is still asleep, they decide to give him a shake before they leave. *'It was only then that we saw that his throat was cut, very neatly, from ear to ear.'*[20]

With HMS *Royalist* undergoing a lengthy refit at Alexandria, and having a new ventilation system installed, the crew would have been encouraged to take leave, to reduce the number on board and under the feet of the dockyardies. Cairo with all its sights and fleshpots was a natural attraction, only 110 miles away, five hours on the train. By the time Alistair and his ship mates were there, the Eighth Army that had fought Rommel and the Africa Corps in North Africa and defeated them was long gone. So Cairo would not have been as full of soldiers as it had once been.

Yet even so in Cairo and back in Aleck, Alistair would have got the scuttlebutt, the buzz on the story of Tobruk, later he would try and tell that story but it was never published.[21] *Tobruk* would have been a book about the capture, the siege and the humiliating surrender of which Churchill wrote: *'It was a bitter moment. Defeat is one thing, disgrace is another.'*[22] And Operation Agreement, the Allied attempt to put the port of Tobruk out of action for the Axis and destroy oil supplies, was another disaster. Of that operation Alistair felt the security *'had been the worst ever'*, mainly because the raid was *'freely discussed in all the best bars in Cairo and Alexandria...by the officers involved'*.

It got even worse when the seaborne landings involved were practised in Alexandria *'under the fascinated eyes of the Royal Egyptian Yacht Club, the loyalty of whose members to the Allies was, to say the least, problematical'*. This was compounded when Lieutenant-Colonel John Haselden's Commando set off from Cairo into the desert observed by the Egyptians accompanied by *'British Sailors carrying limpet mines'* which could only be used against ships. We will return to Alistair's *Tobruk* later.[23]

During February 1945 HMS *Royalist* was 'worked up' testing all the systems and the work of the dockyard in the Mediterranean off Alexandria. Later that month she *'sailed with the Escort Carrier Force for the East Indies Station'*.[24]

Chapter Eleven

March–August 1945, Far East

HMS *Royalist* arrived in Ceylon in March at the East Indies Fleet base of Trincomalee. Even though it was a tropical island it was not overly liked by the matelots. A rating from HMS *Phoebe* expressed his opinion in the ship's newsletter.

*The swaying palms and thundering surf? Yes, and its red ants, the mosquito, the crabs, jelly fish and barracuda. And the ear diseases. The stars and the sun? And the prickly heat, toe rot, sunburn. The flies, smells and everlasting lassitude. The cruises, with lazy hours lounging in deck chairs beneath a tropic sun, and swimming in a sparkling blue sea. The weary sweltering hours in turret, boiler room and Action Stations.....
There we have the exotic East – a la East Indies Fleet.*[1]

Commodore Oliver's force was renamed 21st Aircraft Carrier Squadron; it consisted, along with HMS *Royalist,* of three escort carriers and six destroyers. All battle-hardened from their time in the Aegean, the force would soon be in action supporting the seaborne landings against Rangoon in Burma, Operation Dracula. The original concept of the operation had been proposed in mid-1944 as an Anglo-Indian force was preparing to recover Burma. However there were not enough landing craft available at the time so it was shelved. In March 1945 it was implemented to capture Rangoon to secure the 14th Army's lines of communication before the monsoon season started. At the time the army was being held up by a Japanese force at Pegu.

During April preparations for the landings went ahead. The assault forces from the 26th Indian Division assembled at Akyab and Ramree islands off the Burma coast which had been captured earlier in the year. Six convoys set off south between April 27–29 for the entrance of the Rangoon River. On 2 May troops began landing in the pouring rain, for the monsoon season had broken early. The 21st Aircraft Carrier

Malayan Peninsula and Java Sea. (*The Author*)

Squadron had been reinforced by a fourth escort carrier HMS *Khedive* and by HMS *Phoebe* another *Dido*-class light cruiser, and provided air cover for the assault convoys and over the landing beaches. Their aircraft also attacked airfields and shore installations on the Tenasserim coast; but no enemy surface ships were encountered, and air opposition was light.

In the final phase of Operation Dracula, light forces swept into the Gulf of Martaban to catch any Japanese ships attempting to escape and early on 30 April three destroyers encountered a convoy of about ten small craft carrying Japanese troops. They sank them all.[2]

By 9 May the East Indies Fleet was back at Trincomalee. Alistair was not a great sports man, even though a Glasgow Rangers supporter. He did not take part in the football matches between ships or departments on the same ship, arranged ashore. He was a reluctant player in some of the mess deck games, Uckers, naval slang for Ludo, was a particular favourite, cribbage was another. Some sailors whiled away the hours knitting or making rugs, model making was another made from any materials to hand.[3]

According to Charlie Dunbar, the only witness we have to Alistair and onboard life, was that he was a loner. He insisted: *'Alistair was a clean-living man'* and drank very little alcohol. This confused Dunbar later when he read about his problems with drink. Dunbar continued that Alistair *'had no time for idle chatter, to the point of being abrupt with those who did'*. Nevertheless he was a handy man to have *'in a tight situation'*.[4]

Two submarines on patrol in the Malacca Strait had sighted the Japanese heavy cruiser *Haguro*, escorted by a destroyer and two submarine chasers on a north-westerly course. They were carrying supplies for the Andaman Islands, whose garrison they had been ordered to evacuate. Admiral H.T.C Walker ordered the East Indies Fleet to sea, including the 21st Aircraft Carrier Squadron, on an interception course. However his ships were spotted by a Japanese reconnaissance aircraft. On 11 May *Haguro* and her escorts reversed course. Admiral Walker thought they might try again so took his fleet well to the south to avoid being sighted again. On the night of 14–15 May he ordered the escort carriers and HMS *Royalist* along with the 26th Destroyer Flotilla, to search the waters north of Sumatra, and on the morning of the 15th aircraft sighted the *Haguro*. The Japanese ships had turned back again to the south-east in another attempt to reach the Andamans. Avengers from the carriers attacked but failed to hit any ships.

The 26th Destroyer Flotilla (Captain M.L. Power) set off with five destroyers leaving the carriers with their own destroyers and at 1100 hrs HMS *Venus* located the enemy on radar at 34 miles. The destroyers went into attack formation wondering if they would be able to close that distance. Then suddenly the *Haguro* turned toward the British destroyers bringing on a general engagement. Heavy rainstorms pounded the sea and lightning flashed across the sky. Captain Power wrote to his wife that it was '*the maddest ten minutes of my life*'. Power tried to close the range as the guns opened fire:

The sea was spouting with shell splashes all round us. Our guns firing rapid broadsides into the destroyer (Kamikaze) and hell's delight going on with every salvo screaming over the ship. Before I got to my chosen range we got hit in the boiler room. There was the roar of escaping steam and clouds of smoke and steam.[5]

Torpedoes from the British destroyers stopped the *Haguro*, and they continued to pound the cruiser with gunfire before more torpedoes sent her to the bottom. The *Kamikaze* escaped undamaged. She returned to the scene of the action the next day and picked up 300 survivors; some 900 of the *Haguro's* crew had been lost. Power's ship HMS *Saumarez* lost two men killed and three wounded in the boiler room. The action had taken part a week after most German forces in Europe had surrendered.[6]

Aboard HMS *Royalist* some were disappointed at not being in on the fight against the *Haguro*, a valuable opportunity for glory, although there was a certain amount of sympathy for the Japanese, after all they were sailors too. Their fate in the shark-infested waters was debated on the mess deck about what they might do if their ship was sunk. Charlie Dunbar said most of them favoured going down with the ship, Alistair said he would take his chance with the sharks in the hope of being picked up in time.[7]

By 21 May the fleet was back at Trincomalee. Within a week HMS *Royalist* was back at sea with three Escort Carriers attacking air bases and shipping and carrying out photographic air reconnaissance off the coast of Sumatra in preparation for Operation Zipper, the landings in Malaya.

On 8 June the submarine HMS *Trenchant* sank the Japanese cruiser *Ashigara* in the Banka strait off Sumatra, in spite of the encounter taking place in very shallow and restricted waters. It was virtually the end of the Imperial Japanese Navy in Malaysian waters, the very same waters that would provide the setting for Alistair's third novel and the last directly influenced by his own wartime experiences *South by Java Head* (1958).

It tells the story of a motley collection of people who escape the fall of Singapore on the *Kerry Dancer*, a Clyde built tramp steamer of 500 tons, the last ship in the novel to leave the city before it fell to the Japanese on 15 February 1942.[8]

Chapter Twelve

September–November 1945, Singapore

During July 1945 the Eastern Fleet had continued with preparations for the reoccupation of Malaya. Minesweepers cleared the eastern approaches of mines while heavy units covered them and bombarded shore targets. On the 19th the minesweepers cleared the approaches to Phuket Island, while aircraft from the Escort carriers attacked enemy airfields on shore. On the 26th there took place the only Kamikaze attack carried out in the Indian Ocean. Three of the attacking aircraft were shot down before they could reach their targets, however a fourth hit the minesweeper HMS *Vestal,* she was so badly damaged that she had to be sunk. This proved to be the last war operation for the East Indies Fleet.[1]

Meanwhile, the day before, news reached them that the Labour Party had swept to power in the general election back home. Absentee ballots were distributed amongst the 'floating voters' aboard British warships, it would have been the first time Alistair, at 23, voted in a general election. There is no record of which party he voted for, or if he voted at all, but many of the ships treated the election with indifference and there was a feeling they might have waited until the war against Japan was over. Yet for that they did not have long to wait, for on 6 August 1945 the American B-29 bomber *Enola Gay* dropped the atomic bomb on Hiroshima with devastating effect, killing over 100,000 people. Three days later a second atomic bomb was dropped on Nagasaki with equally huge loss of life. On 15 August Japan surrendered.

On 11 August the 21st Aircraft Carrier Squadron was on its way to attack Penang and Medan when the news was received that Japan had accepted peace terms. Admiral Louis Mountbatten, responsible for a huge area of south-east Asia because of the amount of widely scattered Japanese forces and doubts whether they would obey the surrender order, decided to launch the assault against the west coast of Malaya on 9 September as planned. By the middle of August plans were well advanced when the Supreme Commander Allied forces, General Douglas MacArthur, issued the order that no landings were to take place until the surrender had been signed. At the time virtually the whole East Indies Fleet was at sea steaming toward the Malayan peninsula. Rather than try to return to Ceylon Admiral Walker took most of the fleet under the lee of the Nicobars where there was enough shelter to refuel his larger ships from tankers and the smaller vessels could be provisioned from the larger ones.

On 28 August the main body of the fleet arrived off Penang and on 2 September the local Japanese commander surrendered on the flagship, the battleship HMS *Nelson*. Meanwhile the naval commander-in-chief, Admiral Sir Arthur Power, onboard the cruiser HMS *Cleopatra* with minesweepers clearing the way, entered the great port of Singapore the next day. This was followed over the next twenty-four hours by the 5th Indian Division arriving in transports. Within three days 100,000 men had landed at various points around the Malay Peninsula.[2]

On 9 September HMS *Royalist* and the Escort Carriers supported Allied forces landing on beaches between Port Dickson and Swettenham on the eastern side of the peninsula within the Malacca straits. Two days later she was in Singapore for the surrender ceremony. The next day, 12 September, Admiral Mountbatten as Supreme Commander, Allied Powers South-East Asia, accepted the surrender of the Japanese forces from General Seishiro Itagaki in the Singapore Municipal building. Many of HMS *Royalist's* crew watched the surrender and their own first lieutenant was the right hand guard of one of the high ranking Japanese officers involved in the surrender. Richard Campbell-Begg, a rating from the destroyer HMS *Paladin*, was in the crowd watching the surrender that day:

> *The Japanese top brass then appeared, each man having two senior British Officers as guards one on each side. They were marched to the building to the jeers of the crowd....After the signing the Japanese were led away and Lord Louis appeared and gave a very spirited and apt speech.*[3]

The Union flag was raised before the building and bands played the national anthems of the Allies. Japanese equipment soon found its way on to Allied ships, a favourite was the army cap. Campbell-Begg noted the streets of Singapore were full of former PoWs, *'all as thin as rakes...'*

They were brought onto RN ships to be fed, not a straightforward job, as their systems could not cope with food after months of starvation, so this was done under the supervision of doctors and the sick bay staff.[4]

HMS *Royalist*, like many naval ships, was employed now as a transport carrying personnel, many of them former PoWs between Ceylon, Penang, Port Swettenham and Singapore. The ship also delivered the Governor-General Sir Gerard Gent back to Malaya where they were given a civic reception in Kuala Lumpur.[5]

No doubt Alistair would have talked to some of the PoWs, storing the information away in his memory, especially those that had been prisoners in the notorious Changi Prison. Setting *South by Java Head* during the fall of Singapore in February 1942, there was a wealth of escape stories of the forty-four unescorted ships of reasonable size that left, most on the 13th, only one or two made it. Of the 5,000 people who tried to escape by sea some 1,000 got through, the rest being killed or captured.[6]

The motley collection of people in Alistair's story who escape Singapore were similar to real events. Like Corporal Fraser, [who has the same surname as Alistair's school friend] a former '*Cairngorms Shepherd*', is made clear he is an Argyll and Sutherland Highlander.[7] The 2nd battalion of this famous regiment fought with distinction during the retreat down the Malay Peninsula where they often formed a rear-guard. By the time they crossed the causeway into Singapore their strength was down to 250. They were joined by 210 Royal Marines, survivors from HMS *Prince of Wales* and HMS *Repulse*, both sunk 70 miles off Pahang by Japanese aircraft only three days after the attack on Pearl Harbor. They formed a composite battalion and became known as the Plymouth Argylls; 52 Highlanders and 22 Marines managed to reach Colombo, the others perished or were taken prisoner.

There is a group of nurses, two Chinese, two Malay led by a Eurasian Miss Drachmann. Sixty-five Australian Army nurses set out in the *Vyner Brooke*, a 300-ton patrol vessel, which carried 200 passengers away from Singapore on 12 February, including civilians, women and children and the nursing sisters. The next day in the afternoon she was attacked by dive bombers and went down in fifteen minutes. Some survivors made it ashore to Banka Island but with no food and the children becoming distressed they decided to give themselves up. When the Japanese arrived they separated the men from the women, took the men along the beach and executed them. Vivian Bullwinkel, one of the nurses takes up the story:

> *The Japanese who had gone with the men came back wiping their bayonets…We just looked at each other. We didn't have any emotion about it. I think by this time we'd had shock added to everything else. The Japanese came and stood in front of us and indicated that we should go into the sea…We knew what was going to happen to us… I think I did hear the rat-tat-tat and I suppose it was a machine-gun. I got hit. The force of the bullet, together with the waves, knocked me off my feet…After a while it sort of penetrated that I wasn't dying right there and then. I thought I'd better stay low until I couldn't stay low any longer. The waves brought me right into shallow water. Finally, when I did sit up and look around, there was nothing. The Japanese had gone and none of the girls were to be seen.*

Along with Vivian, 23 of her fellow nurses survived the bombing of the *Vyner Brooke* and capture and internment by the Japanese.[8] The survivors of the *Kerry Dancer* and the *Viroma* face similar sadistic treatment from 'Captain Yamata' in *South by Java Head*.

Miss Drachmann looks after a small English boy, Peter Tallon, they know his name because he had a disc around his neck that tells them: '*He's two years and three months old, he lives in Mysore Road in north Singapore, and he's a member of the Church of England.*'[9]

Lieutenant Parker leads a small detachment of soldiers; their main job to make sure Foster Farnholme survives, for the former brigadier-general is a spy, the counter-espionage chief of South-East Asia who has obtained a copy of the Japanese invasion plans for Australia.[10]

There are others like the mysterious Dutch Van Effen, while Captain Siran and the crew of the *Kerry Dancer* are not to be trusted. This is before these people are picked up by the tanker *Viroma* once the *Kerry Dancer* has been sunk, a 12,000 ton ship of the British-Arabian line, and we meet Captain Francis Findhorn, his first officer, John Nicolson, and the rest of the crew. We will return again to *South by Java Head* later in the book, suffice it to say Alistair knew the setting of the novel well from his time on HMS *Royalist*.

The book was dedicated to his brother Ian who helped with some of the Merchant Navy details, the brothers had stayed in touch by letter throughout the war. Ian's job was equally as dangerous as serving in the Royal Navy was for Alistair; over 30,000 men who served under the Red Ensign lost their lives in the conflict. Ian must have been impressed with his younger brother's writing for he wrote: *'I think your future lies in writing, Alistair. With the description and the way you compose your letters, you should really end up writing books.'*[11]

At sunset on 31 October the flag of Geoffrey Oliver, now a Rear Admiral, was struck on HMS *Royalist* and the ship joined the 5th Cruiser Squadron. Oliver retired from the navy in 1955 a full admiral.[12]

Chapter Thirteen

Demob

In December 1945 the sailing order that HMS *Royalist* was heading to Simonstown via Mombasa for a refit no doubt went down like a lead balloon with the crew. With most thinking of getting home, she sailed from Ceylon on 12 December. However at Mombasa the orders were changed and she was ordered to return home via the Mediterranean.[1] HMS *Royalist* reached Portsmouth on 28 January 1946; why it took five weeks is not known, the cruiser might well have been used as a taxi again. Arriving back at her home port, *'preparations were advanced to pay her off into reserve.'*[2]

One wonders as Alistair went down the gangplank for the last time on 11 December 1945 whether he looked back at his old ship, rust streaked and battered, after all it had been his home nearly three years, though somehow, I doubt it. What of the ship that became *HMS Ulysses* in all but name? HMS *Royalist* remained in the Reserve until 1956 when she was modernised and on completion was transferred to the Royal New Zealand Navy. After ten years as Flagship of the RNZN she was returned to the Royal Navy. Placed on the disposal list after twenty-five years service, in January 1968 she arrived at the breakers yard in Osaka, Japan.[3]

Alistair MacLean left the Royal Navy on 26 March 1946 as a Leading Torpedo Operator, after a brief spell for accommodation on the battleship HMS *Howe* and the barracks at HMS *Victory* where he had joined the Royal Navy five years before. He would have gone home before that date on 'survivor's leave', entitled to fifty-six days paid leave. Demobilisation consisted of handing in his kit and being supplied with a 'Burton' civvy suit, a hat, shoes, two shirts and a tie. Burtons was one of the main suppliers for these suits that became the source of much comedy due to often being a poor fit. He would have been given a rail warrant and his pay.

He stopped off in London first to see his brother Ian on his ship at the King George V Dock on the Thames. The last time they had met Alistair had just left school. Now he was a battle-hardened veteran of 24, a bit gaunt looking. They had a good drink together in Ian's cabin on board and discussed the future. The romantic wish Alistair once had to follow his brother into the Merchant Navy had been dispelled by four years in the Royal Navy. At the time he may well have felt like Charles Causley, that life in the Navy *was an experience I could well have done without*.[4] However for Alistair, and for that matter Charles, they would be able to draw on the wealth of that naval experience in their later writing. Both men had the notions on demob that they would go to university and take a degree. There was a Government scheme to prioritize returning servicemen in universities and colleges.

Next for Alistair it was back to Glasgow and his mother, only to find out his younger brother Gillespie, who had served in the Intelligence Corps in Germany near the end of the war in Europe, had been injured in an explosion. He was shipped back to the UK to a hospital in Surrey where he lay in a coma for six months. Mrs Mary MacLean had had more than her share of heartache over the last decade, losing her husband and eldest son before the war, worrying about the two boys at sea, and now Gillespie lying in a hospital bed hundreds of miles away. However Alistair went down south to see him once a fortnight. On a lighter note, he was soon able to renew his friendship with Alastair Cameron, the son of the minister who had been his father's friend, who had joined the Cameron Highlanders in 1939. His father, the Reverend Hector Cameron, had died in 1940. They resumed their support for Rangers, attending home matches at Ibrox Park. Many of the players on the pitch were the same as them, returning servicemen. Saturday would continue with a few drinks and perhaps a film, often at the Grosvenor cinema in Bynes Road. Glasgow was still largely a Victorian city with slums and old factories polluting the atmosphere, entertainment was provided at the *'Locarno or Green's Playhouse Ballroom, dancing to Joe Loss or Felix Mendelssohn and the Hawaiian Serenaders'*.[5]

In 1946 the intake for servicemen at universities was high. Oxford and Cambridge had around 80 per cent, with the national average around 50 per cent. Some of these students were returning to their courses which only had to be completed. Alistair, as a new student in pursuit of a degree in English language and literature, faced a four year course.[6]

Many of these former-servicemen-students, after up to five or six years of deprivations, were hell-bent on having a good time, while others merely wanted to get a degree as quickly as possible. Alistair had a low profile at the university, he worked doggedly, attended all the classes and the tutorials of his lecturer John Farish but took no part in the university's social life.

Glasgow University students were to grab world headlines in Alistair's last year when in December 1950 four students, Ian Hamilton, Gavin Vernon, Kay Matheson and Alan Stuart took the Stone of Scone from Westminster Abbey. They were all members of the Scottish Covenant Association, a group that supported home rule for Scotland. Edward I of England (Longshanks) in 1296 took the stone as a spoil of war and it was fitted into King Edward's chair in Westminster Abbey on which the subsequent English and British monarchs were crowned.

A few days before Christmas the four students drove to London in two Ford Anglias, they were backed by Glasgow business man Robert Gray. Trying to remove the stone they managed to break it so putting a piece in each car, the larger part was taken to Kent and buried in a field. The other piece remained in one of the cars and was left with a friend in the midlands. The students returned to Scotland, two by car and two by train. On discovering the stone was missing the authorities closed the border between England and Scotland for the first time in 400 years. A fortnight later the students returned for the two parts of the stone and brought them to Glasgow where the stonemason Robert Gray mended the stone. In April 1951 the authorities were told the stone was on the high altar at Arbroath Abbey where in 1320 the Declaration of Arbroath asserting Scottish nationhood was made. In February 1952 the stone was returned to Westminster Abbey. The four were eventually identified but not prosecuted to avoid highlighting their cause and in the interests of the unity of the UK. In 2008 a film was made of the incident, an adventure-comedy.[7]

Alistair was not a Nationalist and thought '*it better to be a good European and a good Scot than just a good Scot, I am not a Scottish Nationalist but do sympathize with many of the nationalistic aspirations*', he wrote in 1972.[8]

To avoid being a burden to his mother, Alistair became a part-time sorter at the post office and a local authority road sweeper. During the long summer holidays, he went to work with Gillespie who had become a forester at the Campbell Estate at Furness in Argyll. They were often joined by the two Cameron boys, Alastair and Ewan in hard physical work, clearing undergrowth from around the trees and bringing in the hay harvest among other jobs.

In his final year, instead of the forestry work Alistair and Alastair Cameron went down south in response to an advert to work as porters and cleaners at the King George V Sanatorium at Godalming in Surrey, a purpose-built TB hospital. It was there Alistair met Gisela Heinrichsen, a German girl, from Schleswig-Holstein. She had come to the UK to learn English and was working on the same ward as Alistair. In general he was shy with women, but with Gisela, a tall good looking girl, it was different: she captivated him. He was close to graduating so Gisela, in order that their romance could continue more easily, applied and got a job at Mearnskirk Hospital to the south of Glasgow, it had started off as a TB Sanatorium and during the war was used by the Navy.

With his final examination looming Alistair was injured in a road traffic accident when he was struck by a brewery truck. It resulted in an injury to his right arm and hand, and there was some concern he might not recover the use of the hand. However, determined as ever he got his hand moving again using a tennis ball and gripping exercises. He would later claim that as his hand was not fully recovered it affected his results in not getting a first, as the examiners found difficulty in reading his writing, yet he still passed with a good second-class degree.

He then took the teaching course at Jordanhill College which led to him obtaining a teaching post at Gallowflat School teaching English, History and Geography. Shortly after this Gisela and Alistair were married on 2 July 1953 at St. Columba Church in Glasgow, the same church as his parents had been married in. His mother was hardly enamoured with the match as Gisela was German and her brother had been killed on the Somme in the Great War. However, it was on a par with Gillespie marrying a Catholic. Ian also voiced his concern over Alistair's match, having met Gisela he told his brother in his opinion they were incompatible, but he was at sea when the wedding took place.

A young Alistair MacLean in naval uniform.
(*Courtesy of Ian MacLean and An Iodhlann–Tiree Historical Centre. 2009.107.3*)

The successful author, Alistair in the 1960s.
(*Courtesy of Ian MacLean and An Iodhlann–Tiree Historical Centre. 2009.107.2*)

On the set of *Force 10 From Navarone* Harrison Ford and Alistair MacLean 1978. (*Everett Collection inc/Alamy*)

Gilleasbuig (Gillespie) MacLean, Alistair's younger brother in the uniform of the Intelligence Corps. The wings indicate he had completed a parachute course. (*Courtesy of Shona Vance/MacLean*)

Sailors undergoing training here at Sunday Divisions. (*Author's Collection*)

Roedean School Brighton used as Torpedo School where Alistair attended a course. Coat of arms HMS *Vernon*. (*RN Research*)

HMS *Diadem* light cruiser, the same class as *Royalist*. (*Author's Collection*)

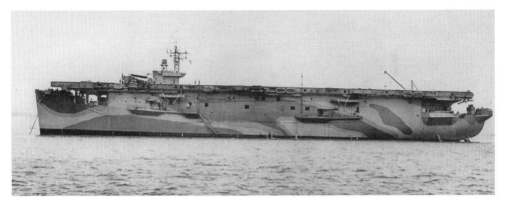

Escort carrier HMS *Attacker*. HMS *Royalist* acted as flag ship to a group of escort carriers like this. (*US Navy Historical Center 7043-42*)

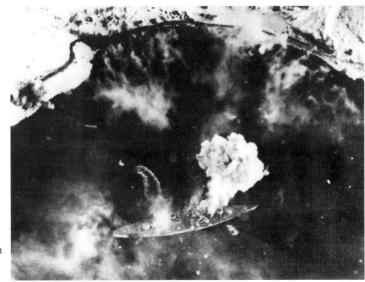

Fleet Air Arm bombs from Barracudas hitting the German battleship *Tirpitz* during Operation Tungsten, 3 April 1944. (*IWM A 22633*)

HMS *Bellona* light cruiser in heavy weather on Arctic Convoy. (*IWM A 27555*)

Meeting of the 'Big Three' – Stalin, Roosevelt and Churchill at the Tehran Conference November–December 1943. (*US National Archives*)

Invasion fleet gathers off Naples for Operation Dragoon, the invasion of the South of France. (*US National Archives*)

View from the flight deck of HMS *Pursuer* shows HMS *Royalist* between the carriers during Operation Dragoon. (*IWM A 19751*)

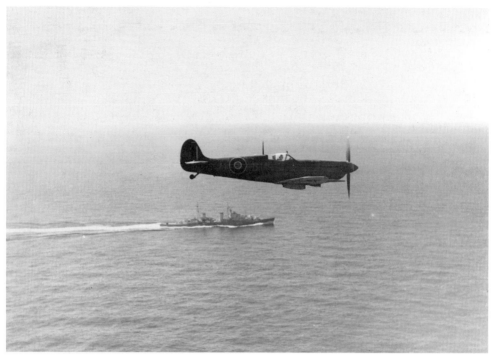

A Seafire fighter flies above HMS *Royalist* near Alexandra 1944. (*IWM A 27758*)

Coastal gun positions once littered the Mediterranean. This is one of the few remaining on Malta, Fort Rinella and its 100-ton Armstrong gun. (*Author's Collection*)

The Guns of Navarone from the 1961 film. (*Moviestore Collection Ltd/ Alamy*)

The Japanese Cruiser *Haguro* here under air attack at Rabaul November 1943. She was sunk in May 1945 by the Royal Navy's 26th Destroyer Flotilla. (*US Navy Historical Centre NH 95558*)

Views of Jamaica Inn near the village of Bolventor on Bodmin Moor. Alistair MacLean bought the pub in 1964 and sold it eleven years later. (*Author's Collection*)

HMS *Belfast*, the last surviving Second World War light cruiser. Although bigger and heavier than *Royalist* she gives a good idea of what conditions would have been like. She is now moored in the Thames as a museum. (*Author's Collection*)

Chapter Fourteen

The Short Stories 1954

The short stories of Alistair MacLean are among his best writing. In the main they got into print because he became the joint owner in a boat.

When he began teaching at Gallowflat School he felt very much the new man and his natural shyness made it difficult for him to find his niche with his colleagues. In the staffroom he would spend most of his time alone smoking, he was a heavy smoker, as many people were at the time. Initially he seems to have got on better with his pupils, he taught the bottom class and although for some of his fellow teachers, discipline was the key problem it was not for Alistair. He kept the 'tawse' or the strap, a leather belt used in Scottish schools for punishment, tucked in his jacket partly on display yet he seldom had to use it. Though strict the boys liked him, he was known as 'Dandy MacLean', after a fictional character of the time. He used a long pointer as much to draw attention to things on the board as to using it as a friendly poke from 'on high' to wake up the inattentive. According to one of his pupils he ran a system of incentives, known as 'correct tick', whereby the class was tested on whatever had been the subject of the week before. If the pupil did not reach eight-out-of-ten they got 100 lines for every point below, which had to read: '*I must remember not to forget to learn my history.*' One of his pupils, Willie McIntosh, felt he was getting fed up writing lines; '*that it dawned on me I had better brush up my performance or I would be doing this for the rest of my schooldays. So for the first time in my life I actually began to study and enjoy it.*'[1] Alistair never conveyed to his pupils his dislike of the job. This was reflected more in his strict nine-to-four attitude; it was as if he could not get out of the school fast enough.

Yet he did find a good friend at Gallowflat, Dougie Seggie who taught technical subjects as he had done before the war, he had spent the war years in the RAF. Dougie came from Cambuslang, a town on the south-eastern outskirts of Glasgow. It was probably hard work for

Dougie, a much more garrulous man, to bring Alistair out of his shell but he saw something special in the former navy man. The great thing they had in common was a love of sailing or the prospect of it. They decided to buy a boat together although neither man was flush with cash. Dougie already owned a rowing boat but what they had in mind was a much bigger craft. Meanwhile Alistair and Gisela moved into Dougie's old shared house as he and his wife Violet moved to Larkhall. So the MacLeans started their married life at No 33 Drumsargard Road, Burnside, Rutherglen, a furnished semi-detached villa which they shared with the owner's son.

Naturally money was tight at the time but Alistair and Dougie managed to raise £200 to buy a 34ft long Loch Fyne Skiff that MacLean had seen advertised in the *Oban Times*. They bought the boat, the *Silver Craig*, from two fishermen on the west coast of Scotland at Loch Gairloch north east of the Isle of Skye. The *Scottish West Coast Pilot* says: '*The main loch is wide and faces the W with a clear fetch of over 30 miles from Harris, so quite a sea can roll in bad weather. Fortunately, though there are two perfectly sheltered anchorages.*'[2]

They needed crew to help them bring the boat south. Alastair Cameron, now a qualified doctor, was back from Canada and he brought along his friend Dr Harvey Miles for the adventure. They headed north in Dougie's old car which would find its way into Alistair's short story '*The cruise of the Golden Girl*' in *Blackwood's Magazine*. As '*a dilapidated and almost springless vehicle of incredible vintage comfort there was none: even before we had clambered aboard the car, its interior had been more than comfortably loaded with provisions, bedding, luggage and equipment. Nor were matters helped by the conditions of the roads during the last four or five hours: it was such as the city or suburban motorist encounters only in nightmares.*'[3]

Although he had spent over four years in the navy Alistair had little knowledge of handling small boats. He would have gone out in the Solent during basic training in a whaler but with an experienced PO at the helm; most of his time on HMS *Royalist* he had spent with torpedoes, his trade, or looking after electrical circuits on board. When the four friends put to sea in the *Silver Craig* they did not even have a radio onboard. They headed straight out into the aftermath of an Atlantic gale as it came roaring in from the west. In his story *The Cruise of the Golden Girl* he changed the name of the boat but not the crew members. Dougie was the engineer, Doctors C. and M. were onboard, and the story is told in the first person whose name is not revealed.

They shot through Kyle Rhea on a spring tide that can '*attain 8 knots*' and '*produce some fierce whirlpools*'.[4] They did take shelter at Kyle which revealed another problem, the ancient Kelvin engine had neither clutch nor reverse which made stopping for the amateur sailors difficult in the extreme and they missed or '*overshot the pier by a hundred and fifty yards*'.

Later they continued on their way south through the Sound of Sleat sheltered by the mass of Skye but:

> *Four hours after leaving Kyle, Dougie and I, blissfully asleep in the fore cabin, were startled into wakefulness by a violent jolt, a loud crash, and water rushing into the cabin above our heads. We knew at once that we were doomed. This was it. Sinking fast, and helplessly trapped below decks. Take to the boats! Only we had no boat.*[5]

They were in open water again and saw through the '*driving rain*' on their beam was Rhum, on the starboard bow Eigg. Their forlorn hope lay in Mallaig Harbour which involved a 180° turn. They make it into the harbour, yet in the harbour their anchor chain begins to drag in a south-westerly gale. They move in closer again to the inner harbour and lay out the complete anchor and chain, but all too soon the anchor begins to drag again. They decide there is no other course but to moor to the pier which takes several attempts. They are lucky, saved, when a '*powerful-fishing boat*' makes fast to them; '*the beautiful purr of those diesels was the loveliest music we had ever heard.*'

They leave twenty-four hours later but chugging out of the harbour the engine stops. By the time Dougie had found and fixed the problem the tide had carried them '*over the sea to Skye*'. At last they make good time, the sea is almost flat calm, they stop at Tobermory, a good night is had on the island of Mull. The next day the *Golden Girl* sails south along the Sound of Mull rounding Duart Point, marked by its castle, they hit white caps in the Firth of Lorne. The narrator mentions '*seas of seething white-caps, so ably depicted by Conrad...*'[6] It was on Mull that two of Alistair's boyhood heroes, David Balfour and Alan Breck, from Robert Louis Stevenson's *Kidnapped,* are shipwrecked when the *Covenant* runs aground on the Torran Rocks:

The reef on which we had struck was close in under the southwest end of Mull, off a little isle they call Earraid, which lay low and black upon the larboard. Sometimes the swell broke clean over us; sometimes it only ground the poor brig upon the reef, so that we could hear her beat herself to pieces; and what with the great noise of the sails, and the singing of the wind, and the flying of the spray in the moonlight, and the sense of danger....[7]

Unlike the *Covenant*, the *Golden Girl* passed Mull safely hugging the east coast and hoping to take advantage of the sea astern when they turned and crossed the Firth of Lorn. Heading for the Pladda Lighthouse and onward for Easdale Sound, they have to enter from the narrower rock strewn south channel: '*Doctors C. and M. stood in the bows, are on either side, sounding desperately for depth and bawling back instructions with a wholly unprofessional lack of restraint.*'

Having taken some advice from two retired fishermen, with the tide turning, who said the crossing to Pladda would be easy as the weather was much improved, '*the sky was now a cloudless blue and the merriest breath of a wind stirred the harbour surface*', thus they did not '*tarry*' long. The locals read the weather wrong. They soon realise the mistake but it was too late to turn back. The *Golden Girl* comes closer to foundering in this stretch than any other even though it is a glorious sunny day. Suffice it to say once into the lee of Pladda it was again calm and still they sailed on to Soarba over a '*translucent blue sea usually associated only with the Aegean and the isles of Greece.*'[8]

The early evening sees the *Golden Girl* at Crinan and they take the canal to Ardrishaig: '*A waterway for smaller vessels saving the passage around the Mull of Kintyre, it has fifteen locks.*'[9] They make their way south and by breakfast-time were far down the calm surface of Loch Fyne. The passage remains calm all the way to the Gareloch, at last they step ashore, home at Shandon. They are '*dirty, weary, unshaven and bloodshot about the eyes*'; their return he likens to '*how Eric the Red felt when he first set foot in the New World, and how Drake felt as he sailed up the Plymouth Sound after his voyage round the world*'.[10]

Alistair also places his short story *They Sweep the Seas* off the West Coast of Scotland, a bleak, cheerless place on an '*early morning of a January day*'.[11] [For the full text of *They Sweep the Seas* see the Appendix at the end of the book.]

The *Silver Craig* was brought ashore to Kilcreggan on the Clyde where Alistair and Dougie began to refit their craft. Dougie brought in another friend, Willie Campbell, a man skilled in woodwork, a big man, strong but mild natured. He had been a Commando during the war and saw service from Dunkirk through to D-Day. Alistair liked him from the start, Dougie and other friends felt he had modelled Andrea on Willie Campbell in *The Guns of Navarone*.[12]

There were many cruises in the *Silver Craig* and they made the rule 'no drinking while underway'. Even so they almost came to grief with a battleship being towed to Faslane to be broken up, passing in front with a good distance to spare, the engine died. Dougie managed to revive it just in time as a *King George V* class battleship threatened to reduce them to matchwood. HMS *Duke of York* and HMS *Anson* were broken up at Faslane about this time. On another occasion they had to call out the Troon life-boat when the magneto got drowned in sea water and they had fare-paying passengers on board. This escapade got into the Glasgow newspapers.

The adventures in the *Silver Craig* brought Alistair out into the limelight with the staff at Gallowflat School. Many members were taken on trips and outings on the boat. The boat gave Alistair the immediate inspiration to start writing his short stories, kicking off with the *Golden Girl* in *Blackwood's* published in the September 1954 issue which was after the *The Dileas* appeared in print. However given the time-lag between submission and publication with magazines it is likely, given the content based on the *Silver Craig's* collection cruise, to have been written first. While another appeared in the *Argosy Magazine,* purely a short story journal published 1926–1974, he was in good company for stories from Ray Bradbury, H.E. Bates and C.S. Forester among others were featured. Later the magazine would review many of Alistair's books.

In February 1954 he began writing a story of a rescue at sea, a tale with Biblical influences, which forces upon its hero a decision that might have tested the Wisdom of Solomon. This time however he entered the story *The Dileas* into a short-story competition run by the *Glasgow Herald,* which won against 942 other entries from all over the world. Yet it was a close-run thing. Six of the *Herald's* journalists formed the judging panel that were evenly divided between Alistair's *The Dileas* and Iris Gibson's *Now Such Light.* The editor, Sir William Robieson, had to use his casting vote to break the deadlock and he voted for *The Dileas* [pronounced Jee-lus]. The title in Gaelic means 'The Faithful'. It was published in the Saturday edition of the *Herald* on 6 March 1954. As it was Alistair might have been disqualified as he had previously submitted stories to the *Herald;* luckily they were rejected as had one been published he would have fallen foul of the rule no entrants to the competition who had written for the paper could enter.

The £100 first prize came at a good time for Alistair and Gisela as they had been given notice to quit by the owners of 33 Drumsargard Road, Mr and Mrs Menzies, although they had offered the property to the MacLeans to buy but they could not afford it. However the prize money gave them the opportunity to buy some furniture for their new home.

His winning story featured *'the Dileas that was old Beumas Grant's boat was a deal better than Eachan made her out to be. When Campbell of Andrishaig built a Loch-Fyner, the timbers came out of the heart of oak.'*[13] Alistair at the time only saw short story writing as a hobby, not as a way out of a job he disliked, a fillip to his other great passion 'messing about in boats'.

At the time Gisela was pregnant so any additional money was handy as his salary after stoppages was around £300 a year. Yet what he did not know, among the thousands of readers who read *The Dileas* in the Saturday edition of the *Glasgow Herald,* was Marjory Chapman who had worked for Collins the publishers in Glasgow as did her husband Ian. She had been moved to tears by the story and showed it to her husband. Ian Chapman wrote to Alistair via the *Herald* asking him to phone him urgently. Alistair, his usually shy self, mulled it over but eventually curiosity got the better of him and he called Chapman at the Collins office in Cathedral Street. Ian invited Alistair and Gisela to dinner with him and Marjory. They met at the grand Royal Restaurant on Nile Street but Alistair was alone as Gisela, heavily pregnant, was suffering and had stayed at home. The Chapmans managed to draw Alistair out of his shell and got him talking about himself. They found out that Marjory and Alistair had been in the same honours class at Glasgow University. As the evening wore on the Chapmans suggested Alistair should write a novel, but he was not enthusiastic, a novel compared to a short story seemed daunting. Yet Ian was not about to give up and the two men had much in common, both were sons of the manse and they stayed in touch.

Francis Ian Chapman, always known as 'Ian' was the son of the Reverend Peter Chapman and had been brought up at Peterhead before moving to Auldearn, not far from Alistair's childhood home at Daviat. He had served in the RAF 1943–44 but was invalided out due to eyesight problems; he then became a Bevan Boy at Plean Colliery near Stirling for three years. He had an ambition to become a concert violinist but he needed to earn a living. He joined Collins as a trainee in 1947 and went to sell Bibles in the USA. In 1951 he returned to the Glasgow Office to head the Bible division, there he met Marjory and they were married in 1953.[14]

Alistair took to the Chapmans and they to him and they met several more times. Although at the time he had other things on his mind, in September Gisela gave birth to their first son, Lachlan. When he told Ian the good news, he also said he was going to try the novel based on his naval war. A remarkable ten weeks later he called Ian: *'So do you want to come and collect the thing?'* Ian drove over straight away to the MacLeans' home, now a small semi-detached bungalow at 343 King's Park Avenue. Alistair gave Ian a brown paper parcel tied up with string at the door. He did not invite him in, embarrassed with nappies drying in the house and the baby crying.

It crossed Ian Chapman's mind that he had no authority to commission anything. But then again could the 'thing' be any good written in such a short time. Yet was this so uncommon? Two years before Ian Fleming had written *Casino Royale* in about the same length of time. However he had been at his bungalow Goldeneye on Jamaica, not working as a teacher with a young wife and baby at home.[15]

At home Ian unwrapped the parcel, the title page on the manuscript said *HMS Ulysses by Alistair S. MacLean.* He and Marjory began to read.

Chapter Fifteen

The First Three War Novels 1955–1958

Ian and Marjory Chapman read that first line: '*Slowly, deliberately, Starr crushed out the butt of his cigarette.*'[1] Over the next few hours they read the book right through. The next day he sent the manuscript with a note to William Collins, the chairman in London who it was doubtful even knew who Ian Chapman was. Three days later Collins rang him, Ian wondered if he was in for a rocket, but no, the chairman liked it and wanted to publish it. He asked him how he had obtained it. Once told about Alistair, he said: '*Go and tell him I'll pay him an advance of a thousand pounds.*'[2]

The same day Ian drove over to King's Park Avenue; once again he was kept on the doorstep but when it dawned on Alistair what he meant he

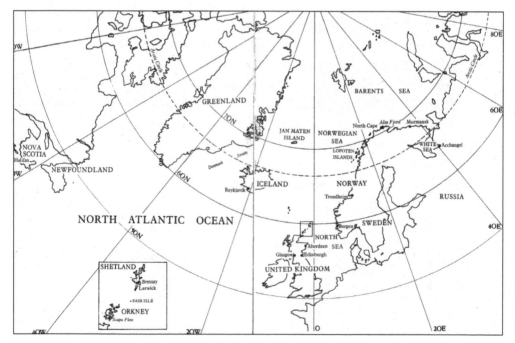

The Arctic and Atlantic Oceans that appear in the front of the first edition of *San Andreas*. (*Courtesy HarperCollins*)

invited him in. There they tried to explain to Gisela what had happened. Ian explained to them an advance was against the royalties the book would earn which was paid to the author. Alistair asked if he would make enough to put a deposit on a house they wanted to buy at Clarkston, a suburban district on the south side of Glasgow. The house was £2,750 and Chapman was pretty sure it would pay much more than the ten per cent deposit usually required at the time.

Sadly, Alistair and Gisela's marriage was coming under strain, possibly due to the fact that they shared the bungalow at Kings Park Avenue with Mrs McAllister. Although they liked her, it was part of the reason he had been reluctant to invite Ian Chapman inside. They only had two small rooms so there was little privacy. The writing process must have been difficult, he came home from school to an early tea, and when it was time to put the baby to bed had to change rooms. The next door neighbours, the Jones, lent him their *old Remington* to type up *HMS Ulysses*.

Another factor in the relationship was that Alistair had a habit of apologising for Gisela being German; even the neighbours noticed how much it hurt her. Mrs McAllister's niece, Elma Nairn, observed this first hand and was not slow in coming forward to tell him: *'After all, he knew she was German when he married her. He had a cruel tongue and I felt sorry for Gisela who was a pet.'*[3]

Collins' marketing department had got behind the book driven on by Ian Chapman and due to launch in the autumn of 1955. The film rights were sold for £30,000 to the Associated British Picture Corporation and the *Picture Post* magazine paid £5,000 for the serial rights. The book was printed with virtually no changes. Alistair explained to the American journalist Jain Johnston in 1972, his method for writing *HMS Ulysses:*

I drew a cross square, lines down representing the characters, lines across representing chapters 1–15. Most of the characters died, in fact only one survived the book, [Johnny Nicholls the young doctor] *but when I came to the end of the graph it looked somewhat lopsided, there were too many people dying in the first, fifth and tenth chapters so I had to rewrite it, giving an even dying space throughout. I suppose it sounds cold blooded and, calculated, but that's the way I did it.*[4]

HMS Ulysses turned out to be one of the most successful British novels of all time. Back then there was no internet to drive sales; most were sold through book shops, by publication day the shops held 134,000 copies, by spring 1956 it had sold 250,000 all in hardback. So what was special about this book?

In some ways it is an odd book. Told in the third person it has a large set of characters but no real key character, the nearest is Captain Richard Vallery, who is heroic. Dying of TB, he rallies the crew after they had mutinied, they were all tired but they set off with the ill-fated FR-77, yet Vallery is dead by page 280. Vice-Admiral Tyndall, known affectionately as Farmer Giles, suffers a nervous breakdown and dies of frostbite and is gone by page 166. Commander Turner, the first lieutenant who takes over command on Vallery's death, is last seen passing a bowline around a seaman, but they are swept away before help could reach them after the *Ulysses* has gone down on page 317.

There are many heroes among the crew and no villains, even the ship has a heroic death trying to ram a German heavy cruiser and dies in the attempt on pages 312–313. Maybe the ship – always called 'she' by sailors – is the key character, a real heroin.

The book has a documentary style, even with a few footnotes, but it does not shy away from the horrors of war, the crews of the ships who are burnt to death, frozen to death in the freezing waters, or just blown apart, as are the crews of the German aircraft and ships. They all do their duty as if they must feed the death machine. The sheer scale of *HMS Ulysses*, with lots of ships involved including three aircraft carriers, is perhaps one of the reasons it has not been filmed to date, although the film rights were quickly snapped up. Robert Clark of the ABFC arranged for R.C. Sheriff, the playwright, best known for *Journey's End*, to write a script, however because of the sheer naval detail involved he found it difficult. Later in the 1970s Rank looked into it but it went no further, whereas Nicholas Monsarrat's *The Cruel Sea* and Herman Wouk's *The Caine Mutiny* are set on a smaller stage. Film makers have tended to shy away from big naval films. Lewis Gilbert's 1960 film *Sink the Bismarck* based on C.S. Forester's book *The Last Nine Days of the Bismarck* is rather the exception to the rule. However a good part of the film and the hero Captain Jonathan Shepard [played by Kenneth More], a director of naval planning, takes part at the Admiralty deep underground in London, giving a more human feel to the story.

Some have accused MacLean of writing to a formula and certainly there are similarities between his novels. His characters tend to be older tired men having to make a super human effort to overcome adversity giving them a sort of epic grandeur. It is true his earlier books tend to be better than the later ones with a few exceptions.

Alistair dedicated the book to Gisela and he acknowledged his debt to Ian, Master Mariner, for his advice on maritime matters. There are no scenes we might equate with Homer's *Odyssey* but all the same it is Ulysses' voyage that gave us that first great sea story so no doubt this influenced Alistair's choice of title.

Ian Chapman had been promoted to the London Head Office of Collins, thus it was his job to get the author to help promote the book. A lavish launch night party was arranged, however that day fell on a school day and Alistair flatly refused to attend. Reluctantly Collins had to change the date and Alistair and Gisela headed south by train for the party. The Book Society at Grosvenor Place hosted the event. A man of few words by nature, Alistair was *'able to circulate widely in the course of the three-hour party'*. Gisela likely had a better time than Alistair, looked after by a small group of friends while her husband endured the limelight. The MacLeans caught the night train back to Glasgow and Alistair was back in front of his Gallowflat School blackboard the next day.[5]

In general *HMS Ulysses* received favourable reviews. In 1982 Alistair wrote an article for the *Glasgow Herald* entitled *Rewards and Responsibilities of Success* in which he voiced his opinion on critics:

> *The first criticism I ever read was of my first book HMS Ulysses. It got two whole pages to itself in a now defunct Scottish newspaper, [Daily Record] with a drawing of the dust jacket wreathed in flames and the headline 'Burn this book.' I had paid the Royal Navy the greatest compliment of which I could conceive: this dolt thought it was an act of denigration. That was the first so-called literary review I ever read: it was also the last.[6]*

In the early summer of 1955 thanks to the £1,000 advance from Collins, the MacLeans fulfilled their dream of a home of their own and moved into No 16 Hillend Road, a five-room detached bungalow, the property bordering onto Renfrewshire farmland. It had a large garden but Alistair proved to be no gardener.

Ian Chapman and Collins were already asking Alistair 'what next', would he be prepared to give up teaching to write full time, but he reasoned it might '*be a flash in the pan*'. He had bought a new car, to replace his 1939 Hillman, his first car, and he had hinted in the school staff-room that he was working hard just to pay the taxman.

In the front room of his new home where the floorboards were still bare, he sat at a card table with a portable typewriter and began to write, to test if it was all just a flash in the pan. Following the route of the *Royalist* from the setting of *HMS Ulysses* in the Arctic Ocean, he was drawn to the Aegean Sea.

His first novel was published with few alterations; this would not be the case with *The Guns of Navarone*, the manuscript of which landed on the desk of the American Milton Waldman, an adviser and editor for London publishers. His report to the Chairman of Collins was that MacLean was a natural teller of adventure stories, however he felt the book needed a re-write with particular attention to tighter sentences, punctuation and a slowdown in the rapidity of events. Three weeks later the manuscript arrived back to Waldman with a surprising note from Alistair given his usual dour take-it-or-leave-it attitude, and general lack of interest in the publishing world. Yet he was beginning to take it seriously as a route out of teaching. He saw that *Navarone* had benefitted from Waldman's editor's pen even praising the American: '*I can see that it is much better-knit, faster-paced and a considerably more convincing book than it was originally. For all this and for all the care and trouble you have taken my very sincere thanks.*'[7]

Later in his 1982 article for the *Glasgow Herald* he was not so gushing but by then he had written twenty-three books: '*I feel some responsibility, though not much, to book editors….I feel moderately competent to attend to revising, cutting, etc, before it reaches the editor. But they can be of help, to some more than others.*'[8]

The dramatic sweep of *HMS Ulysses*, the Arctic convoys desperately fought through to Murmansk to help keep Russia in the war, to tie down the might of the German Armies, is matched by the background of *The Guns of Navarone*. The attempt by both sides in the Second World War to influence neutral Turkey in 1943 to join them, Britain got the worst in the Aegean, yet it produced many tales of courage against the odds which influenced Alistair. *Navarone* with a much smaller cast of characters is crisper and more rounded. It is still told in the third person but there is a distinct key character in Keith Mallory, the well-known mountaineer, who had served in the Long Range Desert Group and who is pulled out of Crete where he was fighting with the resistance.

Then there is Andrea Stavros, a colonel in the Greek Army, a large man, who had been with Mallory in Crete and '*was the complete fighting machine*'.[9] Dusty Miller, the American explosives expert, [he is British in the film played by David Niven] is a cynic who questions everything. Andy Stevens, another experienced climber, racked by self doubt, falls on the cliff face of Navarone breaking a leg. He cannot be left behind so he becomes a burden to the group but redeems himself with an act of heroic self sacrifice.

Casey Brown is the Scots engineer, '*short, dark and compact*', a petty officer from the Clydeside, he will look after the old caique and get them to Navarone. After that he will be the radio operator.[10]

It is often difficult for writers to say just where a plot or even an idea for a story comes from; we know Alistair's naval service provided the setting of the Aegean and the time frame, what happened in 1943 in the same area the year before he got there. He also cites liking the Greeks '*if I didn't*', he wrote, '*I'm quite sure I wouldn't have written the book*.'[11] He had an admiration for the men of the SBS and the LRDG, mavericks in a lot of cases and guerrilla fighters. In 1962 he wrote a biography for younger people of Lawrence of Arabia to coincide with David Lean's film, based on T.E. Lawrence's book of the Arab revolt *Seven Pillars of Wisdom*. Alistair's profile by then was much higher. *Navarone* the film had been released the year before to huge critical acclaim, Richard L. Coe of *The Washington Post* called the film '*a magnificently detailed cliff-hanger of spectacular settings and deeds of impossible derring-do…*'[12]

Navarone is Alistair's best book; reviews on the whole, like *Ulysses* were good. In 1990 the British Crime Writers Association placed *Navarone* at 89 on a list of the top 100 crime novels of all time. An odd choice in some ways being a war-time adventure, yet no doubt Alistair would have been happy to be amongst such august company as Raymond Chandler, who he much admired, who has three books on the list, while John le Carré has two, also there is John Buchan. He would not have been so impressed to see at number 35 Ian Fleming with *From Russia with Love*, whose work he disliked intensely – we shall come back to this later. However, not on the list was Winston Graham who he regarded as the best writer of his generation. The book also confirmed to Alistair that he could leave teaching.

It came as no real surprise to his colleagues in the staff room when he told them he was leaving to pursue his writing career. They had a collection for him and purchased a barometer as a leaving gift. On leaving he gave a short speech of thanks saying he would return. Although he kept in touch with Dougie Seggie he never went back to Gallowflat. Leaving his class was probably more emotional for both teacher and pupils. He had instilled in the boys a love of the wider world and to inspire children is really the best any teacher can hope to do.

He did, over the years, develop a close group of friends, Bill Knox was one. A journalist, the *Evening News* sent him around to interview the author as he lived close to the MacLeans. He knocked at the door and was not turned away, maybe because this was Alistair's own house or equally it might have been because now he was ploughing a lonely furrow as an author.

Over the course of several meetings they developed a friendship that lasted a life-time. When Bill said he was a short-story writer Alistair encouraged him to write a novel which he did and became a thriller writer of some note. His first attempt fell short, it needed to be 60,000 words, and Alistair's advice was to '*stretch it*'. It was published in 1957 *Deadline for a Dream;* he went on to write over fifty novels, often under a pseudonym in the US market. Later he would work in television and presented the STV series *Crimedesk*.

During this brief period Alistair was enjoying his new home, trying to sort out the garden and obtain furniture. He even helped Knox put up a sectional garage. Knox found Alistair brusque in manner but this was just a shield, when he got to know him he enjoyed his company even if Alistair often tried to bait him into an argument loving the cut and thrust of debate, a trick Knox came to learn to avoid.

However by now Alistair was earning quite large sums of money and the punitive tax system in Britain at the time was approaching 90 per cent for top earners. So he discussed with Gisela moving to Switzerland, she was excited by the prospect as she would be closer to home and she had never felt entirely at home in Scotland where '*I always felt a foreigner*'.[13] Plans were made to move to Wilen, near Lake Sarnen in central Switzerland.

Before the MacLeans left Scotland Alistair had completed his third novel *South by Java Head*. Yet Milton Waldman was even more critical of this manuscript than he had been of *Navarone*. Even a re-write did not satisfy him. In his report to Collins he felt Alistair should put *Java* aside and start another book, '*preferably one having nothing to do with the war*'. This seems rather an odd request.

As we have seen *South by Java Head* was inspired by the time Alistair spent in the Far East in 1945–46 on HMS *Royalist*, in the waters around the Malay Peninsula. Once again he set his book in the recent past, set against the fall of Singapore to the Japanese in 1942. In this book he has returned to a bigger cast of characters but unlike in *HMS Ulysses,* does have a key character in the shape of the first officer of the tanker *Viroma*, John Nicolson, yet he does not appear until page 45 along with the rest of the ship's crew. Nicolson is a widower, his wife dying in a car crash due to a drunk who escapes unhurt on Singapore, and as with a lot of Alistair's characters he is tired and world weary. Due to circumstances, he is thrust forward to take command.

The cast of characters includes Captain Francis Findhorn of the *Viroma*, also a widower, who is wounded in a Japanese attack on his ship and Nicolson takes command. The Bosun Mckinnon, twenty years at sea, with his slow Highland voice from the Isle of Lewis, a rock of a man. Then there are the people from the *Kerry Dancer,* soldiers, nurses, even a spy carrying the Japanese invasion plans of Australia. All are trying to escape from Singapore and the Japanese and face ordeal after ordeal, a typhoon and attacks by aircraft that sink both ships, next they are becalmed under a blistering sun with drinking water running low. They fight off a Japanese submarine, and then a captured American PT Boat crewed by the Japanese. There are heroic sacrifices until final rescue by the Australian destroyer HMAS *Kenmore*.

Java is the least convincing of Alistair's three war books based on his own experiences. The plot of sorts is to get the Japanese war plans through, yet it might have been better to make it tighter and based more on the real escape stories. The key character not coming front and centre until about page 100 is a weakness. With *Navarone* we know Mallory is in charge early in the book. The *New York Times* book review said it was '*Crammed with action and realistically sketched backgrounds but there is a patchiness about the escapes from tight fixes that makes South from Java Head a less credible chronicle of daring-do than its remarkable predecessors.*'[14] Yet the book has gone on to sell over a million copies.

Java was not shelved as Waldman had advised but saved by the film producer Danny Angel. It fell to Ian Chapman as the man in the middle to tell Alistair that Collins was not going to publish the book. Chapman had tried hard to convince William Collins that Waldman was blind to a commercial success, but the chairman sided with his advisor. By this time the MacLeans were in Switzerland, Marjory Chapman and her son had gone on ahead to visit them; Ian would join them later after a business trip to Sweden. He was dreading telling Alistair the bad news. On arrival in Switzerland his mail had caught up with him, including a telegram from William Collins which read: *'Have just sold film rights of Java Head to Danny Angel. Wonderful! Tell Alistair it's a great book.'* In the long run it was another book that was never filmed, nevertheless the power of the cinema was such that it eclipsed Waldman's advice, but was he right?

Milton Waldman was a biographer and academic, he wrote historical biographies such as *Elizabeth and Leicester, Queen Elizabeth I,* and *The Lady Mary.* While at Collins he turned down *The Lord of the Rings* as too long, even though he was a friend of J.R.R. Tolkien. One wonders if he was the right sort of editor to assign to Alistair. His advice to write something other than war stories surely was a matter of his own taste, because the war novel continues to sell in large numbers up to the present time.

Yet might there have been a fourth war book after *South by Java Head?* There is a manuscript running to 74 pages and six chapters, *Tobruk,* held by HarperCollins in which there are clues as to when it was written. On page 16 he writes: *Looking back over eighteen years....'* And on page 36, a reference to the South African General Hendrik Klopper – he was the unfortunate commander who surrendered Tobruk to the Axis in June 1942 – Alistair says he was *'interviewed that month'* while making preparations for the 1960 Olympics in Rome being a member of the South African Olympic Committee at the time. The writing of *Tobruk* therefore took place in 1959–1960.[15]

Given that up to this time Alistair had written little non-fiction, and at the time he was writing *South by Java Head* and *The Last Frontier* and moving to Switzerland, on the surface it does seem to be an attempt at non-fiction, but oddly there are some characters that are hard to pin down. On pages 2–4 of *Tobruk* we are introduced to an Italian soldier, Luigi La Farina, who comes from Taormina on Sicily. Now La Farina is certainly a Sicilian name dating back to the middle ages but where did he come from? There is no doubt Alistair had sympathy for the ordinary Italian soldiers '*who could fight as well as the next man when he had a mind to*'.[16] Luigi and his crew man their anti-tank gun in defence of Tobruk facing heavy odds. They fire off four rounds against the advancing Allied tanks bringing '*an 'I' tank grinding to a halt as a shattered track spun off the driving wheel*'. (I tank – Infantry tank generally a British Matilda MKII widely used in the desert war.)

Their gun then receives a direct hit. Luigi gets up '*painfully*', the gun shield is smashed, his face is bleeding. His crew unhurt were lying on the ground and not about to get up. He notices a '*fifth shell was in the breech – and the trigger ready to hand*'. Yet he feels caution is the better part of valour, his position is about to be overrun, he thinks of the '*vineyards at home and hesitated. And then he thought of Paolina, and hesitated more.*' He moves away from the gun, his hands raised in surrender.[17]

Then there is Blackie Gordon, a private of the 2nd Australian Infantry Force. Through his eyes Alistair tells the story of the siege of Tobruk and what the ordinary soldier has to endure. He is a Sydney man, the heat he is used to but not the freezing nights stuck in a fox hole. The sand got everywhere, '*on his skin, clothes and scratchingly imbedded beyond recovery in the fastnesses of his luxuriant black beard…*' It got in the food and water, and jammed up the weapons. The dust storms were like '*moving in a blind world*'. It even worked its way past goggles to inflame '*his eyes and nostrils…*'[18]

The poor water and a diet devoid of vitamins led to desert sores. '*Then there were the Omni-present flies, and the still intolerable and at least equally Omni-present fleas.*' Then there were the '*chafing points*' of equipment which led to festering sores and his boots were torture, brick-hard and rubbing. Yet amazingly he could take his mind off the physical misery from time to time; even off the enemy to consider the sheer boredom.[19]

Worst of all he felt a '*Sucker*' who along with '*his cobbers were the forgotten men of World War II…*' Strangely his '*bitterest feelings*' were not reserved for the generals and politicians that had put him in this position but '*rather for his countrymen back home*'. He heard about political squabbles back home of strikes, he wondered why those back home so patriotically vocal in the papers '*did not volunteer to join the colours and come out to relieve them, in Tobruk*'. So much for the romantic notion of the desert war.[20]

There are other characters that crop up that make me wonder whether *Tobruk* is fiction or non-fiction. Corporal John Fraser of the Cameron Highlanders, is he a remodel of Corporal Fraser in *South by Java Head* or is *Tobruk* the earlier work? There are nurses in the hospital struggling against the odds in the boats in *South by Java Head*. There is a confusing mix of certainly real and what seem fictional characters. There are handwritten notes in Alistair's difficult to read small spidery hand and alterations further indicating this is an earlier work. Later we will see he hated rewriting but he certainly did in *Tobruk*, however at the bottom of page 31–32 he typed an instruction/message:

> *(I had intended going on to the end of this paragraph, but remember your saying that you were going to cut out the reference to Chester Wilmot, so decided to leave it there. I take the liberty of reminding you of the insert we agreed upon for the second paragraph in Page 9. I think it is quite important).*[21]

Who is Alistair talking to here? Is it Waldman? Chester Wilmot, or to give him his full name Reginald Winchester Wilmot, was an Australian war correspondent and was in Tobruk during the siege of 1941. He wrote a book about the siege published in 1945: *Tobruk 1941, Capture – Siege– Relief* published by Angus & Robertson. It may have been extracts from this book that the intended recipient of Alistair's note was not happy with.

Alistair opens his *Tobruk* well by referring to the Encyclopaedia Britannica for the precise location of the small port at 32 degrees North latitude and 24 degrees East longitude. As Ernle Bradford put it, places like Tobruk became important because '*From the Levant to Algeria, the battle rolled back and forth. Derna, Mersa Matruh and Tobruk, places hitherto unknown except to coastal traders, featured in the headlines of the world.*'[22]

So the question is, what is Alistair's *Tobruk* trying to be, what was he trying to achieve? It is too long to be an article and too short to be a book. Is it fiction or non-fiction? It is hard to say, was he trying to bring *HMS Ulysses* – what some people have called '*semi-documentary nature*' – to *Tobruk?* If so it is very different for it is full of real people whereas in *HMS Ulysses* they are few and far between; even most of the ships have fictional names. So we will leave it there.[23]

For his next book Alistair did move away from the Second World War. After all, with *Java* he had, to coin a phrase, cruised through his war. *The Last Frontier* (1959) was a Cold War thriller set against the background of the 1956 Hungarian Uprising. It would be the first of his books to be filmed, launched in April 1961 two months before *Navarone* premiered. It starred Richard Widmark as Reynolds. It was certainly an altogether better constructed and written book than *Java* with more rounded characters, and we will come back to it later.

The problems with *Java* might also be linked to the rush to leave Scotland. The sale of 16 Hillend Road was left to the estate agents. The MacLeans rented a flat in Switzerland until their new home, a purpose built chalet-style villa overlooking Lake Sarnen, was ready.

The relationship between Waldman and Alistair soon came to a head as he told Collins: '*Get that man off my back. I've had enough.*' William Collins was well aware that MacLean was fast becoming a significant commercial asset, and his joking, when annoyed, that could someone send him the address of Heinemann, a rival publisher, might become reality.

Alistair began to believe that when the manuscript left him they needed no revisions and he had no interest in correcting proofs. He took some interest in the dust jackets and the blurb material and enjoyed writing caustic letters to the publishers when they got it wrong. For example, with *When Eight Bells Toll* he wrote:

> *Covers are frequently drawn by artists who have not read the book but it must be a bit unusual to have the blurb-writer prepare himself in the same fashion. Briefly, the complaints are these: the cover depicts a bloke in a scuba suit caught in a searchlight. The artist must have been thinking of some other book. Doesn't happen in mine.*
>
> *In the second paragraph, reference is made to an incredible pursuit at sea. The only incredible thing is the blurb-writer's imaginative power. No pursuit in my book.*
>
> *In the third paragraph, Calvert is alleged to have boarded the Nantesville in the Irish Sea. Somebody must have transferred the Hebrides down there when I wasn't looking.*[24]

It was during the early months in Switzerland that Alistair, Gisela felt, began his drinking. Paul Townend, a local hotelier and new friend, went on some benders. Up until this time he had been a moderate drinker even in the navy, but now it was different, new found wealth had something to do with it and loneliness.

He was soon inviting his friends to come to Switzerland on holidays. Bill Knox, his wife Myra and their two children came over by road in their Ford Consul. Bill viewed Alistair's writing room with some surprise considering his wealth. It was a small room, with an ordinary desk, no drawers and a kitchen chair; no reference books, not even a waste-paper basket, just the table and typewriter now an IBM golf-ball, the latest in electric machines.

His closest friend remained Dougie Seggie; when Alistair left Scotland he had handed over ownership of the *Silver Craig* to him. Soon Dougie, wife Violet, daughter Helen, his brother Tom and big Willie Campbell flew out for a three week holiday.

Alistair did keep a small boat on Lake Sarnen but like a lot of things in his life, it was not quite what he wanted, for he preferred the sea. He revelled in his Mercedes, driving his guests on sightseeing trips. Their conversations were largely about the old days and voyages in the *Silver Craig*. His visitors had noticed that Gisela seemed very quiet and Alistair was drinking a lot. Lachlan had a skin disorder which could result in bad bleeds; the ailment would remain with him for much of his life.

The only trouble for Alistair, with the visits of his friends, was that at some stage they had to go home, fame and success had brought its own rewards but it also had its pitfalls.

Chapter Sixteen

At the Crossroads 1959–1963

In the short time the MacLeans had been in Switzerland, Alistair had become increasingly frustrated with Collins and wrote to his publishers in June 1960 saying he was bored *'to tears and beyond'* with writing the way he had for his first four books. He felt they did not seem to entirely appreciate him or his books even though they had earned them significant sums of money. For number five *Night without End* he turned to *'completely impersonal writing in the first person'*. Yet he denigrated those early books himself calling *Navarone* and *Java 'rubbish'*.[1]

In *Night without End* the setting was a return to the Arctic Circle set on Greenland, where a BOAC airliner crash-lands on the Ice Cap. Nearby is the remote camp of a scientific research team and the people there hear the plane come down. The team is led by Dr Peter Mason, a medical doctor and geologist. Part of the team set out to rescue the survivors but find most of the flight crew dead, the pilots having been shot in the back, while back at the base the radio set is destroyed cutting them off from the outside world. Mason and a small team set out on a 300 kilometre trek to the coast where there is a settlement. In his usual relentless style Alistair piles obstacles and problems on his characters. There had been a USN base near Ivigtut in Arsuk Fjord, codenamed Bluie West 7 or Grondal, during the war from the spring of 1941. It was used for refuelling ships often going on to join the Arctic Convoys.

Still the book received favourable reviews; the *New York Times* called it a *'bang up adventure yarn...'*[2] Again the film rights were sold indirectly through agents to Paramount and Eric Ambler was brought in to write the script. Even so it was another film that was never made.

In that same year Alistair wrote a series of articles for the *Sunday Express* returning to the war, sea stories, most about tragic incidents. Given the events were still shrouded in secrecy at the time, Alistair asked some pointed questions.

In July 1940 the *Arandora Star*, a Blue Star liner, had been taking 1,600 German and Italian internees and some prisoners of war to internment camps in Canada. Two days out of Liverpool she was torpedoed by a U-boat at 0600 hrs. The submarine was *U-47* commanded by Gunther Prien, one of the most successful U-boat commanders of the war. He had managed to get into Scapa Flow and had sunk the battleship HMS *Royal Oak*. Alistair is scathing about the press reports at the time that blamed the large loss of life on the cowardly behaviour of the Germans and Italians. One report even had thirty Italians fighting among themselves *'for the privilege of sliding down a single rope'*. However four survivors were interviewed, two crew members, one Italian, and a British passenger, all agreed there had been no fights or panic to get to the boats.

Alistair asked the question: why the bad reporting? He felt the papers had doctored the information to try and explain the great loss of life, maybe, even under official direction. He then goes on to explain in some detail the reasons for the cover up. The captain of the ship and the CO of the guard had both protested about the overcrowding on board and wanted the passengers cut by half. Naturally the overcrowding meant there were not enough life-jackets; if there were not enough life-jackets there were not enough life-boats and there had been no life-boat drill either. Life rafts that might have saved lives could not be released because the tools needed to do this were not available, so they went down with the ship.

Something that did not come to light until sometime later was that barbed wire compounds had been erected onboard. These partitioned the decks and cut access to the lifeboats. Captain Edgar Wallace Moulton protested but the wire remained. There was little wonder that the story of the *Arandora Star* was placed under a blanket of official secrets. Nevertheless about 1,000 people, guards, crew and prisoners got off the sinking ship. Although July, the Atlantic was bitterly cold and people began to die. Around noon a Sunderland flying boat came on the tragic scene and helped guide the Canadian destroyer *St. Laurent* there. She searched the sea for hours using her boats and keeping on the move, well aware U-boats might still be in the area and they managed to pick up 800 survivors. Alistair called it *'an astonishing feat almost without parallel in the life-saving annals of the sea, almost enough to make one forget, if even only for a moment, the barbed wire and the thousand men who died. Almost, but not quite.'*[3]

These six stories have a similar theme highlighting incompetence, bureaucratic nonsense and interference from Whitehall coupled with heroic self-sacrifice. They would hardly have been looked on favourably by the powers that be at the time, only fifteen years after the war's end.

HMS *Rawalpindi* was a P&O liner built to ply between Britain and the Far East. Pressed into service as an armed merchant ship because of the Royal Navy's lack of cruisers, the 17,000 ton ship had eight old 6-inch guns, a crew of 280 made up of about fifty men who had served on the ship before the war, the rest were RNVR, and there were no regular navy on board. *Rawalpindi* and ships like her were deployed on the Northern Patrol around Iceland and Greenland to stop merchant ships trading with Nazi Germany. She doesn't get the signal to withdraw when two German battle cruisers steam into her patrol area. The *Scharnhorst* signalled HMS *Rawalpindi* to 'Heave to', but Captain Edward Coverley Kennedy, called back by the navy after seventeen years ashore, refused. Within minutes HMS *Rawalpindi* is a flaming wreck but still managed to hit the *Gneisenau*. Yet the sixty-year-old Captain Kennedy, almost like a MacLean character – although this was for real – would never admit defeat, his bridge wrecked around him he leaves looking for some smoke floats to cover the ship's escape: *His ship was holed and sinking, damaged beyond help or repair and visibly dying: his guns were gone, his crew were decimated, but still he fought for survival.*

It was a display of *'courage'* and *'tenacity'* in some ways beyond comprehension.[4] The Germans picked up forty men, 240 went down with HMS *Rawalpindi* including Captain Kennedy.

The story of HMS *Jervis Bay* was another armed merchant ship, the only cover for convoy HX 84 out in the mid Atlantic, before the U-boats had really developed into the threat they were to become. It was 5 November 1940; Britain had survived the threat of invasion. The convoy consisted of thirty-seven ships including eleven tankers. The sole escort had been built in 1922 and was armed with some old 6-inch guns, commanded by the Irish Captain Fogarty Fegen, the 47-year-old son of an admiral.

It is evening and over the horizon comes the German pocket battleship *Admiral Scheer,* 10,000 tons, fast and armed with six 11-inch guns. The convoy is ordered to turn to starboard away from the threat and to scatter and make smoke. Meanwhile HMS *Jervis Bay* turns toward the enemy and puts on speed to close the range; she is soon hit. *Admiral Scheer* moves to bypass HMS *Jervis Bay* but Fegen alters course to intercept to keep his ship between the enemy and the convoy. Pounded by the 11-inch guns she was quickly wrecked as a fighting ship. Again *Admiral Scheer* tries to move around but the impudent ship keeps coming, even though on fire with huge holes in her sides, as if she is attempting to ram the pocket battleship. Fegen by this time had lost an arm; he orders smoke floats to be dropped still trying to cover the escape of the convoy and soon after was killed. He would be awarded a posthumous Victoria Cross.

HMS *Jervis Bay* sinks stern first, the Germans make no attempt to pick up survivors. The *Admiral Scheer* only manages to sink five ships in the convoy. That night the Swedish ship the *Stureholm*, commanded by Captain Sven Olander, goes back to the scene even though the frustrated German ship is cruising around firing star shells trying to find other victims. She manages to pick up sixty-five survivors from the freezing waters.

The *Meknes* was a French ship which had onboard 1,180 French sailors who, since the fall of France in 1940, had elected to go home. She leaves Southampton at 1630 hrs on 5 July en route to Marseilles, steaming down the English Channel lights blazing, for in effect she is a neutral ship. That night an E-boat opens fire on them. Captain Dulroc of the *Meknes* asks 'Who are you?' and the reply is in the shape of a torpedo. The E-boat even machine-gunned the survivors in the water. Almost a thousand men were left in the water and were picked up by British destroyers in the morning. MacLean asks just who was responsible for this disaster that cost 400 lives. The French claimed they had not been informed of the sailing, the British said they had:

> '*What is beyond dispute*', wrote Alistair '*and this is the crux of the matter – no safe conduct or guarantee was given by the Germans. Yet the criminally negligent decision was made to permit the sailing of this unarmed and unescorted vessel into the E-boat and U-boat infested Channel without waiting for a reply from the Germans.*

He goes on to place the blame firmly in the corridors of power and does not mince his words. '*It would be interesting indeed to know what British Service or Government department was responsible for this decision.*'[5]

The RMS *Lancastria* was more a straight Government denial at the time to keep bad news from the British people. She was sunk by German bombers off St. Nazaire during Operation Aerial, the evacuation of British troops and civilians from ports in Western France. Estimates vary of just how many people were on board, it is believed that as many as 3,000 people might have gone down with the ship while another 2,500 were picked up. Churchill himself put a D-notice on the sinking, the worst maritime disaster in British history. In Alistair's article he concentrates more on the personal stories of some of the survivors.

The last of the six was the *City of Benares* perhaps the most tragic of all because it involved children. The *City of Benares* was torpedoed on the night of 17 September 1940 in the North Atlantic and she went down in just over ten minutes. Her total complement was 406 passengers and crew, 100 of which were young children; nearly all of them were being evacuated to Canada under a Government scheme. On the third day out after leaving Liverpool the destroyer escort left their charges as they were past the recognised danger zone.

Many of the children died in the initial explosion or were trapped in their cabins and went down with the ship. In the end only nineteen would survive. '*A pitiful handful*', wrote Alistair. Yet dozens of the crew and passengers gave their own lives willingly to try and save them, like the man who towed a raft of children away from the sinking ship to a lifeboat. He went back for another and again a third time after which he was never seen again. Of this man Alistair wrote:

> *We do not know, nor does it matter. All we know is that this man who selflessly gave his own life would never have thought of recognition nor cared for it had he been given it. An unknown man, a nameless man, but he remains for ever as the symbol of the spirit of the City of Benares.*[6]

In 1960 Carl Foreman, reluctantly, was engaged by Columbia Pictures as writer-producer for *The Guns of Navarone*. He was concerned he might become type-cast as a producer of war films having recently directed *The Bridge over the River Kwai* for the screen (1957). He preferred '*the stories that work best for me involve a loner, out of step or in direct conflict with a group of people.*' One of his most famous films, the Western *High Noon* (1952), fits this model. He tried to get out of the *Navarone* project feeling it was too complicated but head of the company Mike Frankovich would have none of it. One of the things that did appeal to Foreman was working in Britain again.

He had been blacklisted in Hollywood in the 1950s accused of being a communist by the House Committee on un-American Activities. He had been a member of the Communist Party but not for ten years and had served in the US Army during the Second World War. Stanley Kramer tried to get him kicked off *High Noon* but Fred Zinnemann, Gary Cooper and Bruce Church stood by him and he moved to England before the film was released.

Foreman naturally approached the author of *Navarone* who he found to be an enigma, a *'quiet reserved'* man and his Scots accent hard to follow but in time he grew to like him for his *'unbounded courage and tenacity'*. In some ways they were kindred spirits. Alistair made it clear he would take no part in making the film; he also told Foreman that he felt he was the man for the job.

As Foreman began to write his screenplay he came to appreciate MacLean's skill as a writer, and found he had a *'gift for keeping his audience enthralled by the pace and drive of his tale'*. He kept reading Alistair's books: *'I believe that Dumas, if he could, would read MacLean with pleasure, with admiration and, quite often, with a touch of affectionate envy.'*[7]

Initially Alexander Mackendrick, another Scot, was engaged as the director as Columbia wanted a British director; he had worked on the Ealing comedies like *The Ladykillers* and *The Man in the White Suit* before leaving for America where the *Sweet Smell of Success* was well received. However director and producer did not see eye-to-eye and Mackendrick was replaced by J. Lee Thompson who also had Scottish roots.

Thompson had directed *Ice Cold in Alex*, when he arrived Gregory Peck was already engaged and had been influential in his appointment having been impressed with his *Northwest Frontier*. He would have to deal with a galaxy of stars including as well as Peck, Anthony Quinn, David Niven, James Darren, Gia Scala, Richard Harris and Anthony Quayle – a volatile mixture of egos. However Anthony Quinn largely solved the rising tensions on the set as the film was mainly shot on Rhodes from April-July with the temperature rising, by organising a chess tournament. All the tension went into that, as Thompson said *'leaving an atmosphere in which it was a pleasure to film'*.[8]

The filming at Pinewood mainly concerned the storm scenes which David Niven said took '*five weeks in England in November simulating a storm at sea by working nine hours a day in a huge tank of filthy water*'. After this Gregory Peck and Niven had to work for a further two weeks on the final scene blowing up the guns. With only three days left Niven '*picked up a fearsome infection via a split lip….*' He was taken to Guy's Hospital where he lay critically ill for several days while the whole ten million dollar film hung in the balance. Niven was eventually pumped full of drugs and managed to complete the final three days. However after that he suffered a relapse that lasted several more weeks. During this time the 'Big Brass' from Columbia came over in panic to see what could be done if the '*sonofabitch dies?*' Niven bemoaned the fact that having finished the film and back in hospital, '*The Big Brass never even sent me a grape.*'[9]

There were changes made by Foreman to the original story, its two male Greek Partisans became female, the women played by the Greek actress Irene Papas and the Italian Gia Scala. Some of the main male characters had slight changes and some scenes from the book were cut. Columbia had taken a big risk given the film's large budget, which was even bigger than David Lean's *The Bridge on the River Kwai*. Yet *Navarone* proved to be a huge and enduring success. It was the biggest cinema hit of 1961, winning six Oscar nominations and winning for Best Special Effects.

As the opening night for *Navarone* approached in the spring of 1961 the various publicity departments at Columbia and Collins went into overdrive. It is hard to assess just how much Alistair appreciated the fact that Foreman had insisted that he was given top billing. The main title people would first see was *Alistair MacLean's: The Guns of Navarone*, rather than being hidden in the credits, and reading something like, *Based on a novel by Alistair MacLean*. Some actors would fight hard to get top billing and here was Alistair in the title line. It is true that he never really understood the film business.

As the opening night approached, 27 April at the Odeon, Leicester Square, it was down to Ian Chapman to persuade MacLean to be there. As usual he refused to come. Chapman had to use all his ingenuity to get the irascible author there, he pointed out Foreman expected him to be there and after all it was beneficial to his own future. Then Alistair started complaining about having to wear evening dress. Chapman then explained the Queen and Duke of Edinburgh would be there. Alistair seemed to be surprised at that but soon countered with 'could his mother come to be presented to the Queen'. Chapman tactfully explained he did not think it would be possible, Alistair replied if his mother couldn't meet the Queen neither would he.

And so it went on and with the date fast approaching Chapman turned to Alistair's brother Ian who poured oil on troubled waters and at last persuaded him to attend. His mother stayed at Ian's house in Surrey where the family enjoyed some pre-première drinks although Alistair, still in awe of his mother, she having been teetotal for years, did not drink alcohol in front of her. It was a wonderful première and even if Alistair felt out of place Gisela enjoyed the glittering occasion.

It was around this time that Alistair came up with the idea, to the consternation of his publishers, that he wanted to write under the pen-name Ian Stuart, which were also Chapman's son's names; he wanted to prove he could write under any name with the same result. Chapman tried to dissuade him; he would be foregoing all the good publicity built up by his previous work and of the film of *Navarone*. Alistair would not listen and delivered the first manuscript under the name Ian Stuart to the publishers personally on a visit to the UK. It was *The Dark Crusader*, a secret service story. He also engaged the literary agents Curtis Brown to be the representatives for his new name, who he felt would get a better deal for him on the sale of foreign rights. Up until this time he had relied on Collins for these matters.

The year 1961 proved to be a prolific one: Collins could hardly accuse Alistair of sitting on his laurels. *Fear is the Key*, book six, was published first under his own name to be followed by *The Dark Crusader* and as we have seen, Alistair had produced a series of articles for the *Sunday Express*.

Some have divided MacLean's novels into four periods, quite who came up with this theory, who knows? The first four books might be called the epic Second World War books but the theory falls down at the beginning as *The Last Frontier* is a Cold War story, although there are references to the Second World War where, rather like Ian Fleming's James Bond who learnt his trade in that war, as does Michael Reynolds, MacLean's secret agent who had served with the SOE.

The next six novels, *Night without End – Ice Station Zebra*, more hard boiled humorous stories combining thriller and detective traits. Again does this work across them all? We will see.[10]

Fear is the Key is set in Florida. John Talbot is the hero, although for a long period we are not quite sure who he is. Much of the first half of the novel concerns a prolonged car chase. Later Talbot reveals he is working for the British Government to find out what has happened to a plane that has crashed off the coast carrying a fortune in gold and jewels. The mob has stolen a submersible to recover the loot and Talbot foils them. It does display a trait of being overly complicated with many twists and turns.

The Dark Crusader has a similar flavour about an attempt to steal the latest rocket of the Royal Navy which is code-named 'Dark Crusader'. John Bentall, the hero, another secret service agent, sets out for Australia to track down some missing scientists. Here MacLean's hero seems to be trying to out wisecrack Raymond Chandler's Philip Marlowe. Alistair admired Chandler and there may be a veiled tribute to him in the book for we read: '*I heard a couple of words that caught and transfixed my attention the way a tarantula in my soup would have done.*'[11]

Whereas this line appears in *Farewell, My Lovely* (1940): '*Even in Central Avenue, not the quietest dressed street in the world, he looked about as inconspicuous as a tarantula on a slice of angel food.*'[12]

One wonders why Alistair did not develop a single character for at least some of his books, whom he could make more rounded over several adventures. It cannot be because of his dislike of Ian Fleming and not wanting to be seen following his lead as he '*....couldn't stand his basis of sex, sadism and snobbery. If you require those things, you are not a writer.*'[13] What MacLean failed to appreciate was Fleming's skill with the voice of Bond, which was clearly appreciated by his readers, as 007 is a cad and that was part of his appeal. Also, as an admirer of Chandler, was he not impressed with the development of Philip Marlowe over eight books? Although he may have read of Chandler's despair having to keep his hero alive when he wrote to Hamish 'Jamie' Hamilton the British publisher:

I am doing a Marlowe story and frankly I wish it were better. In fact, except for practical reasons I'd like to forget about Mr Marlowe for several years. But I have to keep him alive somehow. There are radio programs in the offing and other low ways of making money.[14]

Ian Fleming tried to kill off James Bond or so it seemed in *You Only Live Twice;* he even has an obituary in *The Times* for his hero. Yet he returns after some public outcry in *The Man with the Golden Gun*.[15] There was even more outcry when Conan Doyle tried to kill off Sherlock Holmes in *The Final Problem;* he was really surprised having to resurrect his hero. Whereas Alistair's hero in *The Last Frontier,* Michael Reynolds, close to the moment of triumph is sure this is his last operation and he's leaving and Philip Calvert in *When Eight Bells Toll* is a typical MacLean character cynical and world-weary who has to battle bureaucracy and the bad guys, more akin to Len Deighton's creation Harry Palmer, who even has to fill in expenses returns.

Even in Switzerland the MacLeans' marriage was still under strain, Lachlan was now seven and they had wanted another child. In the end they decided to adopt. Collins the much maligned publishers, even helped with this and put them in touch with an adoption agency in the UK. They adopted a little boy in Germany, Michael. Alistair told Ian Chapman in October 1961 that he was like him *'well-behaved'* and he *'never cribs about anything'*. He also announced they were going to move back to Britain, shortly before this Gisela found she was pregnant; perhaps the arrival of Michael had helped by releasing some of the tension. Ian MacLean's wife Bunty found them a house to rent in Surrey at Lower Bourne, Farnham. They sold the villa at Sarnen although taxation would soon become a problem again.

The Golden Rendezvous was published in 1962 which was followed by the *Satan Bug* under his pseudonym Ian Stuart. Even with all the disruption of moving and a new baby on the way, Alistair was as prolific as ever, as well as the two novels, he produced a small volume for younger readers *All about Lawrence of Arabia,* a little gem of a book superbly illustrated by Gil Walker. It was listed in the hundred outstanding books for young readers in the *New York Times*.[16]

In October Gisela gave birth to Alistair Stuart MacLean, named after his father. For tax reasons the young family moved to Ireland in 1963 for a short period before returning to their new residence, Sunbiggin, Haslemere in Surrey. An opulent country house with two acres of ground, an orchard and a tennis court, it had a self contained flat which Alistair thought might suit his mother but she refused to leave Scotland. In addition, there were six bedrooms and two bathrooms.

For that year Alistair concentrated on one book. The pseudonym Ian Stuart died a natural death after two books although he insisted he had proved the point, while Collins felt sales had been slow and when later released under the MacLean name they picked up.

The concentration on one book at Sunbiggin paid dividends; *Ice Station Zebra* was a return to the epic stage of the Cold War and his familiar ground of the Arctic. The superpowers are in a race here to obtain a film from a reconnaissance satellite that had photographed every US missile site that had fallen to earth near the weather station Zebra. However contact had been lost with the station and the weather had closed in thus the need of a submarine to reach it. Alistair retained the first person narrative, but cut back on the wisecracks from his key character Dr Carpenter, an MI6 agent. He arrives at Loch Long ready to board the USS *Dolphin* [which becomes the *Tigerfish* in the film] a nuclear powered submarine. Her captain Commander James D. Swanson '*short, plump and crowding forty*', questions the written orders Carpenter presents him with, but higher authority intervenes in the shape of Admiral Garvie confirming the orders. They set off on a wintery night and head for the North Polar Ice Cap, to surface as close as possible to the burnt-out weather station called Zebra. They are not sure what they will find when they get there or that there is a spy on board the *Dolphin*. It is a vintage MacLean story.[17]

The USN asked how MacLean had such a good knowledge of the highly restricted US nuclear submarines. The USS *Nautilus*, the first nuclear-powered submarine came into service in 1955; she did a transit of the North Pole in 1958. The USS *Skate* was the first to surface through the ice of the Arctic in 1959. The USS *Thresher*, the lead submarine of that class was lost off Cape Cod while under sea-trials in 1963 while Alistair was writing *Ice Station Zebra*. HMS *Dreadnought* was the Royal Navy's first nuclear-powered submarine launched in 1960 and commissioned in April 1963. Alistair was happy to reply to the USN request in that he had bought a submarine kit in a US toy shop, which he built [Revell produced a plastic model kit of the USS *Nautilus* at the time] that gave him an excellent plan, and he read some *Time* magazine articles on the subject. His nephew Ian recalled that Uncle Alistair '*quite spooked US intelligence community with his depiction of a US nuclear submarine in Ice Station Zebra to the extent they interviewed him about it.*'[18]

His publishers were excited by the prospect of this story, it was top drawer. In the USA it became a Book Society choice guaranteeing large sales, much to the pleasure of Lee Barker at Alistair's US publisher Doubleday.

However when he delivered *Ice Station Zebra* to Collins' office personally he told Ian Chapman that it would be his last book. A shocked Chapman asked him what he meant. Alistair said he had never enjoyed writing and only did it to make money and now he was going into the hotel business.

Chapter Seventeen

The Hotelier 1963–1966

When Alistair told Ian Chapman he was going into the hotel business he had already purchased the historic Cornish Jamaica Inn high up on Bodmin Moor. Situated near the village of Bolventor that dates back to the Middle Ages, it was built in 1750 as a coaching inn standing on eighty acres of land, mid-way between Launceston and Bodmin on the turnpike, in the shadow of Rough Tor the second highest point on the moor at 1,313 ft.

Jamaica Inn was world famous because of Daphne du Maurier's novel of the same name and the Alfred Hitchcock film of the novel starring Charles Laughton and Maureen O'Hara and subsequent film adaptations. Du Maurier discovered the Inn in 1930 and stayed there to go horse riding on the Moor, during which Daphne and a friend got lost in the mist. They dismounted and allowed the horses to lead them back to the Inn; there she learnt something of its smuggling past. Another visit to the moor in 1935 inspired her to start her story; it would be a *'tale of adventure full of smugglers and steeped in atmosphere'*.[1] She would impress the mood of Cornwall on every page. It was a melodramatic tale in the manner of R.L. Stevenson's *Treasure Island*. In 1936 her novel *Jamaica Inn* was published, set in 1820, a story of murderous wreckers led by Francis Davey, the albino vicar of Altarnun, a Cornish village four miles to the east of the Inn. Within three months it had out sold Daphne's first three novels put together.[2]

On 27 July 1964 Alistair purchased Jamaica Inn for the sum of £27,500 from William and Margaret Palmer who had bought the pub in November 1962. Perhaps the 'Big Freeze' of the winter 1962–63 had put them off ownership although eleven years later when Alistair sold up they did try to buy it back.[3]

Sylvia Kestell who worked at the Inn at the time, found Alistair a *'real gentleman'*. Although he was seldom there, she recalls selling his books which were popular in the Inn shop; however they were removed if

Alistair was visiting as he frowned on his own books being sold in his own Inn.[4]

He went on to buy the Beambridge Inn on the A38 near Wellington in Somerset, another coaching inn built in 1832 nestling amid the Blackdown and Quantock hills, and the Bank House Hotel between Great Malvern and Worcester in the Cotswolds.

He looked at 112 hotels before settling on Jamaica Inn. When Gillespie found out about his brother's intention to venture into the hotel trade he tried to dissuade him, he had been in the hospitality business since 1952 and had managed several hotels. This is when he really took up using the name Gillespie, as so many hotel guests seemed to have trouble pronouncing the Gaelic name Gilleasbuig. Alistair had even bought him a hotel, the Ring Bridge, near Spean Bridge where the Commando memorial looks out over the Scottish Highlands. He argued how Alistair could keep a handle on the business, having three hotels and still living in Surrey. Gillespie was right; living at Sunbiggin, Alistair found he was on the road a lot clocking up the miles in his Lancia on frequent trips to Cornwall.

In the summer of 1964 the *Sunday Express* journalist and book critic Robert Pitman, one of the few Alistair took to, found the author at Jamaica Inn pulling pints and selling souvenirs to the customers and in his element. He told Pitman that he had '*been in more contact with real life in the last hour than during nine years of writing novels*'. Was the irony apparent to him at the time that a large part of the appeal of Jamaica Inn was down to a novel, but he had no qualms in trading on it.

Pitman had no doubt he was enjoying his new found freedom and he explained he was never '*a born writer, I know it and you know it. I don't enjoy writing. In Switzerland I wrote each book in thirty-five days flat – five weeks for seven days a week; plus of course, time for preliminary research. Two days! I wrote like that because I disliked it so much I just wanted to get the damned thing over.*'[5]

Alistair felt now he was dealing with real people whereas writing novels was bordering on the immoral. With only one of his books had he felt pleased with the characters and dialogue and that had been *Fear is the Key*, but sales had been disappointing.

However in less than a year his hotels were losing money at an alarming rate. The Bank House at Worcester was the worst. It didn't help that

Alistair had no idea about stock-taking or much about accounting either. In time his brother Ian and wife Bunty came in and took over the running, forming a company for the process. Even though Ian was high up in the Shell organisation in charge of the tanker fleet, he made time. Ian felt his brother was naive with people and he never made any money from his hotels. Alistair soon became disillusioned and was seldom seen in any of the hotels. The venture lasted six years although one of the hotels was not sold until 1976.

He had kept in touch with the Chapmans who were frequent family visitors to Haslemere and Alistair often met Ian Chapman in London for lunch. In all those meetings Ian never mentioned writing or anything about books, even though it became obvious business was not going well and that Alistair was hitting the bottle again. In the end it was Alistair who raised the subject that since *Ice Station Zebra*, Ian had never mentioned anything about books or writing.

Again Ian did not rise to the bait. Instead indicating that he respected Alistair's decision to give up writing, however if he had had a change of mind he would like to hear about it. Alistair, probably exaggerating, said various people had been after him and in particular he mentioned Elliot Kastner the film producer who wanted him to write a screenplay. This was in 1966.

In 1966 the 36-year-old Elliot Kastner was a New York Jew who had produced his first film the year before, *Bus Riley's Back in Town*. He teamed up with Jerry Gershwin to form Winkast Film Productions based at Pinewood Studios and they would make eleven films together. The first was *Harper*, the third was *Kaleidoscope* starring Warren Beatty and Susannah York, which Kastner and Gershwin sold to Warner Bros. His stepson Cassian Elwes, a former head of the William Morris Agency, praised the inventive nature of the pair: '*That was the beginning of producers taking control creatively by self financing....*'[6]

Here was Alistair at another crossroads of his life. Ian did at last prompt him; if there was to be another book he might be interested in publishing it but would '*have to see if you can still write...*' After all '*you've been away for a long time.*'[7]

It was no fiction or leg-pulling by Alistair that he had been approached by Kastner among other people, however the American was more persistent than most. He had read *HMS Ulysses* and *The Guns of Navarone* and thought them both displayed fine writing. He managed to obtain the phone number of Sunbiggin and caught Alistair at home and told him he was a film producer.

Alistair pointed out that all his books' film rights had been sold and he was wasting his time. However Kastner said that was not what he was after; rather he wanted him to write a screenplay. This intrigued Alistair as he had never been asked this before, and the film world held an attraction for him, so he invited Kastner to come and see him at home.

For two hours on an autumn afternoon in 1966 they batted around the subject. Kastner wanted a war story, a tight story with not too many characters, who face big odds and obstacles to reach their goal; it would need a couple of women and need pace, the clock had to be ticking. What he wanted in essence was another *Navarone*. He had bought with him two screenplays that Alistair could study. They quickly struck a deal, a $10,000 advance, then $100,000 on delivery and they would split the profits 50–50, Alistair could even have the publication rights so that he could write a book. Alistair said he could not start until early in 1967 and they agreed on a delivery date in mid-March.

Later Kastner would say that Alistair, as far as business was concerned, was '*a gentle, generous, naive kind of fool...*' He believed he had been exploited with *The Guns of Navarone* which had been a fine film for which Alistair got peanuts. And he '*allowed himself to be seduced by people, some good, some bad*'. Ironically the two men would later fall out over money.[8]

Chapter Eighteen

Back to the War 1966–1968

The reason why Alistair could not start on the Kastner screenplay until January 1967 was that he was working on another project, a book for Collins, although at the time the publishers knew nothing about it. When he delivered the manuscript to Collins he had not settled on a title. It was another secret service story but this time in many ways much closer to his nemesis Ian Fleming's James Bond. His Philip Calvert might have come out of a similar pod. Fleming had died in August 1964, having written fourteen Bond books and many short stories about 007, yet the film franchise was gathering pace. By 1966 four Bond films had been made and a fifth *You Only Live Twice* would be released that year, the screenplay had been written by Fleming's friend Roald Dahl.[1] Also Len Deighton had introduced his secret agent Harry Palmer to the world in 1962 with the *Ipcress File*, by 1966 there were four books and three had been filmed. There seemed to be an insatiable appetite for spy stories.

The manuscript Alistair delivered to Collins became *When Eight Bells Toll*. The story was set in the Scottish Western Isles, Alistair's old sailing grounds. He bought an MFV in 1965 to sail the area for research.[2]

The book has a cracking opening scene in which Calvert is confronted with a Peacemaker Colt, the famed pistol of so many Westerns. The story is told in the first person and Calvert tells us all about this weapon confronting him and how deadly it could be, with its low velocity and soft nosed bullets, compared to modern guns. It was a bone smasher rather than going straight through and Calvert *'wished to God that Colonel Sam Colt had gone in for inventing something else….'*[3]

Told in the first person, Calvert is on the track of a gang who are taking ships carrying gold, for the United States Treasury, off the British coast. He is under the orders of his boss, head of the secret service Rear Admiral Sir Arthur Arnford-Jason, KCB, known as *'Uncle Arthur'*.[4] Alistair returns to using chapter titles with the day and time as used in his first two books. Again Calvert is in the mould of Philip Marlowe. The plot is over-complicated yet still it was a good return book for Alistair.

With *When Eight Bells Toll* delivered he could turn to the screenplay. It would be set in Germany, he told Kastner in December over lunch, at a castle called the Adler Schloss, often pronounced the other way around as Schloss Adler, and he showed him the location on the map near Salzburg in Austria. There would be no return to the background of HMS *Royalist*'s cruises and his own experiences and no naval background other than the head of the Secret Service would be another admiral. However it is likely that Alistair had the Wewelsburg Castle in mind in Westphalia, Germany. When the Nazis were in power it became the SS cult-site.

Alistair, in *Where Eagles Dare*, calls the Adler Schloss the home of the Gestapo.[5] In 1934 the Gestapo the 'State Secret Police' came under Himmler and the SS and was administered by the Reich Security Main Office [RSHA] and became known as the Amt (dept) 4 of the RSHA. The SD Sicherheitsdienst was the secret service branch of the SS.

Walter Schellenberg who toward the end of the war would become a reluctant head of the SD, wrote about the SS and the Wewelsburg Castle:

> *The SS organisation had been built up by Himmler on the principles of the order of the Jesuits. The service statutes and spiritual exercises prescribed by Ignatius Loyola formed a pattern which Himmler assiduously tried to copy. Absolute obedience was the supreme rule; each and every order had to be accepted without question...*
>
> *A medieval castle near Paderborn in Westphalia was reconstructed and adapted to serve as a kind of SS monastery, the so-called 'Wewelsburg'. Here the secret Chapter of the Order assembled once a year. Each member had his own armchair with an engraved silver name plate, and each had to devote himself to a ritual of spiritual exercises aimed mainly at mental concentration.[6]*

Admiral Canaris is mentioned in *Where Eagles Dare* as the head of the German Secret Service.[7] However, Admiral Wilhelm Canaris was head of the Abwehr, the Armed Forces Intelligence Service. When he was removed from office in 1944 the Abwehr was absorbed by the SD, so there is a confused mix of the various German security services.[8]

There are certainly echoes of the interior of the Wewelsburg castle, redesigned for the SS, in *Eagles*. Everything '*was gold or golden gilt*' and '*The chandeliers were gilded, above the white and gilt-plated fireplace.*' It was a huge room '*at least seventy feet by thirty wide…*'[9]

Eight weeks from 15 January the manuscript arrived on Kastner's desk at Pinewood. He was impressed, he found it '*rich, full, exciting*', but he was not impressed with the title *The Eagles Castle*. He renamed it taking his title from Shakespeare's *Richard III*: Act I Scene III: '*I cannot tell: the world is grown so bad: That wrens may prey where eagles dare not perch.*'

Kastner brought in the young director Brian Hutton for the film, which meant he needed a well-known actor to impress investors; he decided on Richard Burton to play Smith, the only trouble would be to persuade the actor. He had to make a trip to the South of France to see him where he had more trouble convincing Burton's agent Hugh French, than he did the actor. He then brought in Clint Eastwood to play the American Lieutenant Morris Schaffer of the OSS. Next he convinced MGM to take on the film who balked at paying Eastwood $350,000, as he was then a fairly new face, but the redoubtable Kastner persuaded them.

It was Eastwood who observed during filming the action scenes that they blasted away without ever re-loading their machine-pistols, the famous Schmeisser. Brian Hutton the director told Eastwood not to worry, nobody was going to notice. Some 20,000 rounds of blank ammunition were fired off during the filming. Derren Nesbitt who played Major Von Hapen felt his uniform was all wrong, not only that but in the film he is referred to as a Gestapo officer while wearing an SS uniform.

Alistair doesn't seem to give us much detail on the Schmeisser which appears in several of his books. The MP40 machine pistol rate of fire was 500 rounds a minute of nine millimetre ammunition carried in the 32-round magazine. More commonly known as the Schmeisser after Hugo Schmeisser who designed the MP 18, Heinrich Vollmer designed the MP40 as an updated version of the MP18. The weapon was made by Erma Werke who made over a million. In his unpublished book *Tobruk* he has the character Corporal John Fraser use a Schmeisser for '*as a connoisseur of automatic weapons, Fraser preferred this gun to British models….*' Yet even then he does not tell us why Fraser likes it so much.[10]

Another favourite was the Luger pistol often used with a silencer. The P-08, to give the pistol its code name, was first patented by Georg

Luger in 1900 thus it was quite an old weapon in the 1960s. It was first used in action in the Boxer Rebellion of 1908. The toggle-lock action is quite rare. Lugers, manufactured in Germany and Switzerland, carried nine rounds in the butt magazine. Technically it was replaced in 1938 by the Walther P.38. Napoleon Solo in the *Man from Uncle* often used a P-08.

It was the first time Alistair visited the film sets of his books; he went to Austria and Pinewood. When he went to Shepperton, Burton stopped the scene they were working on so that he could talk to the author. Burton was in awe of writers and he took MacLean to his caravan where they had a long chat during which the actor consumed several large Vodkas. At the time he was drinking four bottles a day.

Kastner observed that the film had a really good effect on Alistair; in his usual earthy language he said he was *'as happy as a pig in shit'*. However things soon deteriorated, drink was the root cause. Barry Norman wrote: *'At a post-production party at the Dorchester the two men, both pretty well plastered, had had a drunken altercation that led to fisticuffs and, in MacLean's version anyway, a punch that felled the great movie star. They never spoke to each other again.'*[11]

Nevertheless it was a triumphant comeback for Alistair. *Where Eagles Dare* and *The Guns of Navarone* were and remain classic war films. Also in 1968 *Ice Station Zebra* reached the silver screen starring Rock Hudson, Patrick McGoohan, Ernest Borgnine and Jim Brown. The screenplay was a multiple effort written by Douglas Heyes, Harry Julian Fink and W.R. Burnett. Martin Ransohoff had acquired the film rights and it was released by MGM. It received mixed reviews and was not an initial success, however over the years *Zebra's* popularity has increased and it remains one of the better adaptations of a MacLean story.

Next on the list for Kastner was a film version of *When Eight Bells Toll*. He saw an opportunity to fill a gap with it. Sean Connery, after *You Only Live Twice,* had given up playing James Bond. He hoped Philip Calvert would take up the mantel of the popular secret agent and that Alistair could write a series of stories. He bypassed the usual route of funding using one of the Hollywood studios and opted for a private backer to the tune of $1.85 million. He brought in the young Anthony Hopkins to play Calvert, backed by some older more experienced actors; Jack Hawkins and Robert Morley were two. It was released in 1971 and although profitable it was not a hit. Alistair did not write the screenplay this time as he was busy with another project.

He was flirting with the idea of forming a company to produce his own films, in particular the sequel to *Navarone*. He had met Geoffrey Reeve, a young producer who had suggested the sequel idea. Reeve had been introduced to Alistair by the London Wine Merchant and Lloyds Underwriter, Lewis Jenkins. He in turn had got to know Alistair after seeing the terms for the deal he had got for the film rights to *Ice Station Zebra* in a paper. He wrote to Alistair via Collins and, intrigued by what he said about the bad deal, the two met. These three would form Trio Productions.

During the first meeting over lunch at Sweetings Restaurant, Alistair revealed to Jenkins some of his tax problems. Jenkins put him in touch with Dr John Heyting, a tax consultant based on Jersey, who in turn got the solicitor David Bishop, his London agent, to look at Alistair's affairs. Ian MacLean thought along with Ian Chapman, that David Bishop was the most important contact Alistair ever made.

Geoffrey Reeve found out that Carl Foreman had already registered a title for a sequel *After Navarone*, saying he had done it to protect Alistair's interests. As soon as he was told, an angry Alistair was on the phone to Bishop to take action which he did, forcefully confronting Foreman. After this Bishop began overhauling all Alistair's business affairs and was shocked with what he found. All MacLean's book copyrights had been put into a company called Gilach AG while he was in Switzerland. When Alistair returned to Britain in 1963, that had been transferred into a scheme run by Stanley Gorrie, a tax advisor, the effect of which was Gorrie controlled most of the author's earnings. If Alistair wanted any big item he had to go to Gorrie for the money. It took Bishop until 1969 to untangle this financial web and regain control for Alistair. It cost £100,000 to finish with Gorrie which had to be borrowed and selling the film rights to two books as well to raise the cash. However, it did return the copyrights of Alistair's books to him. Bishop also advised Alistair to return to Switzerland.

They met again in Switzerland. David Bishop found he was taking more responsibility for Alistair's affairs which he was not altogether happy with. So he suggested to Alistair it might be a good idea to do what Ian Fleming had done two years before he died and sell 51 per cent of his copyright company. In that way Fleming had got a sizeable payout and retained 49 per cent. Bishop learned not to mention Fleming to Alistair again, who had flown into a rage saying he was not going to do anything the Bond author had done.

In 1967 Alistair had written *Force 10 from Navarone*. This was a return, at the start, to the Aegean and his time on the *Royalist* which had inspired the first *Navarone* book. It would be his only sequel. It starts where the *Guns of Navarone* ended with the three heroes picked up by the destroyer *Sirdar* just as the guns are destroyed: '*The rumbling was still in their ears, the echoes fading away....*'[12]

Force 10 opens with Captain Vincent Ryan on the bridge of the S-class destroyer *Sirdar*, he had felt somehow the result of the destruction of the guns disappointing, apart from some smoke and a faint glow on the cliffs, the harbour of Navarone looked like it might have done in ancient times.[13]

Alistair in *Force 10*, and for that matter in *Eagles*, had returned to the third person narrative. We are reunited with Captain Keith Mallory, Dusty Miller and Andrea Stavros. Not to forget '*the splendidly piratical figure of Captain Jensen, RN, chief of Allied Intelligence, Mediterranean...*'[14]

Alistair and Geoffrey Reeve had gone to Yugoslavia in 1967 to research the background for *Force 10*. Why did he choose that part of the world? Most likely he was inspired by the exploits of his namesake, Sir Fitzroy MacLean's time in the country, who had been sent by Churchill as envoy to Tito [Josip Broz Tito] the leader of the Communist Partisans in 1943–45. Fitzroy MacLean was a proud Scot, his ancestors had fought at Culloden and the family motto was 'Thank God I Am a MacLean'. He had parachuted into the country in September 1943. His subordinates were a mixed bunch, some good technicians, others like Randolph Churchill and Evelyn Waugh. He found the partisans were tying down a large number of German troops. He spent two years there based on the Adriatic Island of Vis or in the mountains. Fitzroy also acted as the link between Tito and Churchill, although the two never got on.[15]

Merlin Minshall who worked for Naval Intelligence during the war, was another agent sent to Yugoslavia, in his case by Ian Fleming who was the assistant to the Director of Naval Intelligence [DNI]. He arrived there from Bari in an MGB and joined MacLean's mission, although according to Minshall the two men did not hit it off. Especially when he told MacLean '*you must please understand that I come under the direct control of the Admiralty. Not of your military mission.*'[16] He also observed: '*The truth was that Tito's Partisans didn't like, didn't want and didn't trust the British at all. The mere fact that we had supported the Royalist Mihailovic* [General Draza Mihailovic] *could not and would not be easily forgotten.*'[17]

Tito and Mihailovic had started as allies fighting the Germans but soon quarrelled, their two forces becoming embroiled in a civil war. This was a great attraction to Alistair, providing many plot twists and turns with the labyrinth of Yugoslav politics. As soon as Mallory's team arrive they are not trusted and fall into the hands of the Chetniks, the Royalist/ Nationalists, who by then had aligned themselves with the Germans.[18]

The truth and real objective of their mission is only known by Mallory as was the case with Major Smith in *Eagles*. It is to blow up the Neretva dam and thus destroy the bridge over the river, trapping parts of two German Panzer Divisions either side of the river who are destroyed by the Partisans, this in turn forces the Germans to move troops from Italy to Yugoslavia thus weakening the forces facing the Allies.

Force 10 was not as well written as *The Guns of Navarone* had been, there were a lot of repetitive sentences and the attempts at comedy often fell flat. Yet even so the book was successful and spent five months on the *New York Times* best sellers list.

While still in the UK Alistair purchased a sea-going boat the *Ebhora*, a 60-foot former fishing boat, he at first moored it at Shoreham-by-Sea not far from Haslemere. He was back in his element when his friends Dougie Seggie and Willie Campbell came down from Scotland and they set out on a cruise in the waters of the English Channel. He later moved the *Ebhora* to the Clyde, mooring her at Port Bannatyne on the Isle of Bute. From there he was able to take members of his family on voyages along the west coast of Scotland, his favourite waters. Alistair was often the life and soul of the party provided he stayed away from the drink.

It was shortly before the MacLeans left for Switzerland for the second time that his friend Robert Pitman died of leukaemia. His death hit Alistair hard; even so he did as much as he could to help Pitman's children and widow, Pat. With James Leasar he became a trustee for a fund Robert had set up for his children. However, Gisela felt he was becoming too involved with Pat Pitman and she suspected there had been other women, resulting in some blazing rows. According to

Webster, Michael aged 8 at the time saw his father hit his mother. Yet both Lachlan and Ali refused to be interviewed, and indeed Alistair's sons have not responded to my attempts to contact them. However, although Gisela admitted that her marriage went through a long rocky patch only resolved by divorce, in later life she and Alistair would once again be close and on good terms.[19]

Chapter Nineteen

Switzerland 1969–1972

The MacLeans decided to live in Geneva this time. David Bishop had, through the Swiss tax expert Henri-Paul Brechbuhl, made arrangements with the Swiss authorities for Alistair to pay a fixed annual tax payment regardless of earnings. By this time Bishop had become rather more than a tax lawyer, but a close friend to Alistair.

Given the disruption of moving house with young children and moving to rented accommodation, and with his marriage far from ideal, it is remarkable that Alistair could produce a book. Yet right on time *Puppet on a Chain* arrived at Collins. It had come about as an idea that came from a visit to Amsterdam with Geoffrey Reeve when they happened to pass a warehouse and saw a puppet strung up by a chain around its neck.

Puppet on a Chain was a story of the narcotics underworld, a gritty tale that pits his new hero Major Paul Sherman, against a tough gang of smugglers on the streets and canals of Amsterdam. It got favourable reviews. The *New York Times* called the book: *'One of the best in the Greene-Ambler-MacInnes tradition…the writing is as crisp as a sunny winter morning.'*[1] It also made the best sellers list of the same newspaper in January 1970.

As Trio productions had so far failed to make any headway producing *Force 10*, Alistair handed over the film rights of *Puppet* to Geoffrey Reeve. He negotiated a deal with Robert Clark of the Associated British Picture Corporation, who at the time still held the rights to *HMS Ulysses*. They offered £30,000 which would include Alistair's screenplay and the services of Reeve as producer or director. However as often happens in the film world, things did not run smoothly. The film was finally made by the Big City Company and produced by Kurt Unger.

Unger was shown around Amsterdam by Alistair who also invited his brother Ian and Bunty, Ian and Marjory Chapman and David Bishop. Bishop knew the local police chief Piet Cleveringa well whose co-operation was vital in the making of the famous boat chase scenes around the canals of the city. However production ran into trouble, Reeve was replaced as director as he was too inexperienced and Don Sharp was brought in. There were even bigger problems with Alistair's script and Unger brought in Paul Wheeler to put it right.

MacLean flew into a rage when he saw a preview of the film; he complained he should have been informed before *'students armed with hacksaws'* had been allowed to commit *'major surgery'* on his script. The trouble was Alistair was supposed to be a co-producer but he was seldom there and if he was he was drunk. To try and accommodate Alistair some scenes were re-shot. Barry Norman recalled him turning up at the Europa Hotel Amsterdam late for a press conference as he had to 'sleep it off': *'There it became apparent that MacLean was an alcoholic and, like many alcoholics, affable enough at a certain stage in his drinking but inclined to become spiky and unpleasant later on.'*[2]

After this Alistair swore he would have nothing further to do with films or film scripts. It was a pity he did not stick to it. *Puppet* went on to do reasonably well at the box office.

The following year the MacLeans moved into their permanent home, the Villa Murat near the village of Celigny close to Geneva and the Jura Mountains. It was smaller than Sunbiggin although far more expensive to buy. He had got Collins to stump up a £50,000 advance on royalties to help with the purchase. They did not learn until later that one of their near neighbours was Richard Burton. In retrospect it might have been better for Alistair if they had not argued, for he had few friends in Switzerland.

He did not attend his mother's funeral; she had suffered a stroke in 1969 and spent the last few months of her life with Ian and Bunty in Suffolk, where she died at the age of 78. She was buried at Daviot in her beloved highlands. Alistair may have already used up his allowed time to visit the UK and would have been caned for tax, or he might have been on a bender.

During this period he met with Barry Norman, they had seen each other a few times before during which Alistair had agreed to give him an extended interview. Norman arrived at the Villa Murat for a two day visit to find he was alone with Alistair; Gisela and the family had gone away for a few days. Alistair told him he was having trouble with his eyesight so Norman would have to drive, he had the choice of a Rolls Royce or Mercedes: *'I didn't mind acting as chauffeur, unfamiliar though I was with both cars, because he drank so much throughout the day and evening that he would have been a menace behind the steering wheel.'*

To Norman, Alistair's drinking was the result of *'self-contempt'* the success he had achieved he believed was undeserved. He told his guest: *'Basically, I'm a person who tells stories and what does that mean. How much is it worth?'*

That first night Norman drove them to a restaurant on the shores of Lake Geneva where MacLean *'ate little but drank plenty'.* Back at the villa he suggested a night cap which amounted to a bottle of brandy. Norman wanted to go to bed but Alistair kept drinking and then fell asleep. Norman did not know what to do so he waited for him to wake up. He did at about two in the morning and verbally turned on Norman, accusing him of wanting money from him and then he told him to leave, yet where could he go at that time in the morning, he could hardly take one of his cars and anyway he had drunk quite a bit. *'The only thing, I decided, was to enter into the drunken game he was playing.'* He got up, told Alistair he was leaving, and promptly went to bed.

The next morning Alistair brought him breakfast in bed and told him he could get up when he wanted. He had no memory of what had happened the night before. They parted on the best of terms:

Taken drunk he could be a monster, taken sober – or not very drunk – he was likeable and somehow rather sad. He was right about his books: They really aren't very good. But he knew that and was prepared to admit it, to himself most of all. I've met a lot of hugely successful people but I think Alistair MacLean had the most self-awareness of any of them.[3]

The article Barry Norman wrote as a result of his visit for the *Observer* titled *Best-selling Sceptic* was also revealing. He outlined just how successful MacLean had been up to that time:

At the latest reckoning his books have sold nearly 23 million copies and continue to sell at the rate of two million a year. His earnings from his books and films can hardly be less than £200,000 a year and his latest and sixteenth novel Bear Island, had an initial print run of 100,000 copies and will move automatically to the top of the best sellers.

He saw writing as something he '*drifted into*'. Of his time in the navy he had little to say other than '*I spent the war years with a spanner in my hand. And when it was over I tired of mechanical things and having dirt under my finger-nails.*'

He did not like celebrities or being one himself but he did use his wealth to try and help people. Norman again:

> *That he does help people I know for a fact and he does it by stealth and not for self-advertisement. He is an extremely kind and likeable man and also surprisingly vulnerable. A man in search of a cause.*[4]

By now *Caravan to Vaccares* had been published, which had first been written as a screenplay for Elliot Kastner. In 1974 Reeve produced and directed it for the screen, starring David Birney and Charlotte Rampling, but Alistair would have nothing to do with it.

Bear Island [1971] marked a return to one of Alistair's favourite settings, the waters of the Arctic Ocean; the book was dedicated to Ian and Marjory Chapman. A throw back in time to Alistair's time in the navy, in the novel Captain Imrie tells us Bear Island was the 'Gate': '*The gate to the Barents Sea and the White Sea and those places in Russia where we took the convoys through all the long years of the war...*'[5] A character called Captain Imrie also appears in *When Eight Bells Toll*.

The key character is Doctor Christopher Marlowe. Is Alistair tempting us here? Is it some sort of homage to the sixteenth-century poet and playwright, said to have been a great influence on Shakespeare? He was accused of anti-intellectualism for his depictions of violence, cruelty and bloodshed and complicated plot lines. Or did he have Philip Marlowe, Chandler's hero, in mind? It would be the last of his books to be written in the first person. Is it a tribute to *The Long Goodbye*, given the amount of drinking that goes on? Chandler's novel opens with: '*The first time I laid eyes on Terry Lennox he was drunk in a Rolls Royce Silver Wraith outside the terrace of the Dancers.*'[6] Whereas in *Bear Island* on the first page we find two of the characters consuming large amounts of spirits: '*Captain Imrie and Mr Stokes, malt whiskey for the captain, Jamaican rum for Mr Stokes*'.[7]

The plot is based around the premise that Germans, just as the war was ended, shipped vast amounts of gold to the island by submarine and buried it. A film crew sets out to the island, which is used as a cover by the people trying to recover the treasure and get away with it in a submarine that is there as a prop in the film. Marlowe is a British agent that foils this although he's rescued at the end by the timely arrival of the police and army.

Bear Island is the southernmost isle of the Svalbard archipelago. It had huge bird cliffs, well illustrated on the first edition cover by Norman Weaver, and the lack of bays and long spells of bad weather make it an inhospitable landing point. The Germans in the Second World War did establish a weather station there, but in July 1941 the light cruisers HMS *Nigeria* and HMS *Aurora* and two destroyers destroyed the weather station with gunfire. In June 1943, *U-212* landed some troops who destroyed the Allied weather station that had been established there.[8]

Alistair had engaged Jacky Leiper as his private secretary. Another Scot, she had been brought up in Greenock, worked in the USA and Switzerland. She was given her own office in the Villa Murat and had little contact with the family but could tell the atmosphere was strained. Although Alistair was very happy with her work, at this time he had tried to write a book about cancer having lost his friend Robert Pitman to it and Lewis Jenkins had to have treatment for it. He hoped to produce it and give as much to the charities fighting cancer as he could. It had the title *A Layman looks at Cancer;* he produced a 35,000 word manuscript. However it did not pass the scrutiny of the medical profession who felt it would not really be helpful as it was too scientific for the intended reader so it was never published.

About this time Alistair became besotted with Marcelle Georgius, a film producer actress, introduced to him by Lewis Jenkins whose company was interested in buying the film rights to one of his books. All three met for lunch at the Hotel du Lac. The meeting went well and Jenkins and Georgius flew back to London. The story goes that Lewis Jenkins, ten days after that meeting, had to go back to Switzerland on another matter but had arranged with Alistair to meet him at the airport, which he did with Marcelle Georgius on his arm. Quite who had approached who is not known but it had helped that Gisela had been away on a visit to Germany and in her absence Marcelle had moved into the Villa Murat.

Born in Paris in 1935 into a family of actors and entertainers, Marcelle had spent much of her adult life on the fringes of the acting world occasionally getting small parts. She had been married twice. With Stewart Pulver, her first husband, she had her only child Curtis in 1956. When Gisela returned Alistair made sure Marcelle was at a hotel and he told his wife of twenty years he had met someone else and wanted to leave. As the news broke, friends and relatives tried to dissuade him. Ian Chapman implored him not to marry her, yet it all fell on deaf ears. The couple were soon installed at the Hotel du Lac in Coppet not far from the Villa Murat.

For the wedding Alistair asked Ian Chapman to be his best man, which naturally he did, even though he saw no future in it. The wedding strangely took place on Friday, 13 October 1972. Were they cocking a snoot at fate? They were married at Caxton Hall Register Office. The honeymoon was in Amsterdam. Apparently it was only a matter of days and they rowed and Marcelle ended up in a canal; whether Alistair pushed her in or she fell in who knows. She was soon trying to inveigle her way into her husband's financial affairs but they were resolutely defended by David Bishop who stopped her and her cronies. However he had to keep fighting a rear-guard action on this and he could not stop her spending money like water. Alistair basically had the sense to support David on this and he had to admit he would never have done this had his mother still been alive.

Given all that had happened in 1972 it is hardly surprising Alistair did not produce a novel. Yet instead he wrote a short biography of one of his naval heroes, Captain James Cook which was published by Collins. One of the greatest figures in the history of the Royal Navy, it was clearly his three great voyages that circumnavigated the world, taken between 1768–1779, that inspired Alistair and form the bulk of the book. Alistair wrote honestly in his prologue:

Far from being intended to be a definitive biography, what follows is no biography at all. A true biography is a fully-rounded portrait but there are colours missing from my palette. I do not know enough of the man: the material just is not there. This is but a brief account of his early apprenticeship to the sea, his development as a navigator and cartographer, and of his three great voyages, and this is perhaps enough to let us have an inkling of the essential Captain Cook... [9]

It might have been better for Alistair had he concentrated more on non-fiction. He also did a long introduction to *Alistair MacLean Introduces Scotland*, which is a tour-de-force and in just twelve pages reveals a lot about himself and his Scottish background. For this work he used a different publisher, Andre Deutsch.

Chapter Twenty

All is Chaos 1973–1977

To say that Alistair and Marcelle's life together was chaotic would be an understatement. They sometimes stayed in Geneva or the South of France, or the flat in Little Chester Street London and then there was California and back again renting palatial properties or staying in expensive hotels.

Graham Lord, the editor of the *Sunday Express*, managed to catch up with Alistair in the South of France for an extended interview and he got him on to writing screenplays: '*he says, "I detest the film world. Why? I think it is meretricious, cheap. Apart from authors, they're the biggest band of rogues in the world." He says he finds writing a chore and describes himself on his passport as "hotelier" yet has probably made more out of joining words together than anyone except Harold Robbins….*'[1]

It must have been about the same time that Jackie Collins interviewed Alistair, she found him '*lonely and unhappy*' in his '*sumptuous, sixth-floor penthouse in Cannes*'. The interview lasted fourteen hours and she found it difficult to get away. He told her he was '*just a cheapskate writer*'. When at last they did part he said: '*Am I the most difficult b*****d you've ever had to interview?' 'Yes', I said. But he was also without doubt the saddest.*'[2]

When in Switzerland they stayed at the Hotel du Lac at Coppet, Alistair and Marcelle occupied a suite, then there was Lachlan now 18 and Curtis 16 and a secretary to be accommodated. Not far away was Gisela at the Villa Murat with the two younger boys who seems to have treated the whole thing with a sense of relief.

Somewhere, somehow in between all this Alistair managed to write *The Way to Dusty Death*, a thriller set against the background of Formula 1 motor racing. While in Switzerland Alistair became friendly with fellow Scot and racing driver Jackie Stewart. He was world champion three times, the final time in 1973 after which he retired. Alistair was clearly attracted to that world. In *When Eight Bells Toll* Calvert bemoans the loss of his friend Tim Hutchinson a '*rare breed*', no one could be like him. Not anyone could be a great Grand Prix driver and he cites three examples: the German Rudolf Caracciola, the Italian Tazio Nuvolari, whom many regard as the greatest of all time, and Jim Clark, the son of a Scottish farmer.[3] Alistair wrote it as a screenplay first that Marcelle was supposed to produce; the book is dedicated to her. Stewart was sucked into helping with the film, taking them around the Grand Prix circus and filming the Monaco race. He was not even told when the project was shelved, although maybe it became obvious as Marcelle soon became bored with the racing world and went back to London, and she was the one supposed to be the producer. Alistair took to calling Marcelle, Mary; indeed some of his books are dedicated to *Mary Marcelle* whether this was a pet name, or somehow something to do with his mother, also a Mary, is hard to say. Or indeed this may have been done to annoy Marcelle.

Soon Alistair's entourage was joined by Marcelle's secretary Sabrina Carver. He realised the situation was far from ideal so sent Jacky and Sabrina to the South of France to find a suitable rented property. They came up with Casa Estella at Cap d'Antibes, a pleasant villa close to the sea where to a degree, given there was still Marcelle to deal with, he could settle down to write. Throughout his life he seemed to be looking for something, as if there was a path he only had to find to something else, to something better. If only he could get through the chaos. It was a phrase he often used: *'All is chaos'.*[4]

By the end of the writing of *The Way to Dusty Death*, Jacky Leiper left the MacLeans but they followed her to Greece where she had obtained another position, and persuaded her to return to Geneva. Alistair, because of his earnings, could only spend ninety days of the year in the UK, while Marcelle and Sabrina were spending more time in London, which left Alistair more often than not in the South of France, an increasingly lonely figure. The arrangements were far from ideal for the children. Michael and Ali were with Gisela and Lachlan was with his father, but in a self contained apartment. Curtis followed like a lap-dog around the various homes. The boys got whatever they wanted but in the long run it did them no good.

In 1974 while in the United States, Elliot Kastner got hold of Alistair and was appalled by the state of his old friend. He had always wanted to work with him again after *When Eagles Dare*. He was not impressed with Marcelle and called her *'a dunce, a self proclaiming, foolish woman without ability, who had no grace, dignity or class*.[5] Kastner got Alistair a contract with Twentieth Century Fox, and says he gave him the idea for a film, a historical story, a Western set in Nevada in 1873 which would become *Breakheart Pass*. Neither the book nor the film, starring Charles Bronson and Jill Ireland, were very successful.

Alistair had originally gone to California to write a screenplay of *Circus* but stayed on. David Bishop went out there in 1976 to sort out the latest tax position in respect to US laws. He found another mess, for most of the decade average earnings were over £500,000 a year, but either Alistair or other people were spending even more.

Behind with the latest book, Doreen Kern, a friend of Marcelle who had gone out to stay with the MacLeans helped Alistair drying out, and got him back to writing. Marcelle moved out of Alanda Place, Beverly Hills, Bela Lugosi's old home, which reduced the tension. It seems she tried every stratagem and verbal blackmail to keep Alistair in California, even trying to gain control of his finances but failed. Sabrina, who had had enough had gone back to her flat in Notting Hill Gate. Then some time in 1976 there came a ring at her door and there was Alistair, all he said was, *'I've got out.'*[6] He asked her to become his secretary, which after some persuasion she did and would remain in the post for the rest of his life.

The divorce from Marcelle was a messy affair, however unwittingly she introduced Alistair to the Canadian producer Peter Snell. He had produced many films including some adaptions of Shakespeare plays for the screen in the early 1970s. He became producer at British Lion Films, making some highly acclaimed films, *Don't Look Now* from a short story by Daphne du Maurier starring Donald Sutherland and Julie Christie, and the cult classic *The Wicker Man*. Marcelle had tried to get him to produce *The Way to Dusty Death*. He was introduced to Alistair who was naturally wary as he had come through her. Snell looked at *Dusty Death* but it came to nothing as the film world found motor racing films extremely difficult in which to maintain good story lines, with cars flying around tracks. However, Snell was fascinated by Alistair and instead he took on *Bear Island*; the film was backed by Columbia Pictures with a star-studded cast including Donald Sutherland, Richard Widmark, Christopher Lee, Lloyd Bridges, Vanessa Redgrave and Barbara Perkins.

The divorce petition was issued by Alistair on 20 January 1977. David Bishop got her excessive demands down to a payment of £250,000 plus

£150,000 to buy back the rights of *Bear Island* and *The Way to Dusty Death*. The total amount was paid over three years. Through all this Alistair kept producing the books; it has to be said on the whole a pretty rum lot including *Circus* in 1975 in which a trapeze artist has to infiltrate an East German prison. The *Los Angeles Times* felt he '*was going through the motions...*'[7] *Golden Gate* came in 1976, a plot to kidnap the President of the USA. About *Seawitch* in 1977 the *New York Times* said Alistair MacLean '*stumbles badly...*'[8] *Goodbye California* came in the same year, surprisingly all sold fairly well to the army of devoted readers who really deserved better.

Chapter Twenty-One

The Last Decade 1978–1987

T he final deed of divorce between Alistair and Marcelle was signed on 19 December 1977. He had maintained contact with Gisela and was now a welcome visitor to the Villa Murat where she still lived, which was her property after their divorce settlement. Later he would stay with her for extended periods. He was now an altogether far more relaxed man. He even appeared at the Author of the Year party in London and also met one of his literary inspirations. When David Bishop arranged a lunch meeting for him with Denis Wheatley at Justerini and Brooks, the wine merchants in St James Street, Wheatley was just as keen to meet Alistair and it was a great success.

In November, although not overly keen on film-sets, Alistair and David Bishop set off for Opatija in Yugoslavia to watch the shooting of some of the scenes of *Force 10 from Navarone,* which at last had been taken up by Columbia Pictures. It took twelve hours to get there on a ramshackle train. They spent much of their time with Robert Shaw, the actor who was playing Mallory, at his rented villa overlooking the sea, both men knew him. They met other members of the cast and production team including a young Harrison Ford. There were some long drinking bouts with Shaw which Bishop frowned on.

The following year Alistair returned to Yugoslavia in the summer to research the background of another book he had in mind which would become *Partisans,* based on a story he had been told about a female double agent that had come from Mostar. He went on to Dubrovnik, he was enjoying himself, and asked Sabrina to try and find him a property as he wanted to spend more time there. Through her enquiries she came across Avdo Cimic, a hotel worker who had built his own house twelve miles north of the city with panoramic views across the Adriatic. There was room for Alistair in a self-contained flat. On a short visit he was taken by Avdo, who worked on the reception desk at the Hotel Argentina, to his Villa Sandra. It was a self-contained ground floor four-room apartment.

Alistair was pleased with it and booked it on the spot, asked for some minor alterations to be made but did not return until 1978.

When he did come back he soon settled into the flat at the Villa Sandra. This would give him the settled life he had craved, for eight months of the year he would stay there and write. He got to know his landlord Avdo well and would in time employ him full-time as his driver, boatman, handyman and companion. There was no contract merely a handshake. Alistair, generous as always, paid him his salary up front for the next twenty years. Avdo was married to Inge an artist, whom Alistair was fond of, and he was impressed with her skill and bought several of her pictures.

Alistair, for him, led an idyllic life at the Villa Sandra. He liked to rise early and cook himself breakfast, the full English including fried bread, and sometimes kippers, another favourite for a full Scottish. Then it was down to work until the English papers arrived, a break to read them then back to work. Sometimes he would cook himself lunch or Avdo would take him out in the car to a local restaurant or it would be the evening meal. When not going out in the evening he watched old films on video and he liked to watch football.

Sabrina in London dealt with his mail and kept the diary dates. She flew out to Dubrovnik to collect the manuscripts for correction and typing and then delivery to the publishers. *Athabasca* 1980, *River of Death* 1981, *Partisans* 1982, and *Floodgate* 1983 all came off the trusty IBM golf-ball typewriter at the Villa Sandra. *Athabasca* was a return to Alistair's favoured setting of the Arctic environment after Peter Snell suggested he should set a story in the Lake Athabasca area of Alaska and Canada. It was not received well by the critics. *The Los Angeles Times* called it *'ponderous'*.[1]

River of Death marked a return to the Second World War, at least at the start, as the retreating Germans ransack a monastery in Greece. It opens with SS troops looting the monastery carrying away chests full of gold coins and jewels so heavy it takes four men to lift them, which they load onto two Junkers Ju 88 bombers, under the orders of Major-General Wolfgang von Manteuffel, and Colonel Heinrich Spaatz, SS officers.[2]

Von Manteuffel commandeers a U-boat to take the loot to South America cutting Spaatz out of the fortune who in turn vows revenge. Years later, a team of archaeologists in search of a lost civilization in the jungles of Brazil, stumble across a settlement of Nazis living as if the war had not ended, and revenge is taken on von Manteuffel.

Alistair was able to extol the Aegean at the start, the '*sea was calm; the air was still and did indeed, as is so often claimed for it, smells of wine and roses*'.[3] The book was on the *New York Times* best sellers list in 1982.[4]

Jack Higgins author of *The Eagle has Landed* wrote of *River of Death* and about Alistair MacLean for the *Sunday Standard* newspaper:

What is the secret of that incredible success? If we knew, we would all be doing it, for there is no doubt that he is one of the greatest page-turners in the business. I don't think one can analyse the exact gift he possesses which enables him to accomplish the trick, because gift it is, and as impossible to explain as the flair which makes one actor competent and the other a great performer.

One can make an attempt at some kind of assessment, of course, and his latest book, River of Death, is as good a starting point as any. MacLean, more than anyone else in the thriller genre, has always varied his backgrounds. The war story as displayed in the brilliant The Guns of Navarone or the classic Where Eagles Dare, the pure thriller of Puppet on a Chain, the Secret Service exploits of The Last Frontier or When Eight Bells Toll.

He then goes on to explain the opening scenes of the looting in Greece before turning to the present day Brazilian rain forest: '*Maclean gives us the heat and smell of the place, with his unerring eye for time and place and along with the story of a mysterious adventurer... A word of warning. Don't start reading River of Death unless you have time to finish it at a sitting, for the old master is in top form with this one.*'[5]

Partisans had similarities with *Force 10 from Navarone* in that one is never quite sure on which side the main character's loyalties lay. In time it takes place before the Allies have landed in Italy, therefore before *Force 10*. In typical MacLean style the plot submerges into the complicated three-way civil war raging across Yugoslavia at the time between the Communists, Serb Royalists the Chetniks and the Croatian Fascists.

Alistair was missing a boat so Sabrina, master-of-all-trades, found him one, an American Chris Craft, a firm that had been building boats since 1874. She was called *Insan*, a classic built wooden launch powered by a

Volvo engine. Avdo had spent some time as a merchant seaman so proved a good deck hand.

There were often visitors for Alistair at the Villa Sandra. His youngest son Ali was the most frequent, who enjoyed sailing along the coast in the *Insan*. As much as possible, he left other visitors to Avdo to entertain, who took them on sightseeing trips by boat or car.

Somewhat to his surprise Alistair was invited back to the University of Glasgow in 1983 to be invested with an honorary Doctor of Letters degree. Many of his best and most trusted friends were at the occasion. His first wife Gisela, both his brothers and their wives, the Chapmans, Sabrina and Avdo, as usual with Alistair heightened by the flowing drink as the occasion loomed, he began to have doubts that he deserved such an honour.

On the eve-of-graduation dinner he had to be assisted to leave, slurring his words. One of his fellow graduates, the Reverend James Martin, had wanted to talk with Alistair about his books he had enjoyed so much and was disappointed in his behaviour. However later they both went on a tour of a Collins printing works, there he saw a different Alistair chatting freely with the women working there: '*he was so good at talking to them I had seen the two faces of Alistair MacLean and could hardly believe it.*'

Andrew Skinner, Professor of Political Economy, presented Alistair for the degree. He outlined his journey from Highland childhood to sailor on the Russian Convoys. He talked of Alistair graduating from the university in 1950, and later the remarkable success of *HMS Ulysses* and went on to say:

> *In accepting the honour, Mr MacLean reminded us of the fact that, in the Royal Navy, a ranker can be awarded a good-conduct medal for twenty-one years of undiscovered crime. Mr MacLean knows well that the honorary doctorate is not simply a reward for good conduct, although it should not be inconsistent with it. It is rather offered to recognition of the accelerating discovery of a formidable talent to amuse – in the best sense of the word.*[6]

He would spend about eight months of the year in Yugoslavia leaving the rest of the year for travel and research. This left him time to relax in the South of France which he loved, but not to work there. The rest of the time he would spend at the Villa Murat with Gisela and the boys, it soon became normal for him to spend the festive season with them. Gisela still *'had great compassion for him but when he asked me to marry for the second time I knew I couldn't....'* she told Jack Webster.[7]

The following year during a visit to the Villa Sandra, Ali caused a bad accident when he reversed his father's Mercedes out of the awkward drive into the path of an oncoming bus, the driver took avoiding action but there was a truck coming in the opposite direction. The truck ended up hitting the Villa while the bus hit a rock face. It was an extremely serious accident, the bus driver and three passengers were killed. Ali was unhurt.

The police took Ali's passport. Alistair would not accept his son was responsible, and Ali felt he was not in the wrong. However, at the hearing Ali was sentenced to a year in prison near Belgrade. All Alistair's money and influence was useless in the face of Yugoslav authority, however he appealed to Sir Fitzroy MacLean his kinsman who had a special place in the hearts of the Yugoslav people. He had a house on the island of Korcula to the north of Dubrovnik. At the same time Avdo asked the Belgrade publisher Bato Tomasevic to intervene. His older sister had served with the Partisans and with Fitzroy MacLean. Added to this Alistair was a supporter of various charities in the country, including homes for mongol children. All these factors and the annual freedom celebrations resulted in Ali's sentence being reduced to weeks. On his release Alistair chartered a private plane to fly him back to Switzerland.

Shona MacLean, daughter of Gillespie and Margaret, has fond memories of her *'generous'* uncle. He encouraged her to become a writer even though it was something he was not entirely comfortable with himself.[8]

Alistair wrote in an article for the *Glasgow Herald* in 1982, titled *Rewards and Responsibilities of Success*, that he had been called a success, but he felt *'"Success", in its most common usage, is a relative term which has to be applied with great caution, especially in writing.'* He felt he *'did write a couple of books which I thought might be judged as being meaningful or significant but – from readers' reactions I was left in no doubt that the only person who shared this opinion was myself.'*[9]

Shona felt: *'It was as if he was looking for something more. Sometimes he would say I should be a writer and at others he was more concerned that I should be happily married and have children, as if there was a choice of making your mark in the world and being happy.'* He was much happier being her uncle rather than the rich and famous writer.[10]

As to his readers he felt he owed them: *'My greatest responsibility and debt are to those who buy my books, making it possible for me to lead the life I do. Moreover, while deriving a perfectly justifiable satisfaction in pointing out my frequent errors of fact, they never tell me how to write. I am grateful.'*[11]

'He certainly made a big impression on me', said Shona, *'and I think of him still as a very kind and generous man, also astute, but very lonely. He was interested in people for their own sake and liked to have around him those, like Sabrina, who were genuine and not just interested in his name.'*[12]

By this time, the early 1980s, Alistair's health was beginning to cause some concern. He has been called a 'mild diabetic', of course there is no such thing; as he had to take insulin it was rather more serious. Doctors told him to stop drinking the hard liquor, the whiskey and vodka, which he did, only drinking some local Yugoslav wine in the evenings.

One of Alistair's most remarkable books, given the gap in time, was published in 1984; *San Andreas* was a return to the icy waters of the Arctic Ocean where thirty years before they had flowed over the sinking *Ulysses*. The book is again set in the Second World War. First there is a ten page prologue during which he praises the men of the Merchant Navy, outlining as we have seen, the appalling conditions they lived and worked under prior to 1939.

It was these seamen who in the end maintained Britain's lifeline. He then goes on to describe Henry J. Kaiser, yes that was his name, who came up with the miracle of the 'Liberty Ship' bringing prefabrication into ship building. Although the design was based on a ship produced by J.L. Thompson of North Sands, Sunderland, the first ship built under the principles, the *Embassage,* was completed in 1935, just in time to be able to quickly replace the crippling losses. The SS *Patrick Henry* was the first one to be launched in the USA on 27 September 1941. In all, eighteen United States and Canadian shipyards would build 2,710, an average of three ships every two days. A tremendous war winning weapon, some could be and were armed with anti-aircraft guns while a few were converted to carry a catapult-launched Hurricane fighter.

Alistair then turns the coin over to admire the tenacity of the Germans in attacking these Allied life lines. The aircraft first, then the surface ships, and finally the most deadly of them all, the U-boats, it would be that arm of the German armed forces that had the highest losses of them all with 30,000 men lost out of 40,000, a figure of 75 per cent.

The *San Andreas* is a hospital ship converted from a Liberty cargo carrier: '*The hospital area of the San Andreas was remarkably airy and roomy, remarkably but not surprising…well over half the lower deck space had been given over to its medical facilities.*'[13]

San Andreas leaves Murmansk in the North of Russia with casualties on board that need repatriating to Britain. She has one escort yet she should not need one, for under the terms of the Geneva Convention, her red crosses should guarantee immunity from attack. However, hours out from Murmansk they are picked up by a 'Charlie', Captain Bowen knows that engine note: '*Once heard, the desynchronized clamour of a Focke-Wulf 200's engine is not readily forgotten.*'[14]

The escort, *HMS Andover*, is soon sunk by Heinkel torpedo bombers. The *San Andreas* escapes serious damage other than some to the superstructure from Condor bombs. They have to bury some dead, condemning them to the freezing waters of the Barents Sea. The *San Andreas* had originally been the freighter *Ocean Belle*. The Russians had finished off the conversion to hospital ship in Murmansk. She was renamed after the California San Andreas fault, as the shipyard that built her at Richmond was close to the fault line.

The book is told in the third person with lots of twists and turns and with a saboteur spy on board. Even when the *San Andreas* rams and sinks a U-boat on the surface it becomes apparent the Germans want to stop the ship intact for some reason. The reason – she is carrying tons of Russian gold hidden by the unusually eager Russian dockyardies. It is payment for the Russian lend-lease, which means if the Germans cannot stop her and take her over or remove the gold they will sink her. With the Germans closing in the *San Andreas* is saved by bad weather and makes it home.

The following year Collins published a collection of short stories and short pieces of non-fiction, to mark Alistair's thirty years as an author. Remarkable in some ways that they had stayed together that long, given some of the arguments. It was titled *The Lonely Sea* and contains some of Alistair's finest writing, much of it about the Second World War.

After the divorce from Alistair, Marcelle had rapidly degenerated, her settlement, not an insignificant amount of money, was soon squandered.

Appeals to Alistair for funds fell on deaf ears. She descended into a state of poverty and her health deteriorated. Her son Curtis found her at the County Hospital in Los Angeles, a refuge for the poor and homeless in California. Curtis likened her state to *something out of Dickens*. A plea for help was sent to Alistair, via David Bishop, who was in Greece at the time researching another book with Sabrina. The message read that Marcelle was dying of cancer but MacLean would hear none of it and insisted no money was sent. This time it was not a story; she had developed cancer of the pancreas and died on 16 May 1985, four weeks short of her fiftieth birthday. Alistair, maybe in a pang of remorse, paid for her funeral. Curtis brought her ashes back to the UK and scattered them at Lynmouth in Devon beside the sea.

In July of 1986 Alistair travelled home to Scotland for an extended visit with Avdo. In England they met with two of his sons, Lachlan and Ali, and drove north to the Scottish Highlands. He was thrilled to see Gillespie and Margaret and their children; after years in the hotel trade Gillespie had retired. He also met with his old school chum Tom Fraser from the Daviot days. Tom's wife Rena felt Alistair was special: *'yet he was always on your level, never making you feel that you didn't know as much as he did'*. They spent several holidays with Alistair over the years and he always insisted on paying the fares in Switzerland, the South of France and Yugoslavia.

During the visit he looked into getting another boat to moor in Scotland to follow the *Silver Craig* and the *Ebhora*. Alistair, along with Avdo and his sons, visited the boat building firm of Herd and Mckenzie at Buckie and discussed plans and designs. He was looking at a cabin cruiser in the £500,000 range. Alistair took some plans with him as he wanted to go over them with his older brother Ian the 'seaman'. They said farewell to the family at Muir of Ord and to his friend Tom Fraser. Alistair wondered if he would ever see him again as he was suffering from cancer.

They headed for Ross-on-Wye, Herefordshire on the border of England and Wales, Ian and Bunty's home. They had moved there to be closer to their children, son Ian and daughter Margaret. Again Alistair was delighted to see his brother and the family. However there was something of an unnecessary argument over the boat designs. Ali felt the boat should be bigger, however Ian with his vast knowledge of the sea felt they were fine, and anyway he often jibed Alistair, he thought he was *'the cat's pyjamas when it came to navigation. In fact he would have sailed his boat into a brick wall.'* The upshot was Ali went off in a huff saying he had had enough, was bored with the tour and went back to Switzerland.

The rest of the family then went south to Wells in Somerset to see Margaret and her family. They stayed in a local hotel where Alistair hosted a farewell dinner. The next morning, still being early risers, Ian and Alistair took a stroll into the town and visited the twelfth-century Anglican Cathedral dedicated to St. Andrew the Apostle. They said farewell later that day – it was the last time they would speak face to face. Alistair spent the festive season with Gisela and the boys at Hinterzarten, a small village in the Black Forest. He phoned both his brothers in the UK on New Year's Day 1987. He had barely weeks to live.

It was in the January that for some unknown reason, Alistair went on a bender; his doctor had warned him such behaviour might spell disaster. There was a mysterious Irishman, a porter at the hotel he got to know and with whom he got into a drinking spree. Gisela did not seem to notice the deterioration in him. However speaking to him regularly on the phone Sabrina picked up a halting quality in his speech, she contacted Avdo who had gone to Austria skiing with his family.

By this time Alistair and Gisela had moved on to Munich to do some shopping and were staying at the Bayerischer Hof Hotel. Avdo went straight from Austria to Munich, he found Alistair in his hotel room in a bad state with the mini bar empty. However he seemed all right and they watched TV together. The next day Alistair was not up early in the morning as usual. Gisela found him in bed in a dazed state. He was rushed to a local hospital and from there transferred to the University Hospital Munich and placed in intensive care.

Various members of the family rushed to the Bavarian capital. Ian and Bunty were among the first to arrive. Ian was told Alistair had had several strokes and was being kept alive on a life support machine. He clung to life through January and died on Monday, 2 February 1987.

As word of Alistair MacLean's death spread, thousands of words filled the obituary columns, some of it sheer speculation. Like the *Globe and Mail*:

A master of nail-chewing suspense, MacLean met an appropriately mysterious death, when he died in the Bavarian Capital after a brief illness, no one, including the British Embassy, knew what he was doing there.[15]

Another stated that Alistair died as a result of a fatal fall when a broken rib pierced his lung. However, Edwin McDowell, writing in the *New York Times* got the facts right by going to Collins. It was far more of a tribute to the author:

> *Mr. MacLean wrote more than two dozen books, most of them war adventures or thrillers whose action spanned continents and often took place in airplanes, ships, or in nuclear submarines. They sold millions of copies worldwide, selling especially well in the United States, where he has been published since 1956. A new novel, 'Santorini' a story of espionage in the Aegean, is scheduled for publication next month by Doubleday, his long-time American publisher.*
>
> *Although many of his books describe violent action, Mr MacLean, according to Charles Poore, a reviewer for the* New York Times, *also wrote 'passages of wry comedy in the midst of chaos, death and general destruction.'*[16]

Alistair MacLean was 64 when he died; he was buried at the Vieux Cemetery at Celigny, Switzerland, within sight of the grave of his old sparring partner from *Where Eagles Dare*, Richard Burton, who had died in August 1984. On Alistair's gravestone are written the words: '*Come my friends. Tis not too late. To seek a newer world.*' Which is part of the poem *Ulysses* by Alfred Lord Tennyson, that appears fully in the front of *HMS Ulysses*. The theme is a search for adventure, experience and meaning which makes life worth living.

MacLean wrote twenty-seven novels and several outlines for novels, two non-fiction books and numerous articles and short stories. It is estimated his books have sold over 150 million copies. Films adapted from his stories remain popular the world over.

Having lived with Alistair MacLean, or that's what it feels like at times, for two years there is bound to be more. I can hear that broad Scots voice with the dry wit that he never lost, even in all his wanderings: '*Ach mon dinny forget....*'

There was *Santorini* reviewed in the *Washington Post* in April under the headline '*The Final Adventure of Alistair MacLean*'. Heywood Hale

Brown, the writer, waxed lyrical about Alistair, comparing him to Sir Walter Scott as he had a similar *'primitive power of keeping the reader in suspense'*.

Of the novel he wrote:

Maclean's protagonists are unflappable and where many of us might be inclined to gulp and yammer at the discovery that atomic weaponry is making funny noises a few fathoms under us, the officers of HMS Ariadne are ready with classical allusions and light-hearted quips along with a fairly staggering electronic expertise.[17]

A few weeks later on 4 May 1987, Alistair's friends and relatives gathered at Daviot Church near Inverness. On a bright windy day they had come to celebrate his life. His father's old pulpit became the centre of the memorial service taken by the Reverend Lillian Bruce.

His elder brother, Ian and Tom Fraser, his life-long friend, read the lessons. 'The Lord's My Shepherd' the 23rd Psalm was sung to Crimond. The eulogy was delivered by Ian Chapman to a small gathering, Gisela with her sons Lachlan and Ali was there. His old shipmate from HMS *Royalist*, Charlie Dunbar was there. Brothers Ian and Gillespie and their wives Bunty and Margaret, David Bishop, his secretary Sabrina Carver and Ian Chapman, by then chairman of Collins, and his wife Marjory were there.

Alison Rapson from Muir of Ord, another Mod winner, sang in Gaelic *'I Love the Shepherd'*, the same song Alistair's mother had sung when she won the gold medal at the Mod of 1913.

Two granite stones are close to the kirk that recalls the MacLean family. The first is devoted to Alistair's father who was minister there. The second for his mother Mary Lamont MacLean and his brother Lachlan. Another name was added, that of Alistair Stuart MacLean, MA, D.Litt, author born Shettleston Glasgow, 21 April 1922, died Munich, Germany, 2 February 1987. And as in Switzerland, beneath this is part of Tennyson's poem *Ulysses* written in 1833 and published in 1842:
'*Come, my friends,*
Tis not too late to seek a newer world.'

Appendix 1

Alistair MacLean's books and their Second World War Content

Unless otherwise stated all Alistair MacLean's Books were published by Collins and in the United States by Doubleday.

HMS Ulysses
Published October 1955, 320 pages. Cover designed by John Rose, dedicated to Gisela. Entirely based on MacLean's time on the cruiser HMS *Royalist* 1943–1944 in operations supporting Arctic Convoys and against the German battleship *Tirpitz*. Also used material from other ships involved in these operations, most notably HMS *Trinidad* and events surrounding the ill-fated convoy PQ 17.

The film rights were quickly sold but to date *HMS Ulysses* has not been made into a film. The novel sold 250,000 copies in hardback in the UK within six months of publication, a record at the time.

The Guns of Navarone
Published 1957, 318 pages. Cover designed by John Rose, dedicated to Alistair's mother Mary Lamont MacLean. Largely based on events in the eastern Mediterranean in 1943 which Alistair heard about when his ship HMS *Royalist* operated in the same area of the Aegean Sea in 1944. The island of Navarone was created by Alistair, however, probably based on the island of Santorini which he placed close to the Turkish coast.

The film rights were quickly sold. Carl Foreman wrote and produced the 1961 film adaptation of the book starring Gregory Peck, David Niven, and Anthony Quinn.

South by Java Head
Published 1958, 320 pages. Cover designed by John Rose, dedicated to Alistair's brother Ian. Based on events immediately after the fall of Singapore to the Japanese early in 1942. Alistair was there in 1945 when

the Japanese surrendered and his ship HMS *Royalist* sailed the area where the book is set, and repatriated PoWs from camps back to Ceylon and Singapore for on-shipment to the UK.

The film rights were sold before publication and the sale was instrumental in the book being published at all, however it has not been made into a film. The book went on to sell over a million copies in hardback alone.

The Last Frontier

Published 1959, 319 pages. Cover design unknown dedicated to his brother Gilleasbuig. The first MacLean espionage story set in the Cold War. Inspired by the November 1956 Hungarian uprising which was crushed by the Soviet Red Army, however most of the characters have their roots firmly embedded in the Second World War. The hero Michael Reynolds, we are told *'had been the youngest subaltern in the S.O.E.'* p.225. The AVO in the novel the 'Hungarian Secret Police' p25, was clearly based on the AVH, The State Protection Authority, renowned for its brutality; it was dismantled in 1956.

The film rights were soon sold. The film appeared under the title *The Secret Ways*. It starred Richard Widmark, who also produced the film, was directed by Phil Karison and the heroine was played by Sonja Ziemann. It was the first adaptation of a MacLean story to be filmed, being released in April 1961, only weeks before *The Guns of Navarone*.

Night Without End

Published 1960, 256 pages. Cover design unknown dedicated to Bunty his sister-in-law, wife of Ian. A complete change of direction for MacLean set against the background of the growing air travel business, although in one of his favourite locations, the Arctic, this time on the Greenland Ice Cap. Another change is that the story is told in the first person. A BOAC airliner crashes near the base of a Scientific Research Team the IGY, International Geophysical Year Station. The team led by Peter Mason set out to rescue the survivors. However they find out the plane came down as a result of foul play. It is carrying a secret device which the criminals want. After many twists and turns the Navy comes to the rescue.

Again the film rights were sold quickly and Eric Ambler was paid to write a script, but the film was never made.

Fear is the Key

Published 1961, 234 pages. Cover design by John Keay dedicated to W.A. Murray, one of Alistair's fellow teachers at Gallowflat School known as 'WAM'. A fast moving thriller, with MacLean's trade mark of many twists and turns. John Talbot, the hero, has come out of the Second World War tired and embittered, even more so when his wife and child are lost in a Douglas DC-3 piloted by his twin brother. Together they had set up Trans Carib Air Charter, the airliner was shot down by a P.51 Mustang, another Second World War survivor, and crashes into the sea off Florida. Then a race develops to recover the gold the aircraft was carrying. The book and later film has a very long car chase, filmed in rural Louisiana. The film was released in 1972 directed by Michael Tuchner starring Barry Newman and Suzy Kendall.

Harper-Collins released a new edition of *Fear is the Key* in 2019 for which Lee Child wrote a Foreword where he observed that '*The Second World War changed everything....*' Well it certainly did for Alistair MacLean, and for the rest of his life he would remain rooted in it.

The Dark Crusader

The first book Alistair wrote under the pseudonym Ian Stuart. Published 1961, 223 pages. Cover designer unknown dedicated to Douglas and Violet (Dougie Seggie and his wife). MacLean used a pseudonym to prove he could write successfully under another name. The book in later editions was published under his real name. Another espionage thriller, John Bentall is sent to Australia to foil an attempt to steal the British missile Dark Crusader.

The film rights were sold in 1991 but no film has been made.

All about Lawrence of Arabia

Published 1962 by W.H. Allen, 177 pages, illustrated by Gil Walker but not dedicated. A gem of a book designed for the younger reader superbly illustrated. With two quotations from T.E. Lawrence's *Seven Pillars of Wisdom*

The Golden Rendezvous

Published 1962, 223 pages. Cover designer John Heseltine dedicated A.A. Lamont, Alistair's maternal grandfather. A rollicking thriller set onboard the cruise ship SS *Campari* in the West Indies. The ship gets involved in a revolution on a small island where she is moored. Several passengers head home, and when she does sail, sabotage begins to occur. Johnny Carter, the First Officer, and the book's hero turns to and sorts it all out. The book was a bestseller.

The film rights were sold and it came out in 1977 directed by Ashley Lazarus and Freddie Francis starring Richard Harris and Ann Turkel. It did not really follow the novel and was renamed the *Nuclear Terror.*

The Satan Bug

The second book published under the pseudonym Ian Stuart. Published 1962, 256 pages. Cover designer John Heseltine, dedicated to Bill Campbell one of Alistair's sailing friends. The key character Pierre Cavell, a former British soldier, is working undercover at Mordon Microbiological Research Establishment, clearly based on Porton Down, investigating some serious security incidents. It cumulates in a gang trying to poison the population of London, with nerve agents so that they can rob all the banks and museums; the plot is foiled by Cavell. The book was later released under the MacLean name. It would be the last time he used a pseudonym.

The book was loosely adapted as a 1965 film with the research establishment moved to the desert of Southern California. It was produced by John Sturges and James Clavell wrote the screenplay. It starred George Maharis, Richard Basehart and Anne Francis and was noted for an early appearance by Lee Remick as a nightclub waitress.

Ice Station Zebra

Published 1963, 255 pages. Cover designer John Heseltine, dedicated to Lachlan, Michael, and Alistair, MacLean's sons. The book is told in the first person from the point of view Dr Carpenter who is an undercover MI6 agent. The USS *Dolphin,* an atomic submarine, is ordered to take Carpenter under the North Polar ice-cap and surface near a burnt-out weather station called Zebra. A top secret film has been ejected from a satellite and has landed near the station. The film contains all the US launch sites of their missiles. However there are other agents equally keen to get hold of the film. Clearly influenced by the Cuban Missile Crisis and the early years of nuclear submarines, indeed Britain's first nuclear submarine HMS *Dreadnought* was commissioned on 17 April 1963.

In 1968, the film *Ice Station Zebra* was released produced by James C. Pratt, it was loosely based on the novel, the screen writers were Douglas Heyes, Harry Julian Fink, and W.R. Burnett. Even the submarine was renamed the USS *Tigerfish*. There was an all-star cast of Rock Hudson, Ernest Borgnine, Patrick McGoohan, and Jim Brown. Although at first not a great success, it has over the years become a classic Cold War thriller.

The accident/sabotage so vividly portrayed on the USS *Tigerfish* whereby the outer torpedo test cocks register closed when they are open, resulting in the submarine almost being lost. This may have been inspired by the sinking of HMS *Thetis* in June 1939 that sank in Liverpool Bay on trials. The accident happened after the inner hatch on the torpedo tube was opened while the outer hatch to the sea was open. Yet the test cock showed that the outer hatch was closed because it was seized in the closed position by some dried paint. Four men got off the submarine using the escape chamber but 99 were lost. A safety latch was designed known as the Thetis Clip, which allowed a torpedo hatch to open fractionally to check that it was not open to the sea before opening the hatch fully.

In the novel Alistair uses the first attempt to break through the ice cap as the dramatic danger to the submarine. They think they have found a thin spot but the USS *Dolphin* hits a layer of colder water masking thick ice. The attempts to flood the emergency tanks to slow the ascent sends the submarine racing for the bottom and before they can arrest descent she is over 400 feet deep.

This was the novel, after its delivery to Collins that Alistair told his publishers he was giving up writing to go into the hotel business.

When Eight Bells Toll

Published 1966, 223 pages. Cover designer unknown, dedicated to Paul and Xenia Townsend. This was Alistair's comeback novel after his brief fling as an hotelier.

A spy thriller set in the Western Isles of Scotland where Alistair had sailed so much. Vast sums of gold bullion are being hijacked from ships, one of which has disappeared in this area. Phillip Calvert of MI6 along with three other agents is sent to investigate. The other agents are murdered. The chief suspect is a Cypriot shipping magnet Sir Anthony Skouros and his gang. As usual there are lots of twists and turns, a Fleet Air Arm helicopter is shot down and Calvert barely escapes. However he manages to corner the gang alone and is rescued by the timely arrival of a detachment of Royal Marine Commandos put on the job by his boss Rear Admiral Sir Arthur Arnford-Jason, known affectionately as 'Uncle Arthur'. It is found Skouros was acting under duress by the pirates. The book has an excellent opening when Calvert is looking down the barrel of a Colt Peacemaker.

It was released as a film in 1971 produced by Elliot Kastner, which starred Anthony Hopkins as Calvert, Jack Hawkins as Skouros, and Robert Morley as 'Uncle Arthur' and Nathalie Delon as Charlotte. It was not a success.

Where Eagles Dare

Published 1967, 256 pages. Cover designer Ian Robertson, dedicated to Geoffrey and Gina Reeve. In this case Alistair, at the request of Elliot Kastner, wrote the screen play first. Although the novel came out more than a year before the film, none of the background of the screenplay or the novel was based on Alistair's wartime experiences. The novel is less violent than the film, and the characters more rounded, some have different names. Major Von Hapen is instead Captain Von Brauchitsch in the book. Also the group of Commandos are flown in by an RAF Lancaster whereas in the film it is a Junkers Ju 52. Some characters are killed by different people and in different ways.

The hugely successful film was produced by Elliot Kastner and Jerry Gershwin and was directed by Brian G. Hutton. Starred Richard Burton, Clint Eastwood, Mary Ure, Michael Hordern, Patrick Wymark and Derren Nesbitt. It featured outstanding special effects and some of the actors dubbed it 'Where Stuntmen Dare'.

Force 10 from Navarone

Published 1968, 254 pages. Cover design Norman Weaver dedicated to Lewis and Caroline Jenkins. A sequel to *The Guns of Navarone* thus partly based on Alistair's wartime experiences and starts where the first novel ended. It features four of the characters found in the first book: Mallory, Miller, Stavros and Captain Jensen. 'Force 10' is the codename of the operation. The team are joined by three Royal Marine Commandos and they parachute into Yugoslavia. There they aid the Partisans in the fight against the Nazis and their Chetnik Allies. There are lots of twists and turns but the main aim is to tie down as many German troops in Yugoslavia as possible and bring out some British agents.

It was adapted into a film in 1978 directed by Guy Hamilton and starring Robert Shaw, Harrison Ford, Barbara Bach, and Edward Fox. It shared little of the plot from the book and was not a success.

Author Sam Llewellyn wrote two authorised sequels. *Storm force from Navarone* 1996, an operation to destroy secret Nazi U-boat facilities in neutral Spain. And *Thunderbolt from Navarone* 1998, an operation to destroy Nazi experimental rockets the V3, based on the Greek island of Kynthos.

Puppet on a Chain

Published 1969, 255 pages. Cover design Hugh Marshall dedicated to Fred and Ina (?). Inspired by a visit to Amsterdam, with Geoffrey Reeve, the title came to Alistair when he saw a puppet hanging from a chain in a warehouse. The story centres on the drug trade in the Netherlands. Paul Sherman an Interpol Narcotics Bureau agent is brought in to take on a particularly vicious drugs gang. He has two attractive female agents to assist him. Even before he can leave the airport he sees a contact gunned down. The suspense continues at a pace.

Reeve would direct the 1972 film which was produced by Kurt Unger and starred Sven-Bertil Taube, Barbara Parkins, and Alexander Knox. The canal boat chase scenes were directed by Don Sharp. Even so the film was not a success.

Caravan to Vaccares

Published 1970, 304 pages. Cover designer Norman Weaver dedicated to Jean-Andre and Emanuela Charial. Originally written as a screenplay by Alistair for Elliot Kastner, the story's core is about Gypsies making a pilgrimage from all over Europe to Provence in the South of France, to the site of their patron saint, Sarah. There are many unexplained deaths so a British agent investigates and finds out about some age old Gypsy secrets.

In 1974 Geoffrey Reeve adapted it into a film which he directed and produced. It starred David Birney, Charlotte Rampling and Michael Lonsdale. It was not a success.

Bear Island

Published 1971, 288 pages. Cover designer Norman Weaver dedicated to Ian and Marjory Chapman. A murder mystery of the locked room type, but this time a remote island is the room. A film crew set off for Bear Island in the Barents Sea, back to Alistair's favourite location, in a beat-up fishing trawler. En route members of the ship's crew and film crew begin to die under mysterious circumstances. The key character Doctor Marlowe (was this a homage to Raymond Chandler, who Alistair so admired, using his character's name?) investigates but he is not what he seems. There is some Second World War content, as at the centre of the story is looted Nazi gold, brought to the island by a U-boat at the end of the war. It was a hugely successful book.

It was made into a 1979 film loosely based on the novel produced by Peter Snell and William Hill and directed and written by Don Sharp. With a star studded cast Donald Sutherland, Richard Widmark, Christopher Lee, Lloyd Bridges and Vanessa Redgrave. Despite having a hefty budget of almost ten million dollars it was not a success at the box office.

Captain Cook

Published 1972, 192 pages. Cover from the painting by John Webber depicting the death of Captain Cook, the artist accompanied Cook on his final voyage. No dedication. Cook was a boyhood hero to Alistair, although not a comprehensive biography it does cover his most important voyages well, and shows he had a stylish approach to non-fiction.

Alistair MacLean introduces Scotland

Published 1972 by Andre Deutsch edited by Alastair M. Dunnett, 256 pages. Alistair contributes a twelve page introduction to Scotland; it is a prime source for his views on his homeland. Various other writers contribute other sections such as Scotland from 1830, The Political Scene, The Thinking Scot etc. There are sixteen sections altogether.

The Way to Dusty Death

Published 1973, 222 pages. Cover design unknown dedicated to Mary Marcelle. Alistair now took on the world of Formula 1 motor racing, having got to know fellow Scot and world champion Jackie Stewart as they both lived in Switzerland. John Harlow the key character is an F1 champion after a devastating crash which caused the death of his best friend, along with the death of his younger brother earlier in the season. Harlow seems to have lost his nerve and has started to drink. His team boss wonders if he will get over it. However Harlow begins to investigate the accidents and finds they were not accidents. The story was first written as a screenplay to star Jackie Stewart and the film was to be produced by Alistair's second wife Marcelle, but it was not taken up.

Geoffrey Reeve did direct it as a TV Movie in 1995 starring Simon MacCorkindale as Johnny Harlow.

Breakheart Pass

Published 1974, 256 pages. Cover design unknown, dedicated to Mary Marcelle. The story was suggested to Alistair by Elliot Kastner. The story begins with a train moving through the Sierra Nevada Mountains in a blizzard in the 1870s. The mission of those on board is to relieve the garrison at Fort Humboldt where there has been an outbreak of cholera. However it soon becomes apparent this is not the only reason for the mercy mission. It was Alistair's first attempt at historical fiction.

In 1975 it was made into a film starring Charles Bronson, who was reportedly paid a million dollars plus ten per cent of the gross. It also starred Richard Crenna, Ben Johnson, and Jill Ireland and was produced by Kastner.

Circus

Published 1975, 224 pages. Cover design unknown, dedicated to Juan Ignacio. The story of a trapeze artist, whom the CIA persuades to lead a raid on the impregnable East German Lubylan Fortress as a laboratory inside has the formula for a new weapon which the CIA want. By this time Alistair had returned to writing in the third person narrative.

The Golden Gate

Published 1976, 246 pages. Cover design unknown, dedicated to Mary Marcelle. Criminals kidnap the President of the United States on the Golden Gate Bridge. FBI special agent Paul Revson rescues the President and other hostages. This was the first of three books Alistair would set in California. The film rights were sold but to date has not been made.

Seawitch

Published 1977, 286 pages. Cover design unknown, dedicated to Lachlan his son. Criminals in the pay of some unscrupulous oil barons are paid to destroy the offshore oil rig Seawitch in the Gulf of Mexico, which they intend to blow up with a stolen nuclear weapon. Private detectives Roomer and Mitchell set out to foil the plot and rescue the oil rig owner and his daughters, who the criminals intend to leave on the rig when they blow it up. Alistair wrote the novel in Mexico to avoid US taxes.

Goodbye California

Published 1977, 315 pages. Cover design unknown, dedicated to Gisela. Inspired by an earthquake Alistair felt in California he wrote in a preface to the book: *'It was at twenty seconds to six o'clock on the morning of 9 February 1972 that the earth shook. As such tremors go it could hardly even be called noteworthy.'* Yet it registered with him. Nuclear scientists are kidnapped along with radioactive material by Islamic terrorists, they plan to make a device to blow up one of California's cities. Detective Sergeant Ryder sets out to stop them hampered by the fact nobody believes this is happening.

Don Sharp tried to make a film of the book but failed.

Athabasca

Published 1980, 284 pages. Cover design unknown. A return to the Arctic for Alistair, producer Peter Snell who made the film *Bear Island* suggested the location would be a good setting for a novel. Set in the Oil Sands fields of Alaska and Canada. Threats of sabotage to the fields in the Prudhoe Bay area are investigated by Jim Brady when an operations manager is murdered.

River of Death

Published 1981, 192 pages. Cover design, Colin Thomas, dedicated to Gisela. A return to the Aegean and the Second World War, at least at the start when the SS are looting a Greek monastery, but switches to the Brazilian rainforests thirty years later as the key character Hamilton goes in search of ancient ruins deep in the jungle. However they discover a group of Nazis living there as if the Third Reich had never ended.

It was made into a film released in 1989. Produced by Avi Lerner, directed by Steve Carver and screenplay written by Andrew Deutsch and

Edward Simpson, it starred Michael Dudikoff, Robert Vaughn, Donald Pleasence, and Herbert Lom. It was not a success.

Partisans

Published 1982, 224 pages. Cover design Vicente Segrelles, dedicated to Avdo and Inge Cimic. Another book set entirely in the Second World War. Peter Peterson and his team of compatriots must cross war-torn Yugoslavia to deliver a secret message and unmask a double agent. The plot included elements from the screenplay of *Force 10 from Navarone*. However the book is set earlier in time, before the Allies have landed in Italy. It has a good description of Termoli on the Adriatic coast of Italy in the province of Campobasso, the nearest big city is Naples 90 miles to the west. The town also featured in *Force 10 from Navarone*.

Floodgate

Published 1983, 310 pages. Cover design unknown, dedicated to David and Judy Bishop. Terrorists blow up dykes in Holland causing the flooding of Amsterdam's Schiphol Airport; unless their demands are met, the withdrawal of British troops from Northern Ireland, they threaten to blow up more and bigger dykes. Dutch police officers infiltrate the mysterious gang known as the 'FFF'. The key character is police detective Peter Van Effen.

San Andreas

Published 1984, 285 pages. Cover design, Paul Wright, dedicated to David and Judy Bishop. Completely set in the Second World War, Alistair returns to the Arctic seas where *HMS Ulysses* was sunk. There is a long prologue of eleven pages where he pays tribute to the men of the Merchant Navy, and to the design and building of the *Liberty* ships, and he acknowledges the skill and determination of the German sailors, air crews, and U-boat crews who battled to stop the Russian convoys.

The story centres on the *San Andreas*, a former Liberty ship that is converted into a hospital ship. She had sailed to Murmansk to pick up British casualties in hospital there and bring them back to the UK. Some work still needs to be done on the conversion which Russian dockyard workers complete. At sea there are various mysterious breakdowns and her escort frigate is sunk, yet the Germans seem reluctant to fire on the hospital ship. After the captain is injured the key character, Bosun Archie McKinnon, has to take command. After various twists and turns and the uncovering of saboteurs on board, it is found the ship is carrying tons of Russian gold to pay for lend-lease items, which the Germans know about and want to capture, providing *San Andreas* does not get too close to the British coast, then they will sink the ship.

The book was met with critical acclaim that MacLean was back to his very best and was a best seller. In 2016 the film rights were acquired by a London production company hoping to adapt several of Alistair's books into a TV series, the first of which would be *San Andreas*.

The Lonely Sea
Published 1985, 222 pages. Cover design, Paul Wright, undedicated. Collins decided to bring out this book to mark the thirtieth anniversary of the association between Alistair MacLean and William Collins & Sons, they called it *Collected Short Stories*. It might have been more apt as *Collected Short Writings* as it is a mixture of fiction and non-fiction. There can be no denying here is some of Alistair's best writing. From the *Dileas* with which he won the *Glasgow Herald* competition that set him on his writing career, to his outstanding non-fiction pieces he wrote for the *Sunday Express* like *Rawalpindi* and the *City of Benares,* and then there is the comic tour-de-force *McCrimmon and the Blue Moonstones,* clearly taken from his own wartime experiences when HMS *Royalist* was being refitted in Alexandria.

HarperCollins reissued a new edition in 2009 with two more stories added to the collection *The Back Storm* and *The Good Samaritan.* For anybody beginning to read Alistair MacLean this is as good a place as any to begin.

Santorini
Published 1986, 224 pages. Cover design, Paul Wright, dedicated to Tom and Rena Fraser. Set in another of Alistair's favourite areas, the Aegean Sea. The Royal Navy ship HMS *Ariadne* is conducting a hydrographic survey near the island of Santorini when they witness a strategic bomber crash into the sea and, almost at the same time, a luxury cruiser catch fire. The plane is loaded with nuclear weapons. Commander Talbot and his

crew are soon in a race against time to recover one of the bombs that has been activated before it explodes and triggers the Volcano of Santorini.

The novel *Santorini* was still on the *New York Times* best sellers list weeks after Alistair MacLean had passed away.

Other authors have completed stories from Alistair MacLean outlines including:

1980	*Hostage Tower*	John Denis
1981	*Air Force One is Down*	John Denis
1989	*Death Train*	Alastair MacNeill
1989	*Night Watch*	Alastair MacNeill
1990	*Red Alert*	Alastair MacNeill
1991	*Time of the Assassins*	Alastair MacNeill
1992	*Golden Girl*	Simon Gandolfi

Appendix 2

Short Stories

The following two short stories demonstrate Alistair's skill as a story-teller with this most difficult of form. Different in style they nonetheless engage the reader from beginning to end and show him to be a master of the art.

It is not so hard to believe that this fine short story set Alistair MacLean on the road to fame and fortune as an author. It was published on 6 March 1954 in the *Glasgow Herald,* as the winner of the newspaper's short story competition; he received the princely sum of £100 as first prize, a significant amount for those times.

The Dileas

'Three hours gone, Mr MacLean, three hours, and never a word of the lifeboat.'

You can imagine just how it was. There were only the four of us there – Eachan, Torry Mor, old Grant, and myself. Talk? Never a word among the lot of us, nor even the heart of a dram – and there on the table, was a new bottle of Talisker, and Eachan not looking for a penny.

We just sat there like a lot of stookies, Seumas Grant with his expressionless face and yon wicked old pipe of his bubbling away, and the rest of us desperately busy with studying the pattern of the wallpaper. Listening to the screech of the wind we were, and the hail like chuckies battering against the windows of the hotel. *Dhia*! What a night that was! And the worst of it was, we couldn't do a thing but wait. My, but we were a right cheery crowd.

I think we all gave a wee bit jump when the telephone rang. Eachan hurried away and was back in a moment beaming all over. One look at yon great moonface of his and we felt as if the Pladda Lighthouse had been lifted off our backs.

'Four glasses, gentlemen, and see's over the Talisker. That was the lightkeeper at Creag Dearg. The Molly Ann got there in time – just. The puffer's gone, but all the crew were taken off.' He pushed the glasses over and looked straight at old Grant.

'Well, Seumas, what have you to say now? The Molly Ann got there – and Donald Archie and Lachlan away over by Scavaig. Perhaps you would be saying it's a miracle, eh, Seumas?'

There was no love lost between these two. I can tell you. Mind you, most of us were on Eachan's side. He was a hard man, was old Seumas Grant. Well respected right enough, but no one had any affection for him and, by Jove, he had none for us – none for anyone at all, except for Lachlan and Donald, his sons. For old Seumas, the sun rose to shine on them alone. His motherless sons: for them the croft, for them the boat, for them his every waking thought. But a hard man, Mr MacLean. Aloof and – what's the word? – remote. Kept himself to himself, you might say.

'It's a miracle when anyone is saved on a night like this, Eachan.' Old Grant's voice was slow and deep.

'But without Donald and Lachlan?' Eachan pressed. Torry, I remember shifted in his seat, and I looked away. We didn't care for this too much – it wasn't right.

'Big Neil's weel enough in his own way,' Grant said, kind of quiet. 'But he'll never be the lifeboat coxswain Lachie is – he hasn't got the feel of the sea.'

Just then the hotel door crashed open, nearly lifted off its hinges by the wind. Peter the Post came stumbling in, heaved the door shut and stood there glistening in his oilskins. It only required one look at him to see that something was far wrong. 'The lifeboat, Eachan, the Molly Ann!' he jerked out, very quick and urgent. 'Any word of her yet? Hurry man, Hurry!'

Eachan looked at him in surprise. 'Why surely, Peter. We've just heard. She's lying off Creag Dearg and...'

'Creag Dearg! Oh Dhia, Dhia, Dhia!' Peter the Post sank down into a chair and gazed dully into the fire. 'Twenty miles away – twenty miles. And here's Iain Chisholm just in from Tarbert farm – three miles in four minutes on yon big Velocette of his – to say that the Buidhe ferry is out in the middle of the sound, firing distress rockets. And the Molly Ann at Creag Dearg. *Mo chreach, mo chreach!*' He shook his head slowly from side to side.

'The ferry!' I said stupidly. 'The ferry! Big John must be smashed mad to take her out on a night like this!'

'And every boat in the fishing fleet sheltering up by Loch Torridon like enough,' said Torry bitterly.

There was a long silence, then old Grant was on his feet, still puffing away. 'All except mine, Torry Mor,' he said, buttoning up his oilskins. 'It's God's blessing that Donal' and Lachie went to Scavaig to look over the new drifter.' He stopped and looked slowly around. 'I'm thinking I'll be needing a bit hand.'

We just stared at him, and when Eachan spoke it was like a man in a stound. 'You mean you'll take the old tub out in this Seumas?' Eachan was staggered. 'Forty years old if she's a day – and the seas like houses roaring straight down the sound. Why, you'll be smashed to pieces, man before you're right clear of the harbour mouth.'

'Lachie would go.' Old Grant stared at the ground. 'He's the coxswain. He would go – and Dona'. I canna be letting my boys down.'

'It's suicide, Mr Grant,' I urged him. 'Like Eachan says. It's almost certain death.'

'There's no almost about it for the poor souls out on the ferry.' He reached for his sou'wester and turned to the door. 'Maybe I'll be managing right enough.'

Eachan flung the counter-flap up with a crash. 'You're a stiff-necked old fool, Seumas Grant,' he shouted angrily, 'and you'll roast in hell for your infernal pride.' He turned back and snatched a couple of bottles of brandy from the shelves. 'Maybe these'll come in handy,' he muttered to himself then stamped out of the door, growling deep in his throat and scowling something terrible.

Mind you, the *Dileas* – that was old Seumas Grant's boat – was a deal better than Eachan made her out to be. When Campbell of Ardrishaig built a Loch-Fyner, the timbers came out of the heart of the oak. And old Grant had added mild steel frames of his own and installed one of those new-fangled diesels-44 hp Gardner. I remember. But even so.

Outside the harbour wall – you couldn't imagine it and you'll never see the like, not even in your blackest nightmares. Bitter cold it was and the whistling sleet just flying lumps of ice that lanced your face open to the bone. And the Sound itself! Oh *Dhia*, that Sound! The seas were short and desperate steep, with the speed of racehorses, and the whole Sound a great sheet of driven milk gleaming in yon blackness. Man, it makes me shudder even now.

For two hours we headed straight up into it, and, Jove, what a hammering we took. The *Dileas* would totter up on a wave then, like she was falling over a cliff, smash down into the next trough with the crack of a four-inch gun, burying herself right to the gunwales. And at the same time you could hear the fierce clatter of her screw, clawing at the thin air. Why the *Dileas* never broke her back only God knows – or the ghost of Campbell of Ardrishaig.

'Are you seeing anything, boys?' It was old Grant shouting from the doghouse, the wind whipping the words off his lips. 'There's nothing Seumas,' Torry bawled back. 'Just nothing at all.'

I handed the spotlight, an ancient Aldis, over to Eachan and made my way aft. Seumas Grant, his hands light on the wheel, stood there quietly, his face a mask of blood – when yon great, seething comber had buried the *Dileas* and smashed in the window, he hadn't got out of the way quick enough. But the old eyes were calm, steady, and watchful as ever.

'It's no good, Mr Grant,' I shouted at him. 'We'll never find anyone tonight, and nothing could have lived so long in this. It's hopeless, just hopeless – the *Dileas* can't last out much longer. We might as well go back.'

He said something. I couldn't catch it, and bent forward. 'I was just wondering,' he said, like a man in a muse, 'whether Lachie would have turned back.' I backed slowly out of the wheelhouse, and I cursed Seumas Grant, I cursed him for that terrible love he bore for those two sons of his, for Donald Archie and Lachlan. And then – then I felt the shame, black and crawling, welling up inside me. And I cursed myself. Stumbling, I clawed my way for'ard again.

I was only halfway there when I heard Eachan shouting, his voice high and excited. 'There, Torry, look there! Just off the port bow. Somebody in the water – no, by God, two of them!'

When the *Dileas* heaved over the next crest, I looked along the beam of the Aldis. Eachan was right. There sure enough, were two dark forms struggling in the water. In three quick jumps I was back at the doghouse, pointing. Old Grant just nodded, and started edging the *Dileas* across. What a skill he had with him, that old one! Bring the bows too far around and we'd broach to and be gone in a second in yon great gullies between the waves. But old Seumas made never a mistake.

And then a miracle happened. Just that, Mr MacLean – a miracle. It was the Sea of Galilee all over again. Mind you, the waves were as terrible as ever, but just for a moment the wind dropped away to a deathly hush – and suddenly, off to the starboard, a thin, high-pitched wail came keening out of the darkness. In a flash, Torry had whipped his Aldis round, and the beam, plunging up and down, settled on a spot less than a hundred yards away – almost dead ahead. At first I thought it was just some wreckage, then I could see it was a couple of timber baulks and planks tied together. And lying on top of this makeshift raft – no, by God, lashed to it! – were a couple of children. We caught only flying glimpses of them: up one minute, down the next, playthings of the devil in yon madness of a sea. The poor wee souls. Oh *Dhia*! The poor wee souls.

'Mr Grant!' I roared in old Seumas's ear. 'There's a raft dead ahead – two wee children on it.'

The old eyes were quiet as ever. He just stared straight ahead his face was like a stone. 'I canna be picking up both,' he said his voice level and never a touch of feeling in it, damn his flinty heart. 'To come round in this would finish us – I'll have to quarter for the shelter of Seal Point to turn. Can the children be hanging on a while longer, do you think, Calum?'

'The children are near gone,' I said flatly. 'And they're not hanging on – they're lashed on.'

He looked quickly at me, his eyes narrowing. 'Lashed, did you say, Calum?' he asked softly. 'Lashed?'

I nodded without speaking. And then a strange thing happened, Mr MacLean, a strange thing indeed. Yon craggy old face of his broke into a smile – I can see yet the gleam of his teeth and the little rivers of blood running down his face – and he nodded several times as if in satisfaction and understanding...And he gave the wheel a wee bit spin to starboard.

The little raft was drifting down fast on us, and we had only the one chance of picking them up. But with old Seumas at the wheel that was enough, and Torry Mor, with one sweep of his great arm, had the children, raft and all, safely aboard.

We took them below and old Grant worked his way up to Seal Point. Then we came tearing down the Sound, steady as a rock – for in a heavy stern sea there's no boat on earth the equal of a Loch-Fyner – but never a trace of the two men did we see. A mile out from harbour old Seumas handed over to Torry Mor and came below to see the children.

They were sitting up on a bunk before the stove, wrapped in blankets – a lad of nine and a fair-haired wee lass of six. Pale, pale they were, and frightened and exhausted, but a good night's sleep would put them right.

Quietly I told old Grant what I'd learned. They'd been playing in a wee skiff, under the sheltered walls of the Buidhe harbour, when the boy had gone too near the entrance and the wind had plucked them out to the open Sound. But they had been seen, and the two men had come after them in the ferryboat: and then, they couldn't turn back. The rest they couldn't remember: the poor wee souls they'd been scared to death.

I was just finishing when Eachan came below. 'The wind's backing, Seumas, and the sea with it. Perhaps there's a chance for yon two – if they're swimmers at all – of being carried ashore.'

Old Seumas looked up. His face was tired, lined and-all of a sudden-old. 'There's no chance, Eachan, no chance at all.'

'How can you be sure, man?' Eachan argued. 'You never know.'

'I know, Eachan.' The old man's voice was a murmur, a million miles away. 'I know indeed. What was good enough for their old father was good enough for Donal' and Lachie. I never learned to swim – and neither did they.'

We were shocked into silence, I tell you. We looked at him stupidly, unbelievingly, then in horror.

'You mean' – I couldn't get the words out.

'It was Lachie and Donal' all right. I saw them.' Old Grant gazed sightlessly into the fire. 'They must have come back early from Scavaig.'

A whole minute passed before Eachan spoke, his voice wondering, halting. 'But Seumas, Seumas! Your own two boys, How could you –'

For the first and only time old Grant's self-control snapped. He cut in, his voice low and fierce, his eyes masked with pain and tears. 'And what would you have had me do, Eachan? Pick them up and let these wee souls go?'

He went on more slowly now. 'Can't you see, Eachan? They'd used the only bits of wood in yon old ferryboat to make a wee raft for the children. They knew what they were doing – and they knew, by doing it, that there was no hope for themselves. They did it deliberately, man. And if I hadn't picked the wee craturs up, it – it—'

His voice trailed off into silence, then we heard it again, the faintest shadow of a whisper. 'My two boys, Lachie and Donal' – oh Eachan, Eachan, I couldna be letting them down.'

Old Grant straightened, reached out for a bit of waste, and wiped the blood from his face – and, I'm thinking, the tears from his eyes. Then he picked up the wee girl, all wrapped in her blankets, set her on his knee and smiled down gently. 'Well, now, *mo ghaol*, and how would you be fancying a wee drop hot cocoa?'

* * *

This story appeared in the *The Lonely Sea* a collection of short stories published thirty years after *HMS Ulysses* in 1985. This story was a tribute to the men of the Minesweeping service.

They Sweep the Seas

It was still night when we cast off and nosed our way through the outer harbour, crammed with vessels of all sizes and nationalities, riding peacefully at anchor. Cold, grey rain was sluicing down mercilessly, spattering off our deck and churning the murky water to a light foam, and from the bridge, visibility scarcely extended beyond the trawler's bows. We felt, rather than saw, our way out to the open sea, barely making headway. We brushed along the side of a sister trawler, and farther on felt our hull scraping over an anchor cable, the black hulk of the ship's bows looming perilously near. Approaching the entrance, and feeling reasonably safe, we increased speed, and all but collided with a big Finnish freighter, which had worked with the tide across the harbour mouth; it was the word 'SUOMI', painted in six-foot high letters, gleaming whitely through the darkness, that gave us warning. Our skipper cursed fluently, spun the wheel to starboard, and we passed on. But we reached the sea without mishap.

In the harbour, it had been comparatively warm and sheltered, but a very different state of affairs existed beyond the headland. The trawler pitched wickedly in the long, heavy rollers coming in from the Atlantic, drenching itself in spray. Sometimes an exceptionally heavy sea foamed along fo'c'sle high, poured into the well, slid over the deck, and went gurgling through the scuppers; but this did not happen often. The wind was not strong, but possessed that biting quality which makes one raise one's coat collar and withdraw, hurriedly, to the lee-side of the upper deck. There are few bleaker and more cheerless places than the west coast of Scotland in the early morning of a January day.

As the trawler went butting through the seas, in the chill grey of the breaking dawn, to its appointed station, the two officers on the bridge discussed the prospects of the coming sweep. Both agreed that it would be a trying day, that it would be as boring as ever, and that they would, as usual, encounter no mines. They disagreed, however, concerning the weather: the Lieutenant thought there was little chance of the wind dying down or the weather moderating; but the skipper was of the opinion that both would come to pass, although, probably, later in the day.

Neither the Lieutenant nor the skipper was a young man. The Lieutenant (RNR) wore three rows of ribbon, had been in the Dardanelles in the last war, and walked with a pronounced limp – a memento of Zeebrugge. He had retired ten years ago, but at the outbreak of war had left his comfortable, even luxurious, existence for the unknown perils and hardships of a minesweeper's existence. He did not do this as a favour to his country: he did it as his duty.

The Lieutenant, as has been said, was not a young man, but the skipper was at least ten years older. Half a century had passed since he first went down to the sea. He had swept mines in the war of 1914–18, but had considered himself, not unnaturally, too old for such an arduous task in this. Then one day, while trawling in the North Sea, he had been bombed and machine-gunned by a Heinkel. The bombs had missed, but the bullets had literally riddled one of his crew. That man was his son. And so he had changed his mind about being too old.

An hour after clearing the harbour mouth, we reached the beginning of our beat and cut the engines until the trawler had barely enough way to keep head on to the seas. We were awaiting the arrival of our companion sweeper, who made her appearance some ten minutes later, pitching heavily up on our starboard quarter, a vague shape in the dim half-light.

We drifted a light line astern and she altered her course to port, to pick it up. A wire was attached to this; we hauled it aboard our own trawler, attached the sweep wire to it, and paid it out astern again. At regular intervals, peculiarly shaped objects, professionally known as 'Kites', were shackled to the hawser by two seamen, whose stoic features betrayed no signs of the extreme discomfort they must have been experiencing from their raw hands and stiff, cold-benumbed fingers. These 'Kites' acted as weights upon the sweep wire, keeping it at the requisite distance beneath the surface of the water.

No landlubber or 'freshwater' man could have performed this task of paying out the sweep wire; it was an operation that demanded the very highest standards of seamanship. The co-ordination and sense of timing of the man at the wheel, the two 'shacklers', and, above all, the winch-driver, were marvellous to a degree. They worked as smoothly and as swiftly as the well-oiled, correlated cogs of an intricate machine.

Everything adjusted to his satisfaction, our Lieutenant signalled, by siren, to the other trawler that he was ready to commence his sweep. She acknowledged his signal, swept round to our starboard beam, and off we went, beating southwards. It was becoming rougher, and the Lieutenant, studiously avoiding the skipper's eye, was smiling with ill-concealed satisfaction. It was not often that the skipper's weather forecasts proved false, but this time, for once, he seemed to have slipped up.

We were broadside on to the seas now, one moment lifting over a sullen, spume-capped crest, the next sliding along a shallow trough, clouds of icy spray cascading inboard. The pitching had given place to a rather unpleasant rolling motion, the latter being a decided change for the worse. It was now that the genius – and genius it was – of the winch-driver asserted itself. His job was to see that the sweep wire did not become too slack, which would have been bad enough, or become too taut, which might have resulted in tragedy. Sailors have, with good reason, a holy dread of overstrained hawsers. A snapped wire is a lethal weapon, and its power of destruction is rather terrifying; such a wire can slice off a man's head far more efficiently than the sharpest axe. But, judging from our winch-driver's nonchalance and the deceptively careless ease with which he manipulated the levers, one would have thought that no such unpleasant possibility had ever occurred to him.

On the bridge, the Lieutenant was poring over a minutely detailed Admiralty chart spread open before him. Also consulting it, but with a much lesser degree of concentration, was the skipper, who only did it that he might not hurt the feelings of the Lieutenant, for whom he entertained a very high regard. Privately, however, he held Admiralty charts and all such inessentials in a mighty contempt, and considered them unworthy of a real sailor. He had never needed a chart; a torn, finger-stained school atlas had served his purpose equally well.

When the Lieutenant judged we had reached the end of our beat, he pulled on the siren lanyard, and the other trawler cut her speed down to a mere crawl; whereas we continued at full speed and came sweeping round in a full half-circle, a manoeuvre which, though apparently simple, like all else in minesweeping, was, in actuality, a brilliantly executed bit of seamanship. One might have been excused for thinking that we had been hauled round by centripetal force, our companion trawler acting as the pivot and the sweep wire as the connecting link, so high a state of perfection had the co-ordination existing between the two trawlers reached.

All morning we continued in this fashion, beating up and down and gradually working our way westward. The wind, in the meantime, had veered from the west to north-by-west, and, though not becoming any stronger, had become exceedingly cold. At this juncture, we began to feel truly sorry for the winchman, exposed, as he was, to the full force of the elements, but consoled ourselves with the thought that he was specially adapted for resisting the cold, owing to his enormous girth.   We were surprised to learn, however, that he was of normal proportions but wore no fewer than five overcoats under his oilskins and life jacket. But this may merely have been malicious rumour and we never received any confirmation as to its truth. Suffice it to say that his attitude, regarding the weather, of the completest unconcern, was Spartan to a degree.

If he was, undeniably, the most important member of the crew, the second most, equally without doubt, was the cook. Balancing himself with a marvellous agility, born of long and arduous practice, he made his appearance at regular intervals – never exceeding three-quarters of an hour – bearing, in the one hand, a large and much-battered iron kettle, and in the other, a motley assortment of tin mugs, joined together by a strand of wire passed through their handles. The kettle was filled, alternately, with strong, sweet tea and cocoa, and the contents surpassed, we were of the opinion, anything we had ever experienced in the finest of city restaurants. Apparently coffee does not find favour in the eyes of the crews of minesweepers.

Minesweeping is a dreadfully monotonous business, but we managed to pass the time tolerably well by smoking, spinning yarns, and drinking the cook's concoctions. In the early morning, a huge, four-engined flying boat of the Coastal Command passed directly overhead, acknowledging our humble presence by dipping graciously in salute, at which we felt highly flattered. About noon, a small convoy appeared on the southern horizon, but was gone within half an hour. Occasionally, gulls or wild duck flew overhead, and twice we saw the round, black, glistening head of a particularly venturesome seal emerge from a nearby wave, stare at us coldly and dispassionately, after the manner of its kind, then sink beneath the waves with an expression of disgust on its face. But noteworthy incidents were non-existent, and we gradually settled down into a state of wakeful boredom.

About two o'clock in the afternoon, when conversation had languished and died, and we were conjuring up fanciful visions of what we should have for our evening meal, our dreams were abruptly shattered by a loud, incoherent, but unmistakably triumphant cry from our indefatigable winch-driver. We dashed to the starboard side of our vessel and scanned the stretch of water under which the sweep wire was passing, eagerly awaiting the first appearance of the mine – as mine it must be. We could see nothing: neither had our winch-driver seen anything, but he had felt some foreign body making contact with the sweep wire – and he was far too experienced a man to make a mistake.

It was a tense moment, holding, as it did, two distinct possibilities regarding the immediate future of the mine – one unpleasant, the other not so. (Parenthetically, it speaks well for our faith in our winch-driver that we never doubted the existence of the mine.) In the first case, our sweep wire might foul the detonating mechanism of the mine, which would forthwith blow up, in which event our sweep wire would be almost inevitably destroyed. Moreover, we had no means of knowing how close the mine was to one or other of our trawlers, and it was far from improbable that the explosion of the mine would entail our own or our companion sweeper's destruction. Such things had happened before. The other and infinitely more pleasing possibility was that the mine would be drawn on to one of the cutters, be severed from its anchorage, and float harmlessly to the surface. To our immense relief, it was the latter that came to pass.

At a spot that was almost mathematically equidistant between the two trawlers, the mine rose slowly to the surface and remained there, rising and falling sluggishly with the seas, an evil-looking, murderous spheroid of black steel, about three feet in diameter, liberally covered with knobs. These knobs, when broken, set the detonating mechanism in action and explode the mine. We steamed on for some distance farther, in order to carry the sweep well out of the mine's reach, and, almost before we had stopped, two of the crew had their rifles out and were firing at the mine, patently bent on its early despatch and eager to witness the explosion and its spectacular after-effects. In their laudable efforts they were nobly supported by the crew of the other trawler.

After about a score of ineffectual shots had been fired by each trawler, it became evident that the disposal of the mine was going to be a by no means simple matter. The heaving decks of the trawlers, combined with the fact that the target was not static, made for very inaccurate shooting. Still, persistency had its own due, if not very satisfying, reward, for, after another ten minutes, the mine sank to the floor of the sea, riddled with bullets, none of which had the luck to impinge on any of the detonators. Although our object had been accomplished and the mine rendered harmless to shipping, one and all were grievously disappointed at the mine's inglorious end, having been pardonably desirous of witnessing a more dramatic finale. With a glow of inward satisfaction, not unmixed with a slight feeling of frustration, we returned to our posts and resumed operations.

Contrary to popular conception, minesweepers do not sweep up and explode dozens of mines every day. Long weeks may pass without so much as the sight of a mine; this was, accordingly, a red-letter day for the crew of our trawler. We had already nine white-painted chevrons adorning our long black funnel, signifying that we had destroyed that number of mines; already the ship's artist was ferreting out his paint and brush, preparatory to painting our tenth chevron when we should reach port or the weather moderate sufficiently to permit of it.

Towards evening the skies began to clear, the wind backed round to the westward again, and the rough, wind-swept seas gradually calmed down to a gentle swell. If the Lieutenant felt chagrined at his interrupted success as a weather prophet, he concealed his feelings remarkably well; probably, however, the excitement and success of the early afternoon had driven all thought of it from his mind. Some time later the cloudbanks to the west lifted, and, for the first time that day, we saw the sun, an enormous ball of dull red, its circumference very clearly etched through the low-lying winter haze.

Half an hour later, the sun dipped slowly below the south-western horizon, laying a broken path of crimson over the sea to our ship. Soon after, as the light was failing and we had the better part of twenty miles to go before we reached our home port, the Lieutenant signalled to our companion trawler to cease operations and disconnect the sweep wire. We hauled it aboard; unshackled the 'Kites' and stowed them carefully away, we then turned the trawler's bows towards the east, for the first time that day, and set course for home through the swiftly gathering darkness.

The day's work was done. The skipper, his hands gently caressing the wheel, was talking quietly to the Lieutenant, relaxed on a disreputable camp stool, his back against the bulkhead, his hands behind his head. Down below, the cook, his labours over, was lying on his bunk, reading a detective novelette. The winch-driver, impervious, as ever, to the icy wind which still blew, had not stirred from his post, but was dreamily regarding our slightly phosphorescent wake, watching it recede gradually into the darkness. A couple of men were sheltering from the following wind in the well-deck before the bridge, quietly smoking. Yet another two men were on the bridge-deck, steadying a ladder, on the top of which was perched a man for whom the slight pitching of the ship, the insufficient light, and the chilly night wind were proving no deterrent in the execution of his task. To him, art was all. He was painting our tenth chevron on the funnel...

Words cannot adequately express what we owe to these men – fishermen all, from the Hebrides and Mallaig, Wick and Peterhead, Aberdeen and Grimsby, Lowestoft and Yarmouth. Call them heroes, and they would jeer at you: yet they are nothing else. Theirs is, at once, the most lonely, monotonous, and dangerous of all our Empire Forces' tasks, and one indispensable for the maintenance of danger-free sea-lanes for the Merchant Service, our lifeline with the world beyond. They put to sea in the morning, gay or grave according to their wont...and some to not return. But they close their ranks, and carry on.

Notes

The following abbreviations have been used:

Imperial War Museum IWM
Naval History Net NHN
The National Archives KEW TNA
National Museum of the Royal Navy Portsmouth NMRN
Royal Navy Research Archive RNRA

All references to Alistair MacLean's books are taken from Collins 1st Editions, unless otherwise stated.

Chapter One: Life before the Navy

1. Alistair MacLean, *Introduces Scotland*, pp.9–10, 'This land...'
2. Jack Webster, *Alistair MacLean*, pp.16–17, 'The approval of...'
3. Alan Ereira, *The Invergordon Mutiny*, pp.31–32, 'Included in the...'
4. Max Arthur, *Lost Voices of the Royal Navy*, pp.172–174, 'I joined HMS...'
5. Alistair MacLean, *HMS Ulysses*, p.246, 'To officer commanding...'
6. Ereira, pp.90–92, 'According to...'
7. Admiral-of-the-Fleet Andrew Browne Cunningham, *A Sailor's Odyssey...*' pp.150–151, 'At Chatham...
8. MacLean, *HMS Ulysses*, p.246, 'To officer commanding...'
9. Fred de Vries, alistairmaclean.blog
10. Webster, p.24, 'Meanwhile the boys...'
11. MacLean, *Introduces Scotland*, pp.10–11, 'You're no better...'

Chapter Two: Joining up

1. MacLean, *Introduces Scotland*, p.15, 'As my father...
2. Ibid, p.11, 'To me, the...'
3. Charles Causley, *Hands to Dance and Skylark*, p.38, 'During the first...'
4. TNA/INF 1/293, 5 December 1941
5. BBC Peoples' War Article A7469157 2/2/2005
6. NMRN Bowman 7/8/1940
7. RNRA HMS *Vernon* November 1942 & *Naval Ratings Handbook*, pp.42–46, 'Hammocks...'
8. MacLean, *San Andreas*, p.243, 'You know all right...'
9. MacLean. *The Lonely Sea, They Sweep the Seas*, p. 150, 'Neither the Lieutenant...'
10. Kenneth Poolman, *The British Sailor*, pp.85–86, 'We formed convoy...'
11. MacLean, *HMS Ulysses*, p.239, 'Me? Ach, there's...'
12. oldglasgow.tumbir.com

Chapter Three: HMS Royalist

1. TNA/ADM 196/119/164
2. Glyn Prysor, *Citizen Sailor*, p.122, 'When they joined...'
3. M.J. Whiteley, *Cruisers of WWII*, pp.118–119, 'Modified Dido Class...'
4. MacLean, *HMS Ulysses*, p.35, 'Technically...'
5. Alan Raven and John Roberts, *British Cruisers of WWII*, pp.294–324
6. MacLean, *HMS Ulysses*, p.24, 'Easy, boy, easy...'
7. NHN, Geoffrey B. Mason, HMS *Royalist*
8. BR. 1938, *Naval Ratings Hand Book*, pp.58–60, 'Advancement.'
9. Ibid, p.47, 'Leave & Liberty'.
10. MacLean, *Introduces Scotland*, p.17, 'In more recent...'
11. MacLean, *The Lonely Sea*, Bismarck, p.66, 'She was indeed...'
12. S.W. Roskill, *The War at Sea Volume II*, p.115–116, 'The readiness for...'
13. Winston Churchill, *The Second World War Volume 3, The Grand Alliance*, p.461, 'On August 25...'
14. *The Times*, 4 April 1942.
15. MacLean, *HMS Ulysses*, pp.56–58, 'This is the...'
16. Ibid, p.127, 'The padre had...'
17. Henry Denham, *Inside the Nazi Ring*, pp.91–92, 'Telegram 'C'...'
18. Donald McLachlan, *Room 39*, p.283, 'A further complication...'
19. MacLean, *HMS Ulysses*, p.260 'Why all the...'
20. Ibid, p.261, 'Authors note....'
21. TNA/ADM, Battle summary No 29 attack on *Tirpitz* by midget submarines, 22/9/1943

Chapter Four: March–May 1944, Northern Waters

1. MacLean, *HMS Ulysses*, p.12, 'Tyndall-universally...'
2. TNA/ADM 116/5468 29/1/1944 & John Sweetman, *Tirpitz*, p.85, 'On 9 February...'
3. IWM, Department Documents, Lieutenant Richard Walker 1–3 April 1944
4. TNA/ADM 116/5468 4/4/1944
5. Kenneth Poolman, *Escort Carrier*, p.129, 'JW 58 in fact...'
6. Prysor, *Citizen Sailors*, p.340, 'The Royal Navy...'
7. Webster, *Alistair MacLean*, p.39, 'Though he did...'
8. NHN, April 1944
9. Webster, *Alistair MacLean*, p.38, 'Tom Brown, an...'
10. NHN, May 1944
11. MacLean, *San Andreas*, p.17, 'But, oddly enough...'
12. NHN, May 1944
13. MacLean, *HMS Ulysses*, p.75, 'We're for it...'
14. Ibid, pp.75–76, 'It was a...'
15. Frank Pearce, *The Ship that Torpedoed Itself*, pp.58–59, 'The sea rose...'
16. Arthur, *Lost Voices of the Royal Navy*, pp.385–392, 'I joined Impulsive...'
17. MacLean, *HMS Ulysses*, p.125 'Tyndall opened...'
18. Ibid, p.65, 'And so the...'
19. MacLean, *San Andreas*, p.11, 'The foregoing may...'
20. MacLean, *HMS Ulysses*, p.55, 'Old Socrates says...'
21. Ibid, p.277, 'The water level...'
22. Arthur, *Lost Voices of the Royal Navy*, p.337, 'I was one...'
23. Pearce, *The Ship that Torpedoed Itself*, pp.77–81, 'The disaster was...'
24. IWM/ Department Documents, Peter Cockrell February 1945

25. MacLean, *HMS Ulysses*, p.56, 'This is the...'
26. TNA/ADM 196/119/164

Chapter Five: July–September 1944, Western Mediterranean

1. Norman Lewis, *Naples 44*, p.26, 'October 6 ...'
2. Ibid, pp.157–158, 'July 24...'
3. MacLean, *The Lonely Sea*, pp.183–184, 'I knocked and...'
4. John Steinbeck, *Once there was a War*, pp.145–146, 'The Lady Packs...'
5. Churchill, *The Second World War Vol 5, Closing the Ring*, pp.75–77, 'I emphasised that...'
6. MacLean, *Force 10 from Navarone*, pp.38–39, 'Of course I ...'
7. Anthony Tucker-Jones, *Operation Dragoon*, pp.11–12, 'Stalin approved of...'
8. MacLean, *San Andreas*, p.16, 'The Heinkel III...'
9. Fitzroy MacLean, *Eastern Approaches*, p.465, 'The Prime Minister....'
10. Ibid, p.467 'It was then...
11. Winston S. Churchill to Clementine Churchill 17 August 1944, Tucker-Jones, *Operation Dragoon*, p.107, 'Always with an eye...'
12. S.W. Roskill, *The War at Sea Vol III*, p.99, 'Admiral Troubridge's escort...' & IWM/ 10818 p.2 August 1944
13. MacLean, *Partisans*, pp.38–39, 'Some twelve kilometres...'
14. MacLean, *Force 10 from Navarone*, pp.26–27, 'Miller was given...'
15. Ibid, p. 28, 'The room was...'
16. Major J.C. Beadle, *The Light Blue Lanyard*, pp.55–72, 'The Battle for Termoli...'
17. MacLean, *Partisans*, pp.40–41, 'That'll do...'

Chapter Six: Churchill's Folly

1. Sir Hughe Knatchbull-Hugessen, *Diplomat in Peace and War*, p. 186, 'I reached Ankara...'
2. Ibid, p.185, 'The purpose...'
3. Ibid, p.190, 'It seemed to be...'
4. TNA/KV 6/8 p3-4
5. Franz von Papen, *Memoirs*, p.511, 'It needed...'
6. Mark Simmons see, *Agent Cicero*, for a fuller explanation of the case & TNA/KV 6/8 16
7. Churchill, *The Second World War Vol 5, Closing the Ring*, p.182
8. Gavin Mortimer, *The SBS in World War II*, pp.80–82, 'Middle East HQ...'
9. MacLean, *The Guns of Navarone*, p.224, 'Even if he...'
10. TNA/AIR 41/53
11. TNA/FO 954132
12. Anthony Rogers, *Churchill's Folly*, p.80, 'Next day...'
13. Ibid, pp.164–165, 'Meanwhile, at....'
14. Ibid, pp.165–166, 'At the range...'
15. Ibid, pp.126–128, 'Fortress Headquarters...'
16. MacLean, *The Guns of Navarone*, p.14, 'I don't have...'
17. Rogers, *Churchill's Folly*, p.133, 'On vendetta...'
18. Ibid, p.81, 'Two days later...'
19. MacLean, *The Guns of Navarone*, p.17, 'But the Navy...'

Chapter Seven: September–October 1944, The Aegean

1. IWM/ Ships Orders p.2, September 1944
2. MacLean, *The Lonely Sea*, p.133, 'HMS Ilara had...'
3. Ibid, p.144, 'About 7 am...'

4. Poolman, *The British Sailor*, p.153, '*Leaving a care...*'
5. Roskill, *The War at Sea Vol III*, pp.115–116, '*Between the end...*'
6. IWM/ Ships orders p.2, October 1944
7. Roskill, *The War at Sea Vol III*, p.116, '*Nor did air...*'
8. Max Arthur, *Men of the Red Beret*, p.263, '*Our task was...*'
9. Ibid, p.268, '*Soon after...*'

Chapter Eight: Navarone

1. MacLean, Companion Book Club introduction to *The Guns of Navarone*.
2. Ibid, *The Guns of Navarone*, p.21, '*There are others...*'
3. Ibid, Companion Book Club introduction
4. Ibid, *The Guns of Navarone*, p.19, '*These guns are...*'
5. Peter Schenk, *The Invasion of England*, pp.324–325, [ranges on German Artillery]
6. MacLean, Companion Book Club introduction
7. Ibid, *The Guns of Navarone*, pp.13–14, '*Neither of them...*'
8. Ibid, p.33, '*The clamour of...*' The island of Castellorizo was used as the setting for the 1991 Italian war comedy film *Mediterraneo* directed by Gabriele Salvatores and set during World War II, about a group of Italian soldiers stranded on a Greek Island and bypassed by the war.
9. MacLean, *The Guns of Navarone*, p.46, '*But-but those...*'
10. Ibid, p.49, '*Three hours later...*'
11. Ibid, p.71, '*I asked you...*'
12. Ibid, Companion Book Club introduction
13. Ibid, *The Guns of Navarone*, pp. 23, 135, 138–139, There are plenty of details of the geography in the novel
14. Mortimer, *The SBS in World War II*, p. 158–160, '*Sutherland told Lassen...*'
15. MacLean, *Introduces Scotland*, p.9, '*This last prerequisite...*'

Chapter Nine: Portsmouth, November 1944

1. IWM/Ships orders p.2, October-November 1944.
2. Bob Hind, *The Portsmouth News*, 21 January 2021.
3. Charles Owen, *Plain Yarns from the Fleet*, pp.92–95, '*It would have...*'
4. Webster, *Alistair MacLean*, p.40, '*Before the Royalist...*'
5. IWM/Ships orders p.2, November 1944.
6. MacLean, *HMS Ulysses*, p.58, '*I know what...*'
7. Ibid, p.130, '*The first shell...*'
8. Webster, *Alistair MacLean*, pp.40–41, '*When the ship...*'
9. Alistair MacLean, *Captain Cook*, p.18, '*Only two things...*'

Chapter Ten: Alexandria, December 1944–February 1945

1. Cunningham, *A Sailor's Odyssey*, p.297, '*Only two things...*'
2. Causley, *Hands to Dance and Skylark*, p.29, '*A night in Alex...*'
3. Ernle Bradford, *Ulysses Found*, p.vii, '*My guest for...*'
4. MacLean, *The Lonely Sea, McCrimmon and the Blue Moonstones*, p.134, '*The information...*'
5. Ibid, p.133, '*The wind was...*'
6. Christopher Landon, *Ice Cold in Alex*, p.1, '*They served it...*'
7. MacLean, *The Guns of Navarone*, p.22, '*They travelled in...*'
8. MacLean, *The Lonely Sea*, pp.134–135, '*His appointment...*'
9. Ibid, pp.135–136, '*An hour passed...*'

10. *The Observer,* 5 September 1971.
11. MacLean, *The Lonely Sea,* p.137, '*As the street...*'
12. Ibid, p.138, '*Mohammed Ali...*'
13. Webster, *Alistair MacLean,* p.42, '*In south-west...*'
14. MacLean, *The Lonely Sea,* p.141, '*Satisfied that...*'
15. Ibid, p.141, '*On arrival at...*'
16. Ibid, p.141, '*McCrimmon ground...*'
17. Ibid, p.142, '*McCrimmon, who probably...*'
18. Ibid, pp.143–144, '*Some time after...*'
19. Ibid, pp.144–145, '*On the following...*'
20. Causley, *Hands to Dance and Skylark,* pp.30–32, '*Have you ever...*'
21. Scuttlebutt: term for Gossip; the original scuttlebutt was an open fresh water cask located between decks which served as a focal point for sailors to talk and exchange gossip; used more in the United States Navy.
22. Churchill, *The Second World War Vol 4, The Hinge of Fate,* p.219, '*I did not attempt...*'
23. MacLean, *Tobruk,* p.67, '*It wasn't only...*'
24. IWM/ Ships orders February–March 1945.

Chapter Eleven: March-August 1945, Far East

1. IWM/ Department of Documents, Pollard, '*Trincomalee a dump...*'
2. Roskill, *The War at Sea Vol III,* p.317, '*Throughout April...*' & NHN Eastern Fleet March–April 1945.
3. Rick Jolly, *Jackspeak: A Guide to British Naval Slang and Usage,* p. 485, '*Uckers. The old family game of ludo, modified by Jack to include strategy and tactics, and played at all levels throughout the Royal Navy.....*'
4. Webster, *Alistair MacLean,* pp.41–42 '*On shore visits...*'
5. IWM/ Department of Documents Captain M.L. Power 20 May 1945.
6. Ibid, Power 20 May 1945.
7. Webster, *Alistair MacLean,* p.42, '*Sailing into shark...*'
8. MacLean, *South by Java Head,* p.51, '*You're right sir...*'

Chapter Twelve: September–November 1945, Singapore

1. Roskill, *The War at Sea Vol III,* pp.366–367, '*Meanwhile the...*'
2. Ibid, pp.382–383, '*On the 15th...*'
3. Prysor, *Citizen Sailors,* p.460, '*Two days...*'
4. Ibid, p.460, '*The streets of..*'
5. IWM/ Ships orders October–November 1945.
6. Geoffrey Brooke, *Singapore's Dunkirk,* p.1, '*Much is known...*'
7. MacLean, *South By Java Head,* p.30, '*At ease corporal...*'
8. Brooke, *Singapore's Dunkirk,* pp.135–146, '*A few sinkings...*'
9. MacLean, *South by Java Head,* pp.260–265, '*When Nicolson awoke...*'
10. Ibid, p.18, '*The Colonel didn't...*'
11. Webster, *Alistair MacLean,* p.45, '*Though there were...*'
12. IWM/ Ships orders October 1945.

Chapter Thirteen: Demob

1. IWM/ Ships orders December 1945.
2. Ibid, January 1946.
3. NHN/ HMS *Royalist* p.3 Postwar notes.

4. Causley, *Hands to Dance and Skylark*, p.164, '*I disliked life…*'
5. Webster, *Alistair MacLean*, p.48, '*After the match…*'
6. BHO, British History Centre the University of Cambridge Epilogue 1939–1956.
7. *The Scotsman* 29/3/2004 & *Daily Telegraph*, 14/12/2008, Ian Hamilton, *Stone of Destiny*.
8. MacLean, *Introducing Scotland*, p.20–21, '*One can hardly…*'

Chapter Fourteen: The Short Stories 1954

1. Webster, *Alistair MacLean*, pp.55–56, '*He wasted his…*'
2. Mark Brackenbury, *Scottish West Coast Pilot*, p.122, '*Loch Gairloch…*'
3. MacLean, *Blackwood Magazine*, 1953, *The Cruise of the Golden Girl*.
4. Ibid, '*The first problem…*'
5. Ibid, '*Four hours after…*'
6. Ibid, '*As we rounded…*'
7. Robert Louis Stevenson, *Kidnapped*, p.118, '*I was on my feet…*'
8. MacLean, *Blackwood Magazine*, *The Cruise of the Golden Girl*, '*In the three…*'
9. Brackenbury, *Scottish West Coast Pilot*, p.26, '*The Crinan Canal…*'
10. MacLean, *Blackwood Magazine*, *The Cruise of the Golden Girl*, '*Our anchor rattled…*'
11. MacLean, *The Lonely Sea, They Sweep the Seas*, pp.149–150, '*In the harbour…*'
12. Webster, *Alistair MacLean*, pp.59–60, '*MacLean and Seggie…*'
13. MacLean, *The Lonely Sea, The Dileas*, p.12, '*Mind you, the…*'
14. *The Glasgow Herald*, Ian Chapman obituary 9 December 2019.
15. Mark Simmons, *Ian Fleming's War*, pp.233–234, '*His biographers disagree…*'

Chapter Fifteen: The First Three War Novels 1955–1958

1. MacLean, *HMS Ulysses*, p.9, '*Prelude, Sunday afternoon…*'
2. Webster, *Alistair MacLean*, p.70, '*The Chapmans…*'
3. Ibid, p.72, '*What grated more…*'
4. *Los Angeles Times*, 17 December 1972, Jain Johnston, '*War is hell but it pays off for MacLean…*'
5. Webster, *Alistair MacLean*, p.74, '*The party to…*'
6. *The Glasgow Herald*, Alistair MacLean article 19 June 1982, '*Rewards and Responsibilities of Success:* Also reprinted in *The Lonely Sea*.
7. Webster, *Alistair MacLean*, pp.91–92, '*Waldham three weeks…*'
8. *The Glasgow Herald*, Alistair MacLean article 19 June 1982.
9. MacLean, *The Guns of Navarone*, p. 31, '*Mallory turned back…*'
10. Ibid, p.30, '*The fifth and last…*'
11. Ibid, Companion Book Club Introduction.
12. *Washington Post*, June 1961 Richard. L. Coe.
13. Webster, *Alistair MacLean*, p.93, '*To me it…*'
14. *The New York Times*, 5 January 1959 Rex Lander.
15. MacLean, *Tobruk*, p.16, '*Looking back over…*' & p.46, '*Who was responsible…*'
16. Ibid, p.4, '*History has recalled…*'
17. Ibid, p.3, '*To his eternal…*'
18. Ibid, p.29, '*The days were…*'
19. Ibid, p.30, '*And then there…*'
20. Ibid, p.31, '*And, for Blackie…*'
21. Ibid, pp.31–32, '*I had intended…*'
22. Bradford, Ernle, *Mediterranean*, pp.541–542, '*Never before had…*'

23. Lee Robert. A, *Alistair MacLean: The Key is Fear*, p.5 'MacLean's first novel...'
24. Webster, *Alistair MacLean*, pp.95–97, 'His tenacious snapping...'

Chapter Sixteen: At the Crossroads 1959–1963

1. Webster, *Alistair MacLean*, pp.112–113, 'In June 1960...'
2. *New York Times*, 21 February 1960 Rex Lander, *Mayhem on the Greenland Ice Cap*.
3. *Sunday Express*, 1960, *The Arandora Star*.
4. Ibid, 1960, *Rawalpindi*.
5. Ibid, 1960, *The Meknes*.
6. Ibid, 1960, *City of Benares*.
7. *Los Angeles Times*, 15 January 1978 Marshall Berges.
8. Robert Niemi, *100 Great War Movies*, pp.147–148, 'The Guns of Navarone...'
9. David Niven, *The Moon's a Balloon*, p.300, 'The Big picture...'
10. Books & Boots, Reflections on books, astrofella.wordpress.com
11. MacLean, *The Dark Crusader*, p.131, 'I refrained from...'
12. Raymond Chandler, *Farewell my Lovely*, p.7, 'Slim quiet negroes...'
13. Webster, *Alistair MacLean*, p.179, 'I think he's...'
14. Tom Hiney & Frank MacShane, *The Raymond Chandler Papers*, p. 61, 'I am doing...'
15. Ian Fleming, *You Only Live Twice*, p.200, 'The Times Obituary...'
16. *New York Times*, 11 November 1962.
17. MacLean, *Ice Station Zebra*, p.9, 'Commander James D....'
18. Letter to the author, Ian MacLean 26 October 2020.

Chapter Seventeen: The Hotelier 1963–1966

1. Margaret Forster, *Daphne du Maurier*, p.120, 'Jamaica Inn was...'
2. Ibid, p.121, 'Even nastier is...'
3. Rose Mullins, *The Inn on the Moor*, p.74, 'Peter Mositano and...'
4. Ibid, p.74, 'A diffident man...'
5. *Sunday Express*, August 1964 Robert Pitman.
6. *Variety Magazine*, 1 July 2010, Obituary of Elliot Kastner, Shalini Dore.
7. Webster, *Alistair MacLean*, pp.126–127, 'Chapman's avoidance...'
8. Ibid, p.130–131, 'Kastner agreed...'

Chapter Eighteen: Back to the War 1966–1968

1. Simmons, *Ian Fleming's War*, p.181, 'After Ian's death...'
2. Tiree's Historical Centre.
3. MacLean, *When Eight Bells Toll*, pp.5–6, 'Another thing...'
4. Ibid, p.21, 'So that's the...'
5. MacLean, *Where Eagles Dare*, pp.62–63, 'What lay below...'
6. Walter Schellenberg, *The Memoirs of Hitler's Spymaster*, pp.32–33, 'The SS organization...'
7. MacLean, *Where Eagles Dare*, p.208, 'You know that...'
8. See Ian Colvin, *Canaris Chief of Intelligence*.
9. MacLean, *Where Eagles Dare*, pp.177–179, 'Two floors higher...'
10. MacLean, *Tobruk*, p.50, 'At half-past five...'
11. Barry Norman, *And Why Not*, p.213, 'It was drink...'
12. MacLean, *The Guns of Navarone*, p.318, 'The rumbling...'
13. MacLean, *Force 10 from Navarone*, pp.7–9, 'It was odd...'
14. Ibid, pp.28–29, 'But what caught...'

15. See Fitzroy MacLean, *Eastern Approaches*.
16. Merlin Minshall, Autobiography, pp.254–255, '*Fitzroy Maclean...*'
17. Ibid, p.257, '*The truth...*'
18. MacLean, *Force 10 from Navarone*, p.59, '*You will forgive...*'
19. Webster, *Alistair MacLean*, pp.150–151, '*The vibrations of...*'

Chapter Nineteen: Switzerland 1969–1972
1. *New York Times*, 4 November 1969, James Lisk '*End Papers*'.
2. Norman, *And Why Not*, p.211, '*Diana took against...*'
3. Ibid, pp.212–214, '*When I arrived...*'
4. *The Observer*, 5 September 1971, Barry Norman, '*The best selling Sceptic*'.
5. MacLean, *Bear Island*, p.122, '*We called it...*'
6. Chandler, *The Long Goodbye*, first line.
7. MacLean, *Bear Island*, p.7, '*The morning Rose...*'
8. www.U.boat.net
9. MacLean, *Captain Cook*, p.11, '*Far from being...*'

Chapter Twenty: All is Chaos 1973–1977
1. *Sunday Express*, Graham Lord interview Alistair MacLean 1972.
2. *Daily Mail*, Graham Lord interview Jackie Collins 4 August 2012.
3. MacLean, *When Eight Bells Toll*, pp.162–163, '*He was sure...*'
4. Webster, *Alistair MacLean*, p.183, '*His basic...*'
5. Ibid, p.207, '*Elliot Kastner...*'
6. Ibid, p.211, '*Though the mystery...*'
7. *Los Angeles Times*, 12 September 1976, Edward M. White.
8. *New York Times*, 23 October 1977, Tom Buckley.

Chapter Twenty-One: The Last Decade 1978–1987
1. *The Los Angeles Times*, 19 October 1980, Dick Boraback.
2. MacLean, *River of Death*, Prologue.
3. Ibid, p.7, '*Darkness was falling...*'
4. *The New York Times*, 25 April 1982 No 380.
5. *Sunday Standard*, Jack Higgins' review *River of Death*.
6. The History of the University of Glasgow, Doctor of Letters p.203.
7. Webster, *Alistair MacLean*, p.282, '*Once settled...*'
8. Letter to the Author, Shona MacLean 9 June 2021.
9. *The Glasgow Herald*, April 1982
10. Webster, *Alistair MacLean*, p.200, '*The effect of...*'
11. *The Glasgow Herald*, April 1982
12. Webster, *Alistair MacLean*, p.262, '*Uncle Alistair...*'
13. MacLean, *San Andreas*, p.32, '*The hospital area...*'
14. Ibid, p.41, '*It's a Condor...*'
15. *The Globe & Mail*, 3 February 1987, Margaret Cannon '*Alistair MacLean's Mysterious Death*'.
16. *The New York Times*, 3 February 1987.
17. *The Washington Post*, 12 April 1987 Heywood Hale Broun.

Bibliography

Alistair MacLean's Books all published by William Collins unless otherwise stated.

Fiction
HMS Ulysses (1955)
The Guns of Navarone (1957)
South by Java Head (1958)
The Last Frontier (1959)
Night without End (1960)
Fear is the Key (1961)
The Dark Crusader (1961)
The Golden Rendezvous (1962)
The Satan Bug (1962)
Ice Station Zebra (1963)
When Eight Bells Toll (1966)
Where Eagles Dare (1967)
Force 10 from Navarone (1968)
Puppet on a Chain (1969)
Caravan to Vaccares (1970)
Bear Island (1971)
The Way to Dusty Death (1973)
Breakheart Pass (1974)
Circus (1975)
The Golden Gate (1976)
Seawitch (1977)
Goodbye California (1977)
Athabasca (1980)
River of Death (1981)
Partisans (1982)
Floodgate (1983)
San Andreas (1984)
The Lonely Sea (1985)
Santorini (1986)

Non-Fiction
All about Lawrence of Arabia (1962) published by W.H. Allen
Captain Cook (1972)
Alistair MacLean introduces Scotland (1972) published by Andre Deutsch

Books

Arthur, Max, *Lost Voices of the Royal Navy* (Hodder and Stoughton, 1996)

——, *Men of the Red Beret* (Hutchinson, 1990)

Beadle, Major J.C., *The Light Blue Lanyard* (Square One, 1992)

Brackenbury, Mark, *Scottish West Coast Pilot* (Stanford Maritime, 1982)

Bradford, Ernle, *Mediterranean: Portrait of a Sea* (Penguin, 2000)

Causley, Charles, *Hands to Dance and Skylark* (Robson Books, 1979)

Chandler, Raymond, *Farewell my Lovely* (Penguin Books, 1949)

——, *The Long Goodbye* (Hamish Hamilton 1953)

Churchill, Winston, *The Second World War* (Reprint Society, 1948)

Colvin, Ian, *Canaris Chief of Intelligence* (George Mann, 1973)

Cunningham A.B., *A Sailor's Odyssey* (Hutchinson, 1951)

De Bernieres, Louis, *Captain Corelli's Mandolin* (Secker and Warburg, 1994)

Denham, H.M. *The Aegean* (John Murray, 1983)

——, *Inside the Nazi Ring* (John Murray, 1984)

Denniston, Robin, *Churchill's Secret War* (Chancellor Press, 1997)

Ereira, Alan, *The Invergordon Mutiny* (Rutledge and Kegan, 1981)

Fleming, Ian, *You only Live Twice* (Jonathan Cape, 1964)

Forczyk, Robert, *We March against England* (Osprey, 2016)

Forster, Margaret, *Daphne du Maurier* (Chatto and Windus, 1993)

Green, Laurence, *All Cornwall Thunders at my Door: A biography of Charles Causley* (Cornevia Press, 2013)

Gulliver, Doris, *Dame Agnes Weston* (Phillimore, 1971)

Hiney, Tom, & MacShane, Frank, *The Raymond Chandler Papers* (Hamish Hamilton, 2000)

Jolly, Rick, *Jackspeak: A Guide to British Naval Slang and Usage* (Conway, 2011)

Knatchbull-Hugessen, Hughe, *Diplomat in Peace and War* (John Murray, 1949)

Landon, Christopher, *Ice Cold in Alex* (William Heinemann, 1957)

Lee, Robert. A, *Alistair Maclean: The Key is Fear* (Borgo Press, 1976)

Lewis, Norman, *Naples 44* (Collins 1978)

MacLean, Fitzroy, *Eastern Approaches,* (Jonathan Cape, 1949)

Minsall, Merlin, *Guilt Edged* (Bachman and Turner, 1975)

Mortimer, Gavin, *The SBS* (Osprey, 2013)

Mullins, Rose, *The Inn on the Moor* (PR Publishing 2009)

Niemi, Robert, *100 Great War Movies* (ABC-CLIO, 2018)

Niven, David, *The Moon's a Balloon* (Hamish Hamilton, 1971)

Norman, Barry, *And Why Not: Memoirs of a Film Lover* (Simon and Schuster, 2002)

Owen, Charles, *Plain Yarns from the Fleet* (Wrens Park, 1999)

Pearce, Frank, *The Ship that Torpedoed Herself* (Baron Jay, 1975)

Poolman, Kenneth, *The British Sailor* (Arms and Armour press, 1989)

——, *Escort Carrier 1941–1945* (Ian Allen, 1972)

Prysor, Glyn, *Citizen Sailors* (Viking, 2011)

Rogers, Anthony, *Churchill's Folly: The Battles for Kos and Leros 1943* (Cassell, 2003)

Roskill, S.W., *The War at Sea: Volume II The Period of Balance* (Naval and Military Press, 2004

——, *The War at Sea: Volume III The Offensive* (Naval and Military Press, 2004)

Schellenberg, Walter, *The Memoirs of Hitler's Spymaster* (Andre Deutsch, 2006)

Simmons, Mark, *Agent Cicero: Hitler's most successful Spy* (Spellmount, 2014)

——, *Ian Fleming's War* (The History Press, 2020)

Steinbeck, John, *Once There Was a War* (The Folio Society, 2013)
Stewart, Jackie, *Winning is not Enough* (Headline, 2007)
Sweetman, John, *Tirpitz: Hunting the Beast* (Sutton Publishing, 2000)
Tucker-Jones, Anthony, *Operation Dragoon* (Pen and Sword, 2009)
Webster, Jack, *Alistair MacLean a Life* (Chapmans, 1991)

Archives
BBC Archives
British History Centre the University of Cambridge
Imperial War Museum (UK)
National Archives (USA)
The National Archives, Kew (UK)
Navy Command Secretariat 4 Navy Search
Naval History Net
National Museum of the Royal Navy Portsmouth
Royal Navy Research Archive
Tiree Historical Centre
United States Navy Historical Centre

Journals and Newspapers
Blackwood Magazine
Daily Mail
Daily Telegraph
Glasgow Herald
Globe & Mail
International Fleet Review Magazine
Los Angeles Times
Sunday Express
Sunday Standard
The Observer
The Portsmouth News
The New York Times
The Scotsman
The Times
Variety Magazine
Washington Post

Websites
Fred de Vries, alistairmaclean.blog
oldglasgow.tumblr.com
www.U.boat.net

Acknowledgements

I am grateful for the help given to me by members of the MacLean family, in particular Shona Vance/MacLean, Alistair's niece, and Ian MacLean his nephew.

Sincere thanks to Lee Child for writing the foreword and to Ian Rankin for allowing me to quote him. And to David Brawn of HarperCollins who is the guardian of the Alistair MacLean literary legacy, for his enthusiastic support for this project and allowing me access to unpublished Alistair MacLean material. Also many thanks to Gareth Shannon, Business Affairs Director at HarperCollins.

The staffs at various libraries and museums as always have been helpful including: the BBC People's War Archive, Imperial War Museum London, department of documents and photographs, Navy Command Secretariat, P & O Heritage, and the Public Records Office at Kew, Royal Navy Museum Portsmouth, Royal Navy Research Archive, and Tiree's Historical Centre.

Overseas museums and libraries have been equally helpful including: Embassy of the Federal Republic of Germany, London, The United States National Archives and the United States Navy Historical Center.

For help and support with the manuscript I would like to thank Iain Ballantyne, Tom Cull, Fred de Vries, and John Sherress. Jack Webster's biography of Alistair MacLean has provided a wealth of information given that most of the people who knew Alistair are no longer with us.

Also the work and memories of the following have been most helpful Max Arthur, J.C. Beadle, Mark Brackenbury, Geoffrey Brooke, Charles Causley, H.M. Denham, Margaret Forster, Laurence Green, Lew Lind, Norman Lewis, Gavin Mortimer, David Niven, Barry Norman, Frank Pearce, Kenneth Poolman, Glyn Prysor, Anthony Rogers, S.W. Roskill, Jackie Stewart, Walter Schellenberg, John Steinbeck, John Sweetman, Anthony Tucker-Jones.

Finally, as always and most important, my wife, Margaret, gave her wholehearted support to the nuts and bolts of building a book, with proofreading, finding her way through the labyrinth of strange and unfamiliar names, and my creative misspelling of them. Thanks to all. Any mistakes or errors are mine alone.

Index